IMAGES
of America

WARREN COUNTY

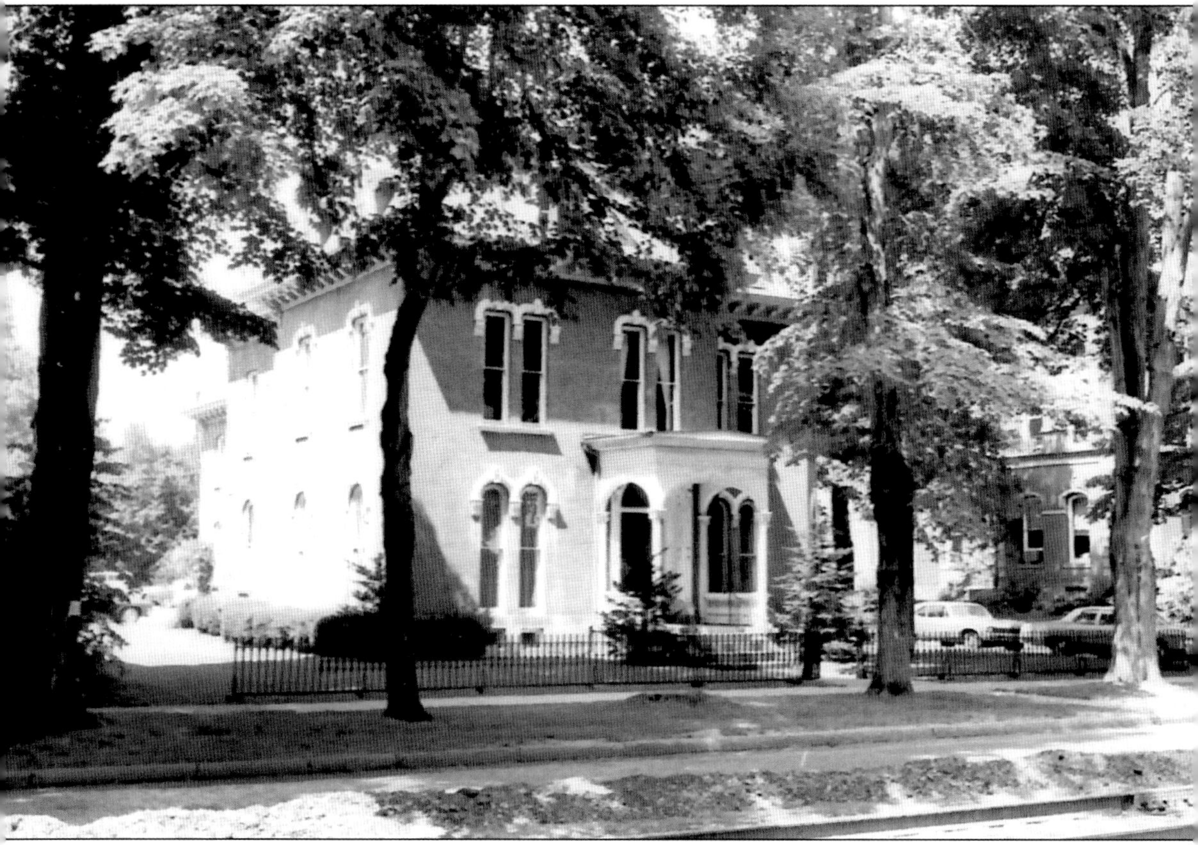

The Struthers-Wetmore-Schimmelfeng House, located at 210 Fourth Avenue in Warren, has been home to the Warren County Historical Society for 50 years. The structure was completed in 1873 and built in the modern Italian Renaissance style, with red brick and a white wood trim and a mansard roof. The walls are double layers of brick separated by an air space, and the woodwork is solid walnut. The house has the traditional wide central hall with a handsome staircase. Today, the formal parlor is dressed in an elegant Victorian motif, the dining room serves as the library, and the smaller sitting room is the front office. This photograph was taken in 1980. (Photograph by and courtesy of Chase Putnam.)

On the Cover: In 1866, when Philip Bucher bought Jacob Knoph's 1849 mill on the West Bank of the Tionesta Creek, both the mill and the area became known as Bucher's Mill. The mill sawed and sent mostly pine boards downstream to Brown Run and thence to the Allegheny River. In 1882, the new owners, Brown Brothers of Clarendon, installed a steam-powered circular saw to cut hemlock. (Courtesy of the Warren County Historical Society.)

IMAGES
of America

WARREN COUNTY

Warren County Historical Society

ARCADIA
PUBLISHING

ISBN 978-1-4671-2251-1
Published by Arcadia Publishing
Charleston, South Carolina

Printed in the United States of America

Library of Congress Control Number: 2014937955

For all general information, please contact Arcadia Publishing:
Telephone 843-853-2070
Fax 843-853-0044
E-mail sales@arcadiapublishing.com
For customer service and orders:
Toll-Free 1-888-313-2665

Visit us on the Internet at www.arcadiapublishing.com

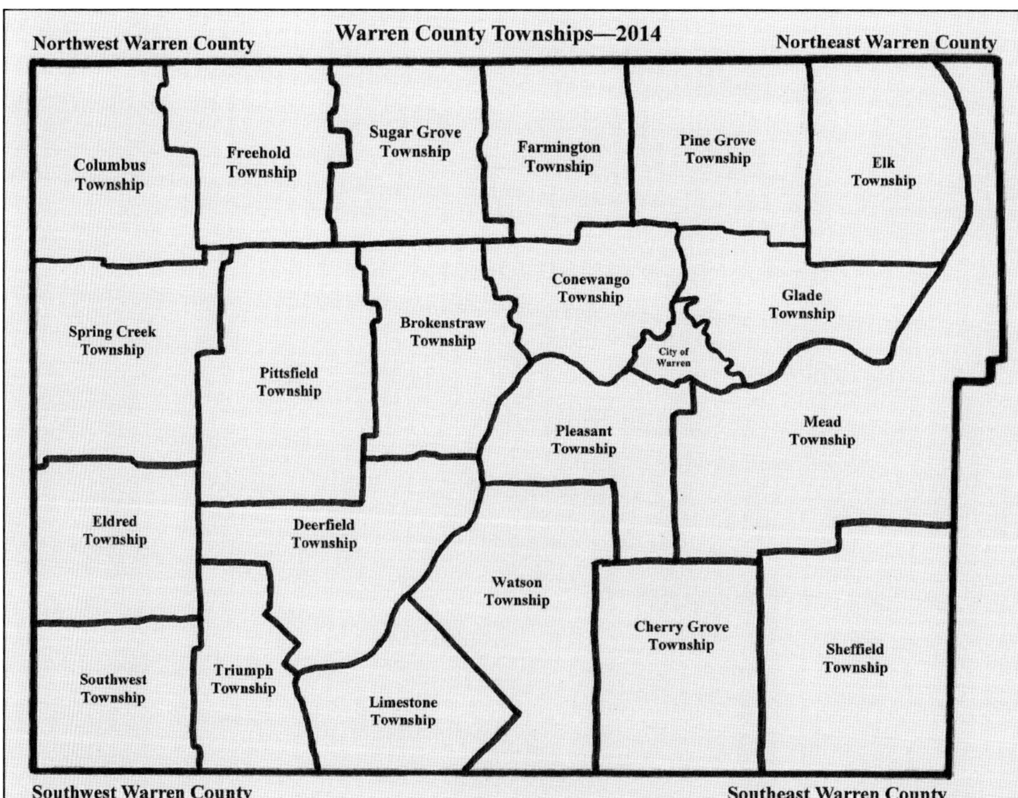

Pictured is a 2014 map of Warren County townships. (Courtesy of the Warren County Historical Society.)

Contents

ACKNOWLEDGMENTS

This publication is a compilation of images and information collected from people and organizations who treasure Warren County history. The Warren County Historical Society maintains extensive archives from many resources, and it is our privilege to share these carefully selected images with you. Unless otherwise noted, all images are from the Warren County Historical Society.

A special thank-you goes to local historians Dr. Julie Boozer, Laura Brainard, Hannah Fry, Nancy Gabel, Sandy Kick, Linda Knapp, Allen McIntosh, James Morrison, Keith Oviatt, Chase Putnam, Mary Putnam, Nicki Tremblay, Doris Trumbull, Marcy White, Jeanette Walter, Carl E. Wolf, and Edward Yaegle.

Thank you, to the staff of the Warren County Historical Society for the numerous hours of research on this book project: Michelle Gray, managing director; Casey Ferry, event coordinator; Jude W. Harter, education curator; Lucille McJunkin, collections manager; and Kara N. Spade, intern.

Thank you, to the board of directors of the Warren County Historical Society for supporting this book project and your dedication to the organization: Keith Oviatt, president; Stephanie Scutella, vice president; Wallace E. Blyth, treasurer; Sue Curtin, secretary; Dr. Karen Black; Ron Bosworth; Cynthia DeChano; Pat Evans; attorney H. Robert Hampson; Lisa Huya; Mike Lewis; and Carl E. Wolf.

Introduction

Warren County, Pennsylvania, is 902 square miles in area and was formed out of Lycoming and Allegheny Counties by an act of the legislature in 1800. In 1805, it was attached to Venango for judicial purposes, but in 1819, after a sufficient increase in population, it was organized as a full-fledged county. It is bordered on the north by New York State, on the east by McKean County, on the west by Crawford and Erie Counties, and on the south by Venango and Forest Counties.

The Allegheny River and its three major tributaries—Conewango, Brokenstraw, and Kinzua Creeks—were natural waterways for the rafting of lumber, which was the county's main industry for many years. Sawing and rafting of lumber continued to be a major activity late in the 1800s.

As the rafting of lumber declined, and as the arable land was cleared of its timber, farming began to flourish, particularly in the northwest section of the county. In addition, manufacturing of furniture and other wood products expanded, the availability of hemlock bark led to the establishment of a large tanning operation in the Sheffield area, and the fabrication of products from iron began.

In the later half of the 19th century, concurrent with the arrival of the railroad, an oil boom developed in Warren County. It added yet another major industry, and by the early 1900s, there were 13 refineries within a six-mile radius of Warren. Sensational oil finds occurred in numerous locations, including Tidioute, Cherry Grove, and Clarendon. Oil production and refining still hold an important position in the county.

Heart's Content and Tionesta Scenic Area are the only appreciable stands of virgin timber remaining in Pennsylvania. With their 300-year-old trees, they are breathtaking evidence of the splendor that greeted the settlers as they moved westward. These tracts are within the Allegheny National Forest, a large portion of which is included in Warren County and which provides vistas of beauty unequaled in any other part of the state.

The construction of the Kinzua Dam and Allegheny Reservoir, a flood control project 12 miles above Warren, has been the impetus for the development of outdoor recreation. Campgrounds, boat-launching ramps, swimming areas, and scenic overlooks have been incorporated into the overall development of the reservoir shoreline.

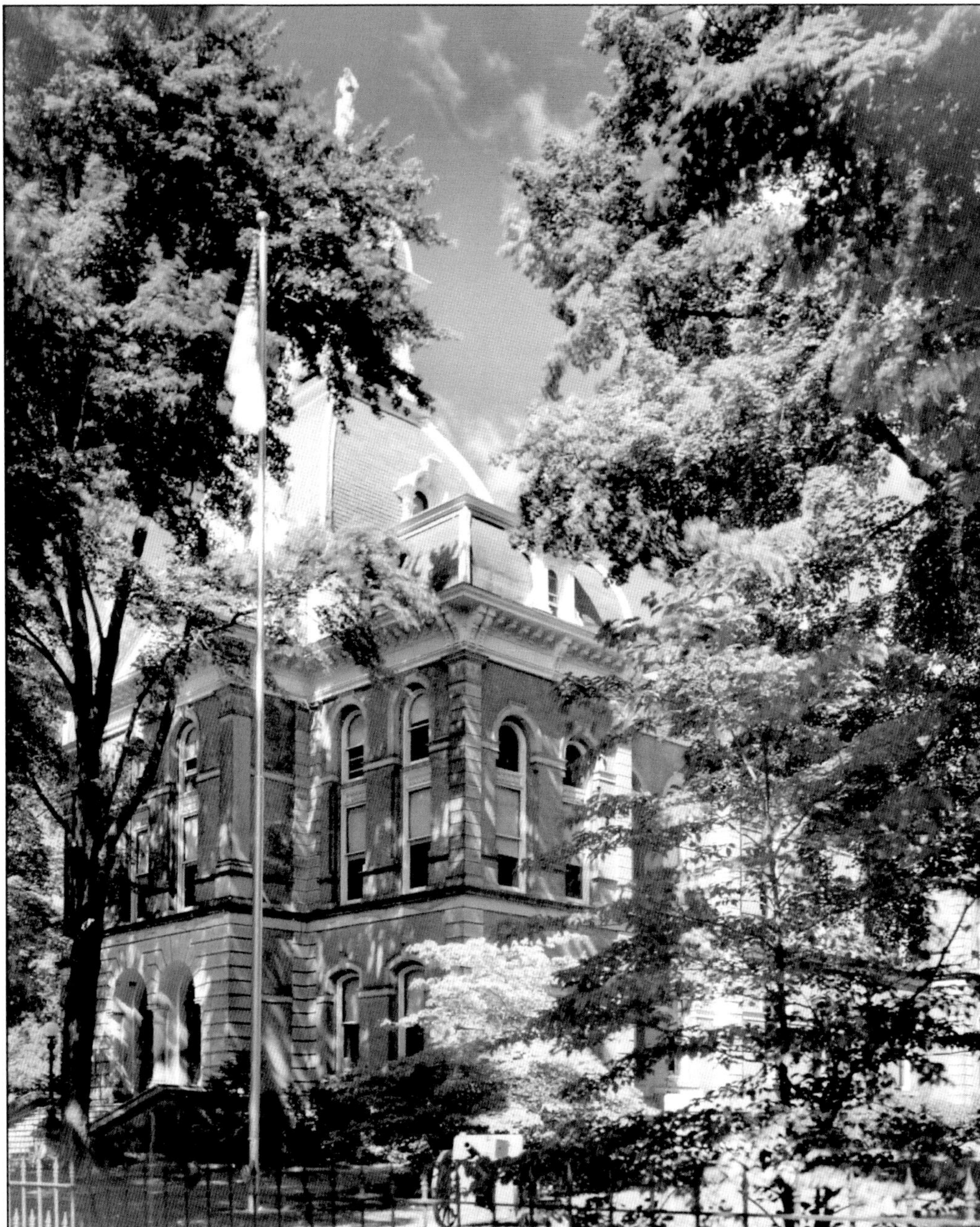

The current Warren County courthouse was completed in 1877 and commended as a "model courthouse of the state." The building is in the Italian Renaissance style, with Georgia pine courtroom floors and marble tile hallways that have elegant woodwork done in walnut and chestnut. (Photograph by Carl E. Wolf)

One

Northwest Warren County

Columbus, Freehold, Sugar Grove, Spring Creek, Pittsfield, and Brokenstraw Townships

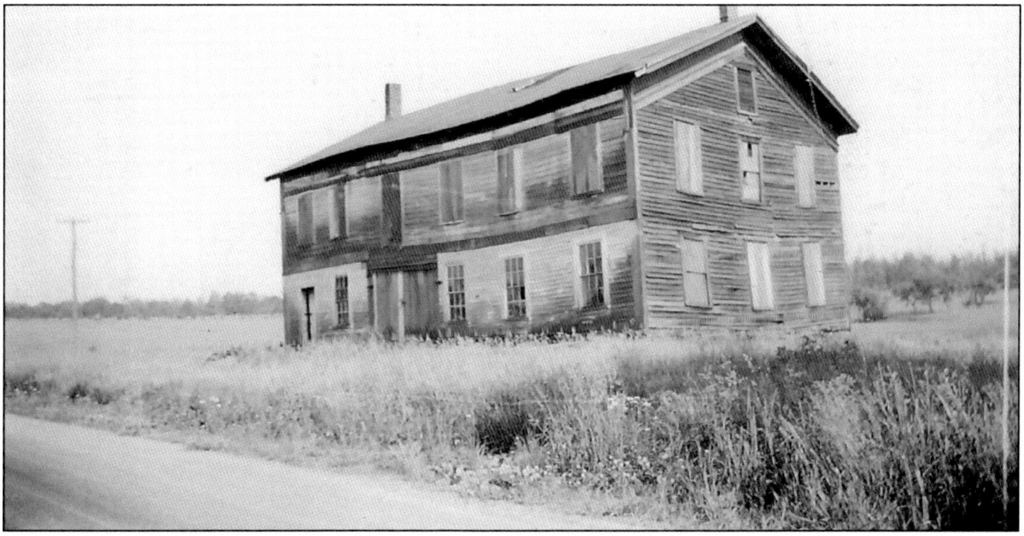

In Columbus Township, the Kansas House Hotel was erected by Seth Webber in 1858 primarily to accommodate drovers. Large corrals were built at the back of the house to take care of the cattle. Located on the Old State Road between Columbus and Lottsville, its tavern kept bottles cool in a spring in the barroom. The dance floor was hung on springs and swayed with the swinging of the dancers. People came to the Saturday night dances from miles around. When Byron Boardman operated the hotel, he held a party that netted him his rent. The house had two large porches, and Byron's sons sold popcorn and candy on one porch and lemonade on the other. After the turn of the century, the hotel was used for storage.

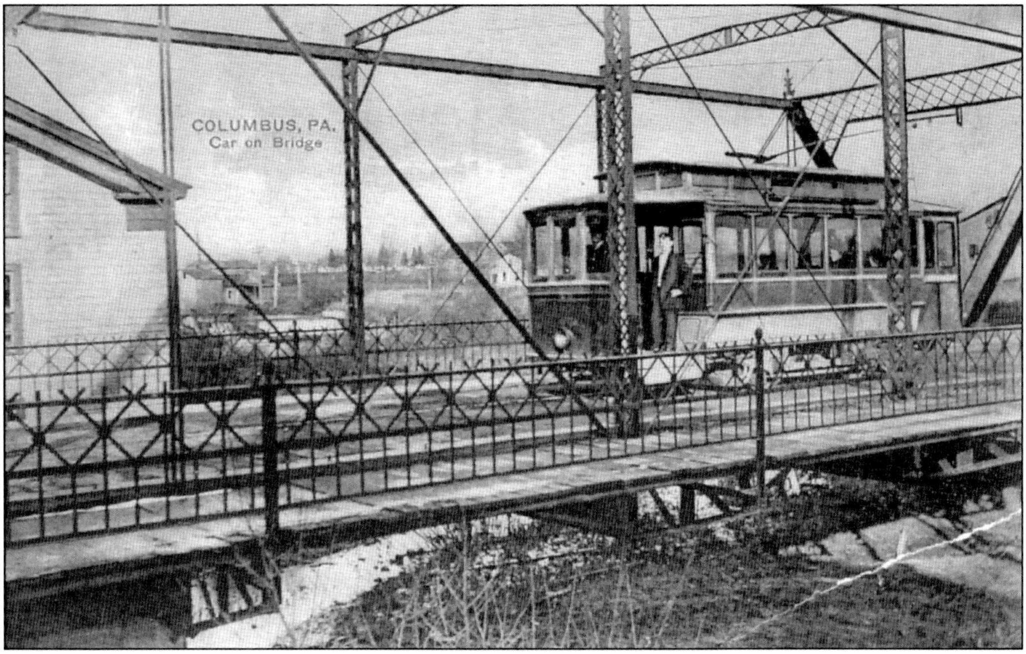

These are early views of the Corry and Columbus Street Railway cars traveling across the Columbus Bridge over the Brokenstraw Creek. The railway line grew out of a syndicate organized in 1903 and opened for business on September 4, 1906, with runs from Corry to the fairgrounds nearby. In July 1907, service commenced to Columbus in Warren County. The five-mile line shut down on August 22, 1923.

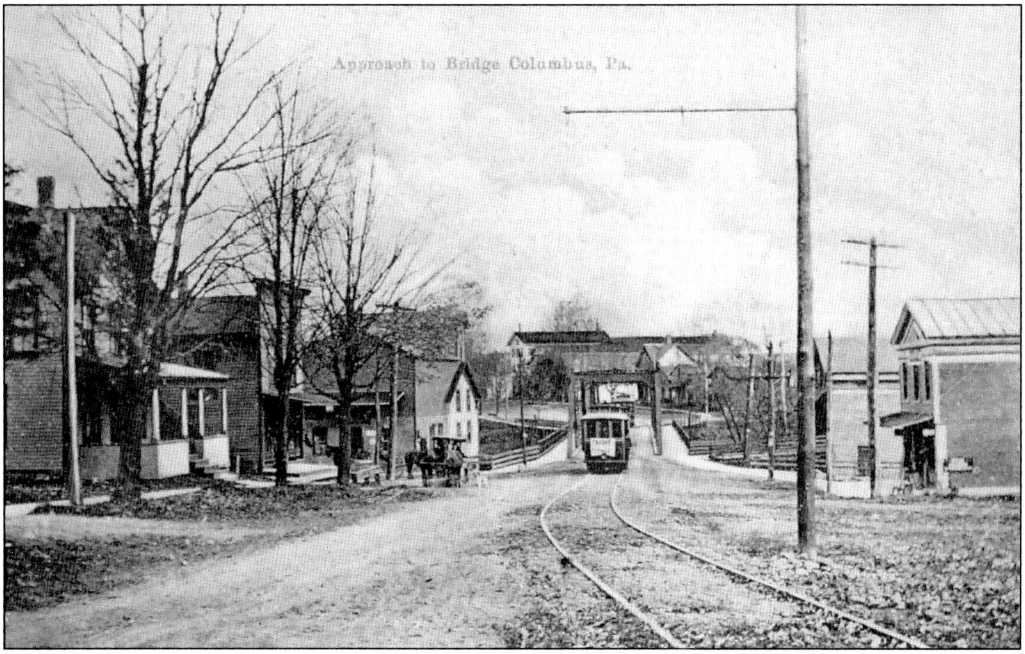

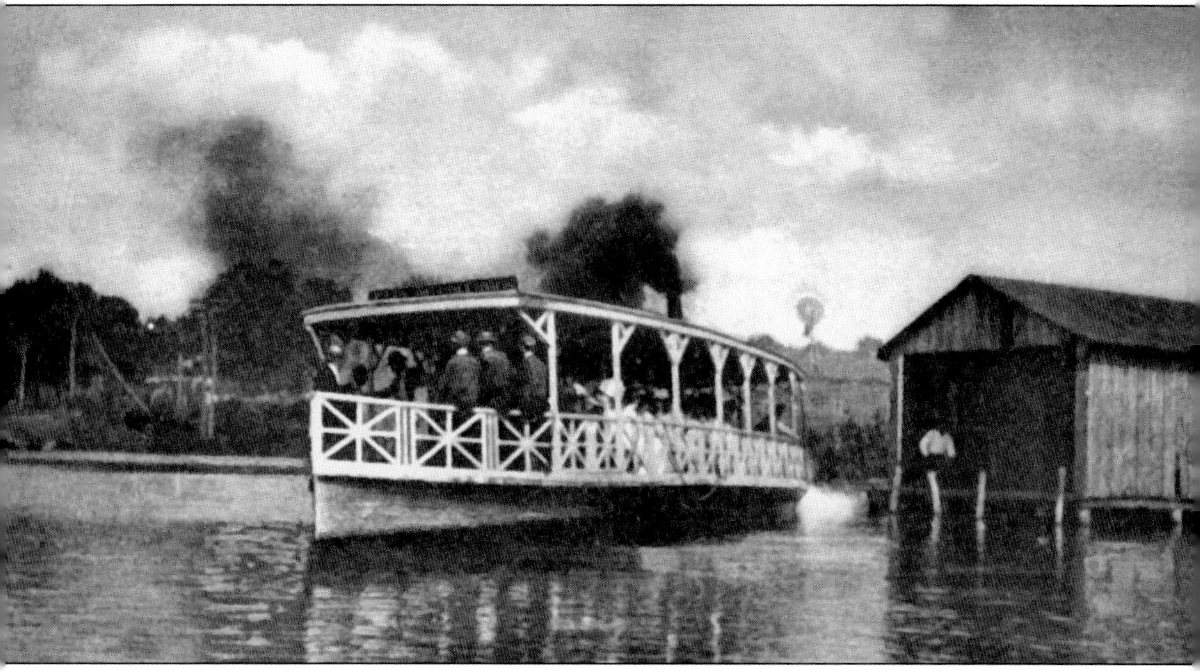

In this 1910 photograph, a cruise departs the boathouse on Columbus Lake. The lake attracted visitors to the area for fishing, boating, swimming, and camping until 1947, when spring high waters washed out the dam. The towns of Columbus and Corry fought to rebuild the dam for its family recreational value; however, by 1955, the project had become a political football, and Columbus Lake became a distant memory.

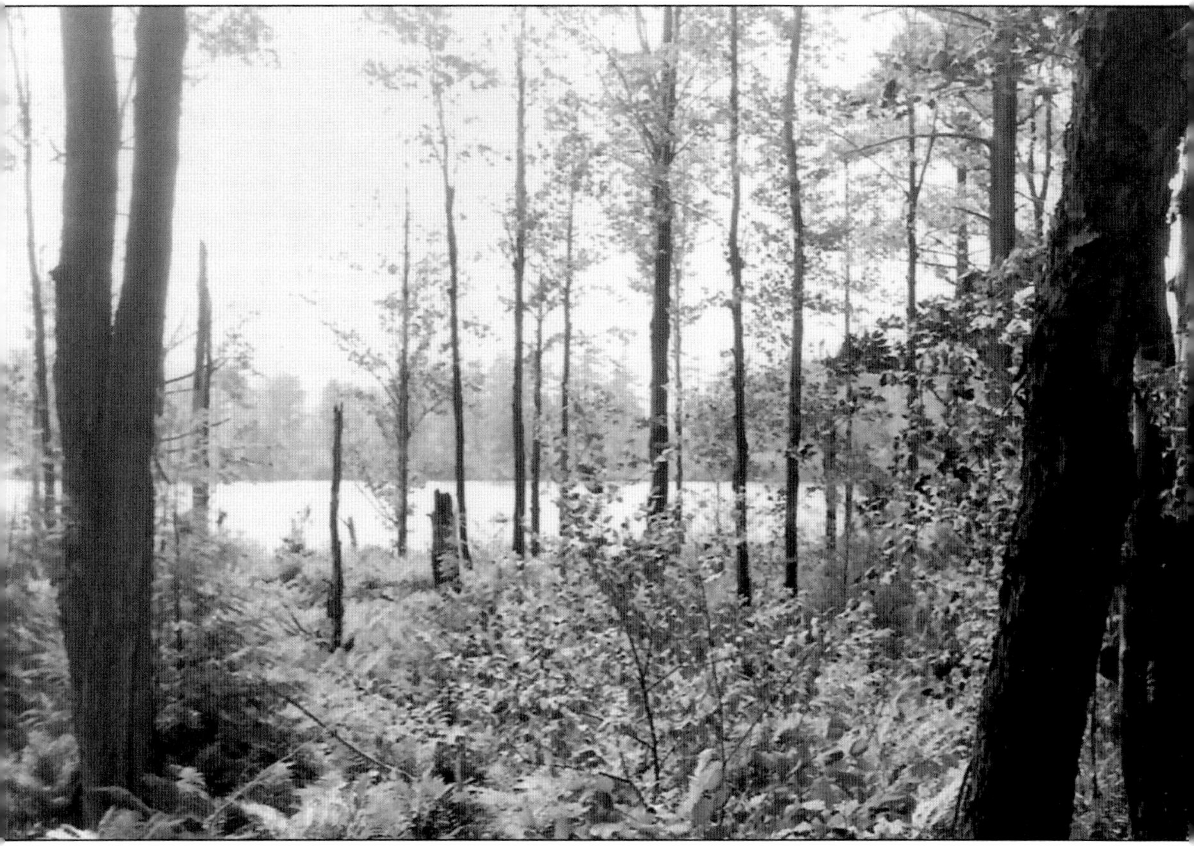

In Freehold Township, the tiny lake is located about one mile from the town of Bear Lake but still considered a very important part of the town. It is around one mile in circumference and has been used for winter skating, small boats, and swimmers. This photograph of the lake was taken in 1972.

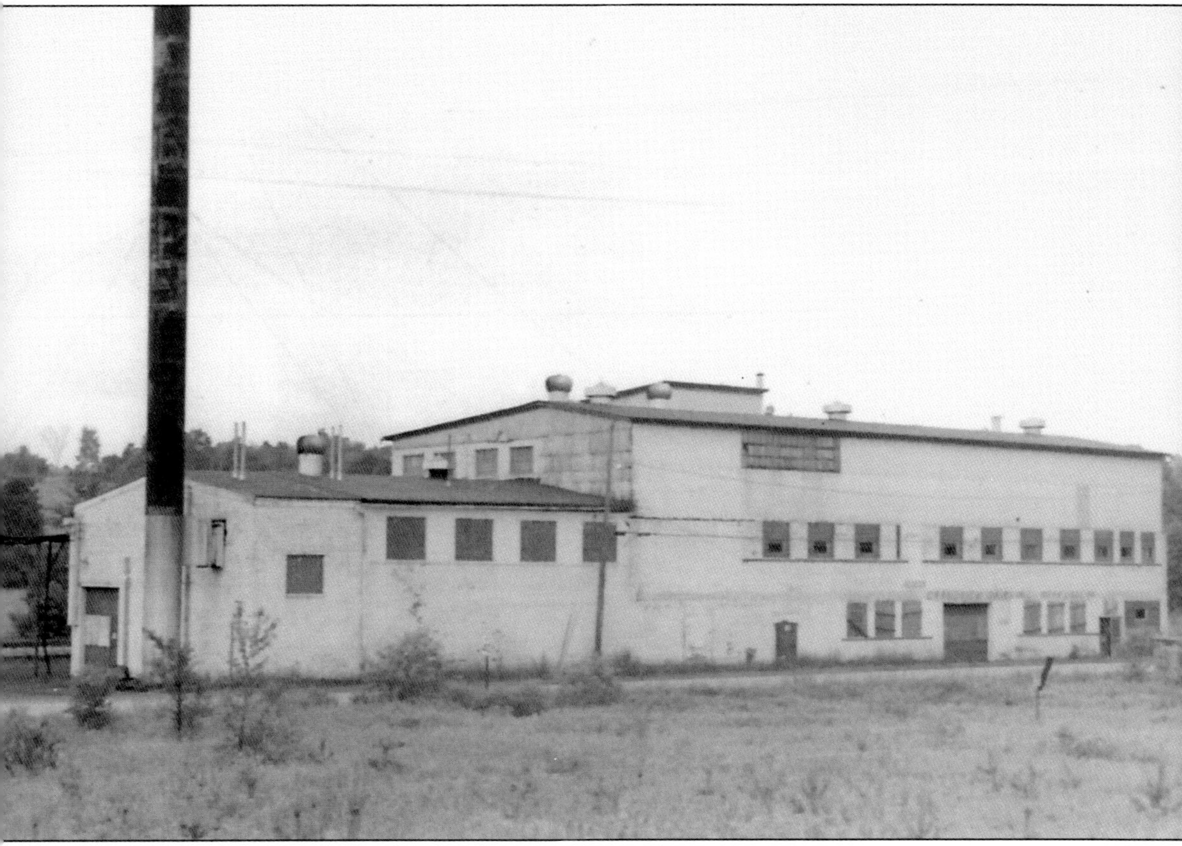

The Mohawk Condensery was built in Bear Lake around 1917. The facility was initially a receiving station for milk that was taken to Clymer, New York, but after two years, the company began producing condensed milk to be used during World War I. The plant closed for a time and was reopened and operated by Grandview Dairies and eventually Roselake Dairies. Over the years, butter, cheese, and powdered milk were also made at the plant.

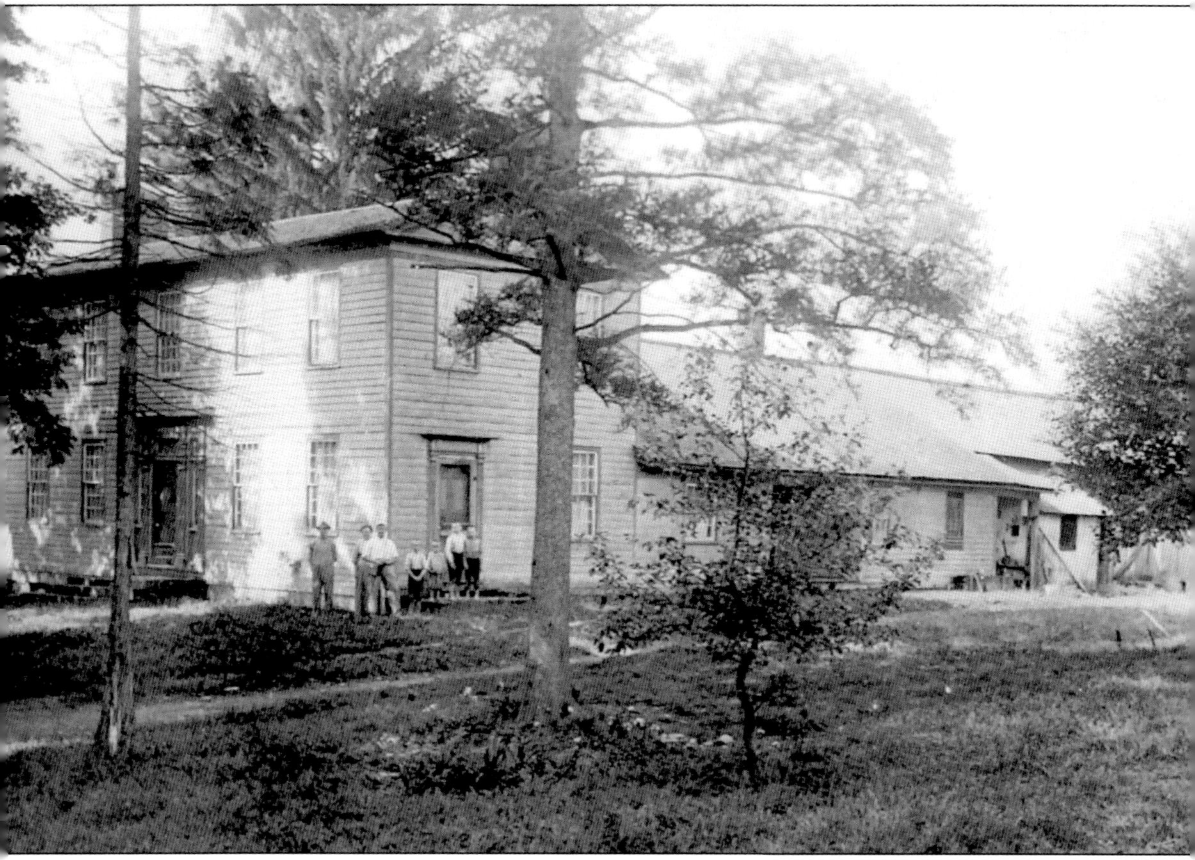

In Sugar Grove Township, the Miller Mansion is located on Big Tree Road. It is the most noted Underground Railroad station in Warren County. The house was built in 1821 by abolitionists Richard Bishop Miller and his wife, Cynthia Catlin Miller. The Millers entertained Frederick Douglass during the 1854 Abolitionists Convention. The Millers considered harboring escaped slaves and helping them to freedom to be "God's work" and utilized many groups to serve their missions, including the Female Assisting Society and the Ladies Fugitive Aid Society. This photograph is from around 1910.

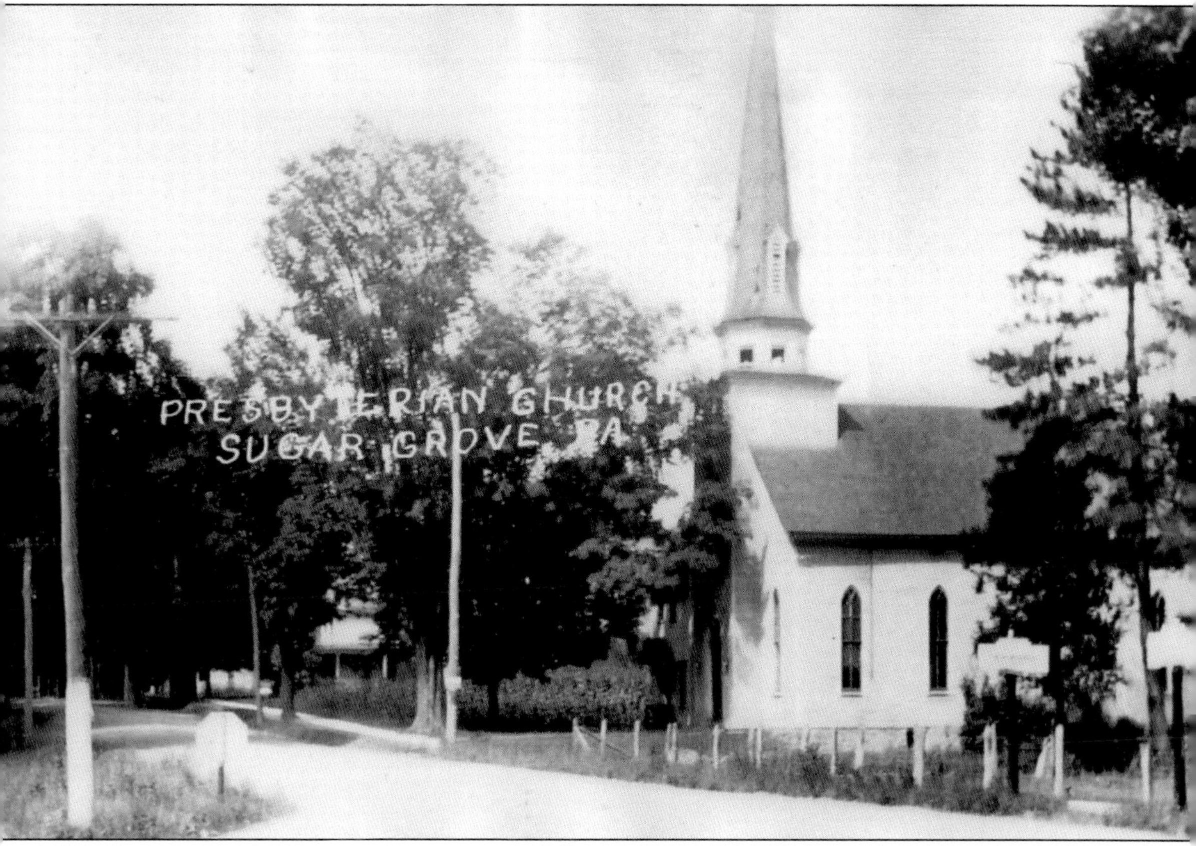

The Sugar Grove Presbyterian Church steeple was taken off this church by J. Ed Abbott and son Norman on Friday, April 14, 1933, under instruction from the trustees of the church. This church was built about 1833 and stood on a lot on the north side of West Main Street. Information about this image was provided by Frank Miller.

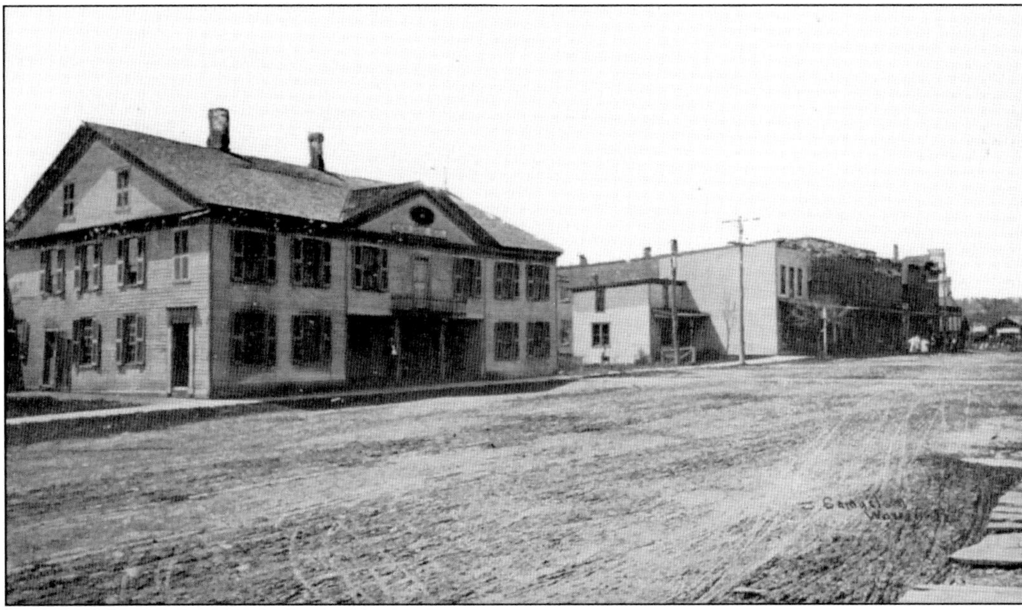

The Sugar Grove Hotel was built and first operated in 1821 by Capt. John I. Willson, who had a deed to the land for $450 in 1825. The Willsons were there until the 1850s. John was originally from Canada and became a steamboat captain on the Great Lakes. His wife, Mary, took care of the hotel while he was away. Mary was a sister of Eliza Elliott, first wife of Robert Falconer. The hotel burned November 1912 while operated by R.H. Buckley.

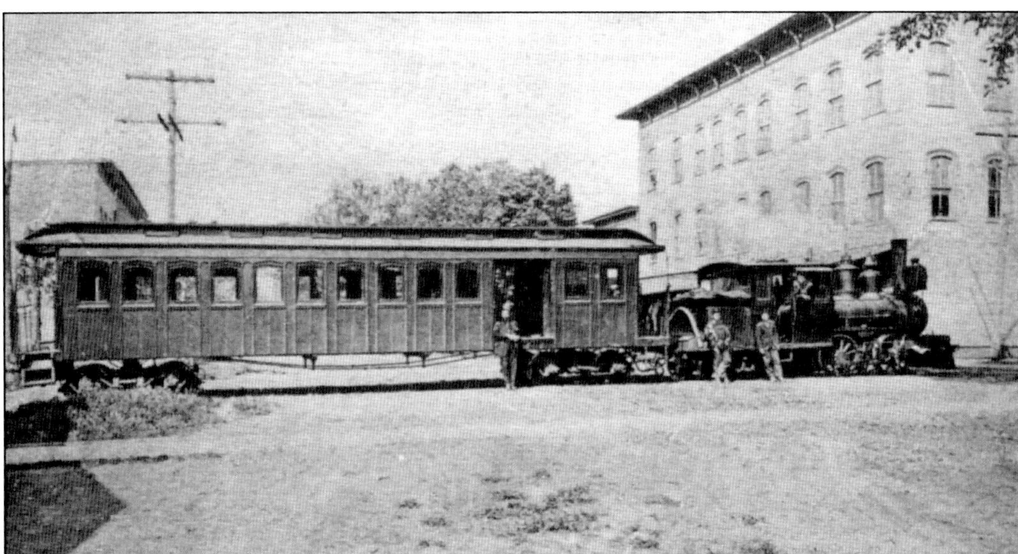

Starting in 1903, the Youngsville & Sugar Grove Train track ran out of Youngsville, up Matthews Run, and into Sugar Grove. It was only 10 miles long but had 22 stations along the beautiful valleys and Stillwater Creek. The Y&SG Train had the capacity to transport 40 passengers per trip, as well as haul coal, merchandise, bricks, apples, lumber, potatoes, and other produce.

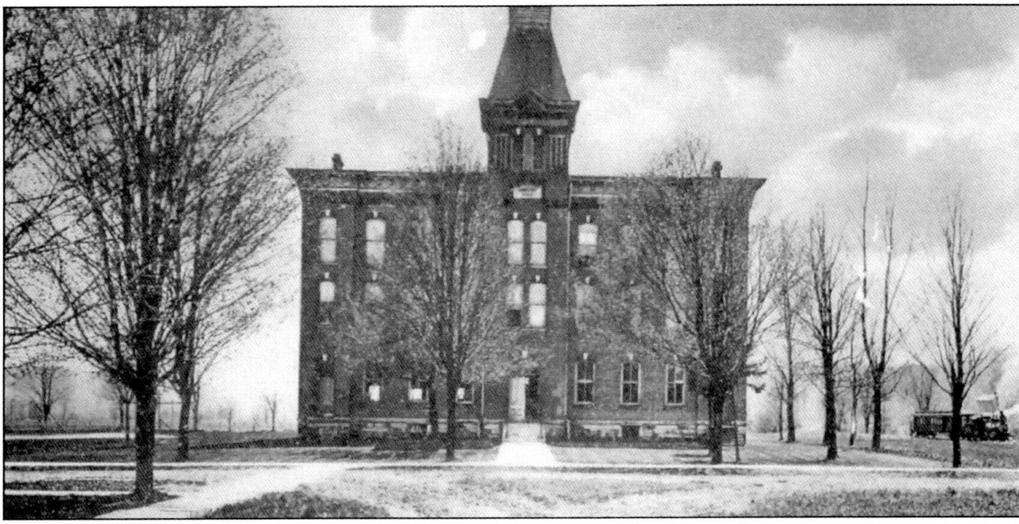

Sugar Grove's most notable institution of learning was the United Brethren Seminary, built in 1883. The aim of the seminary, as stated in many of the annual catalogs, was to create a Christian atmosphere while providing the best possible academic program. The seminary was never intended to compete with the public school system but to supplement and enhance it. In 1914, due to financial difficulties, the seminary closed its doors. Beginning in 1917 and continuing until 1963 when it was demolished, the seminary assumed a new role as the largest public school building in Sugar Grove. Today, the seminary's bell is mounted on the lawn of Sugar Grove's elementary school.

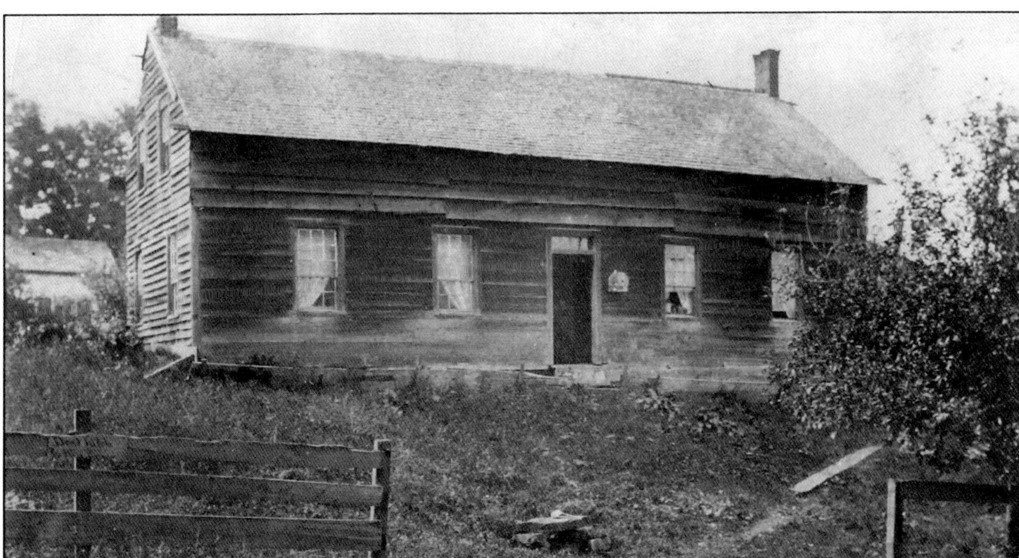

The first framed home in Warren County was erected by the Honorable David Brown, the first representative from Warren County to the Pennsylvania House, and was the birthplace of his son, Judge William D. Brown, in 1823. A sign on the fence reads, "Do not hitch to this fence."

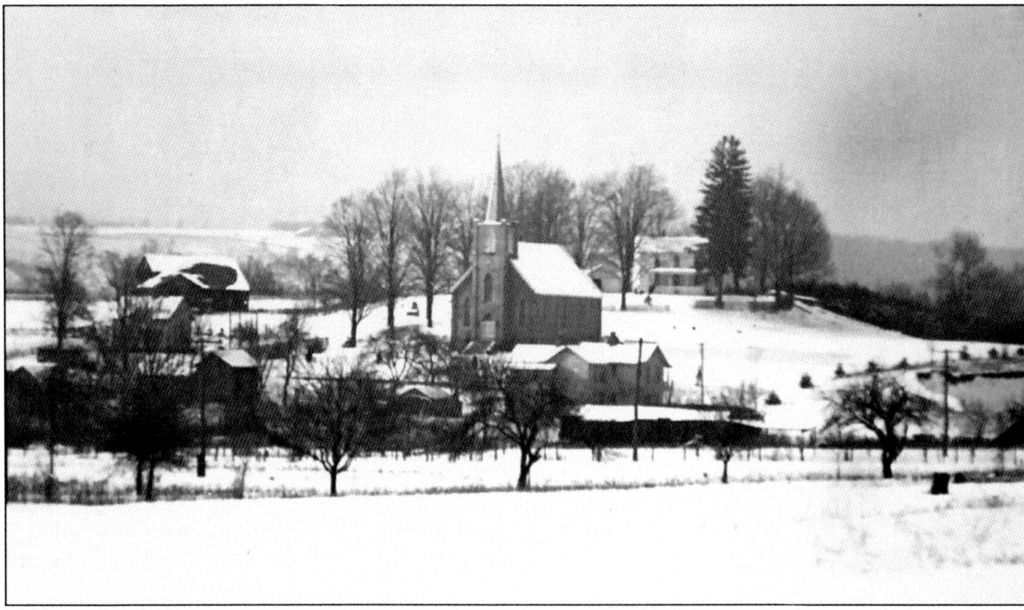

The village of Chandlers Valley is located in Sugar Grove Township. It was named for a Revolutionary War veteran, John Chandler, who settled there in 1815. A considerable number of Swedish families immigrated to the area, which was also known as Swedesburg. Chandlers Valley is considered the oldest Swedish settlement in the eastern United States.

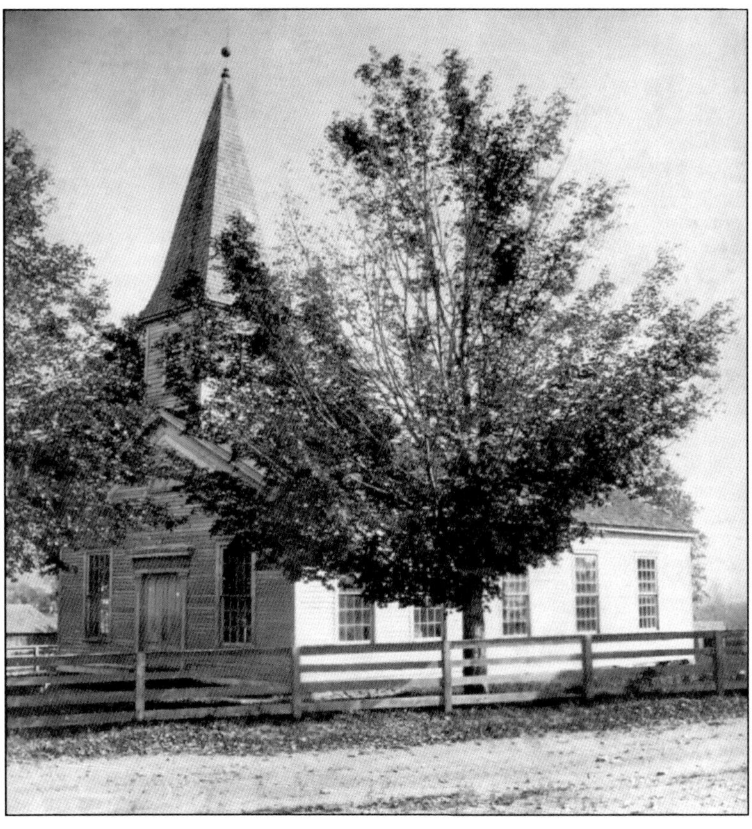

Just west of the village, the Reverend Jonas Swenson organized a Lutheran church. The first church of the growing Swedish settlement started in 1853 and was situated at the junction of Sugar Grove and Matthew's Run Roads. In 1885, this church building was finished and named the Hessel Valley Lutheran Church. Until 1933, services were held in the Swedish language.

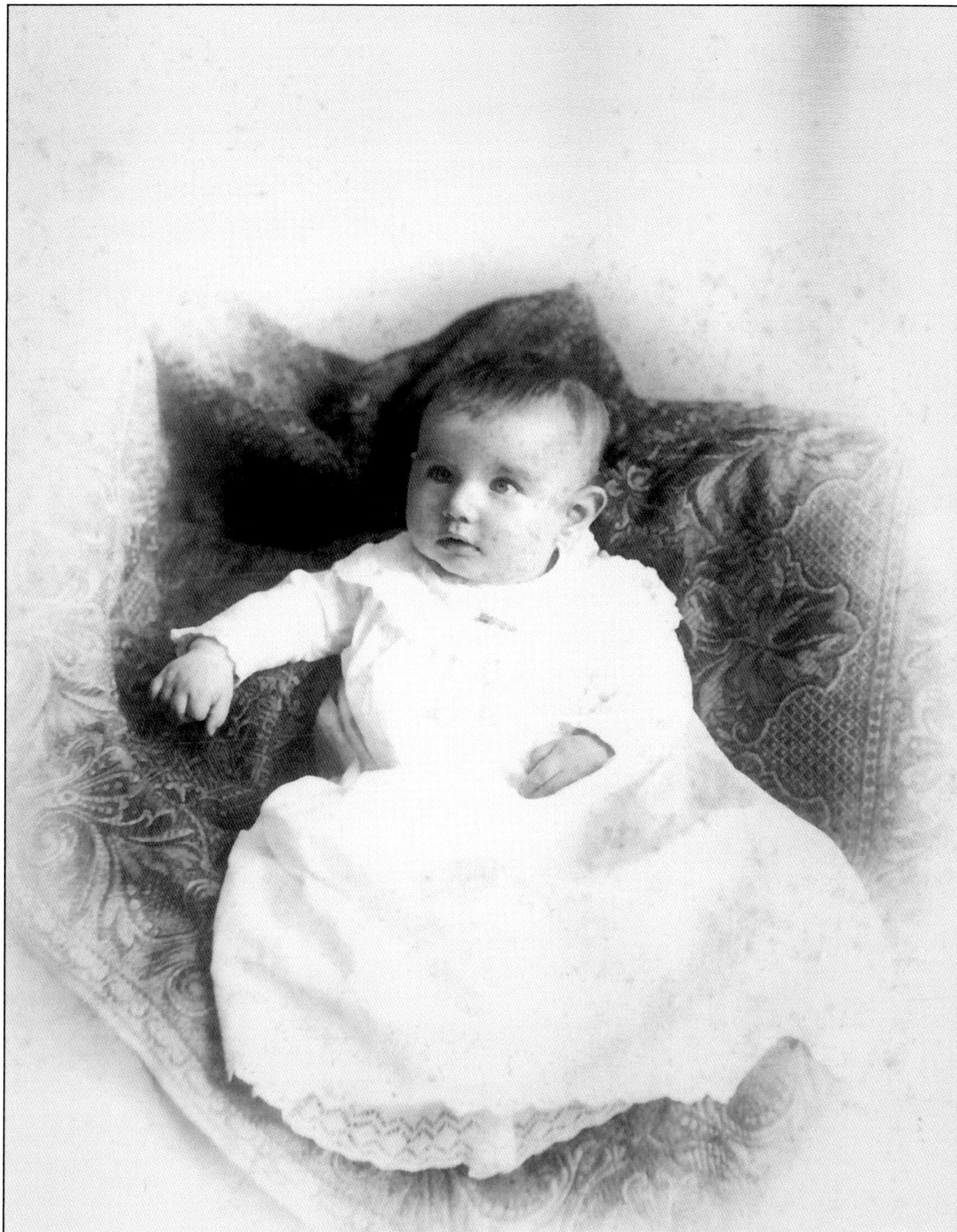

In Spring Creek Township on February 13, 1892, Robert Houghwout Jackson was born in the Jackson family farmhouse. Jackson became a Supreme Court justice and chief prosecutor at the World War II Nuremberg War Trials. He was known as the "country lawyer" and was the last Supreme Court justice to not hold a formal law degree. Jackson was viewed as one of the finest writers to ever serve on the Supreme Court.

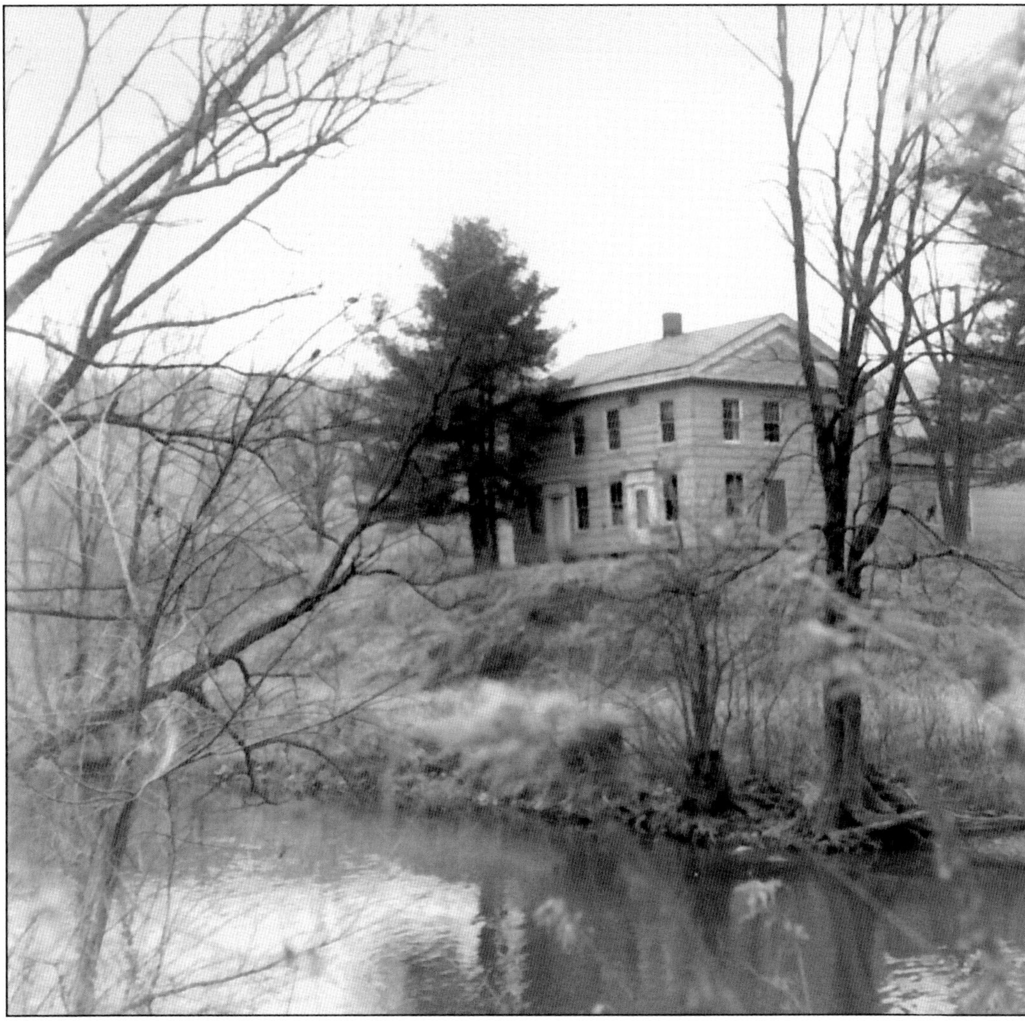

This house is the birthplace of Robert H. Jackson, native-born son of Spring Creek Township. Jackson radically changed the face of international law by utilizing his opportunities to practice his ethical and moral values of justice, fairness, and human decency. Jackson died in 1954, but not before exercising his final opportunity to let justice prevail in *Brown v. Board of Education* on May 17, 1954, marking the beginning of the first step to the elimination of "separate but equal" and the desegregation of public life.

The Clough Farm is located along Old Route 77 in Spring Creek Township. The farm was built by timber baron Levi S. Clough in the early 1900s. Clough was a very powerful man in pursuit of a lifestyle for the rich and famous. The property was more than 1,000 acres and had at least seven small farmhouses at any given time. The dairy operation was one of the most noteworthy in northwestern Pennsylvania, with the larger of the two barns housing 260 milk cows. Clough's company was known as Spring Valley Farms.

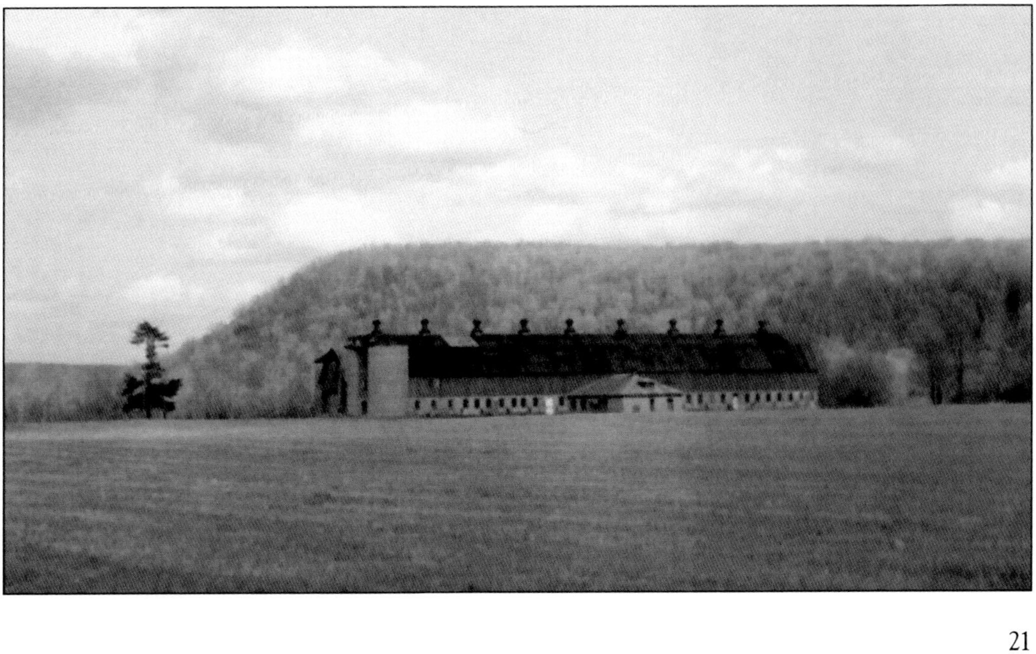

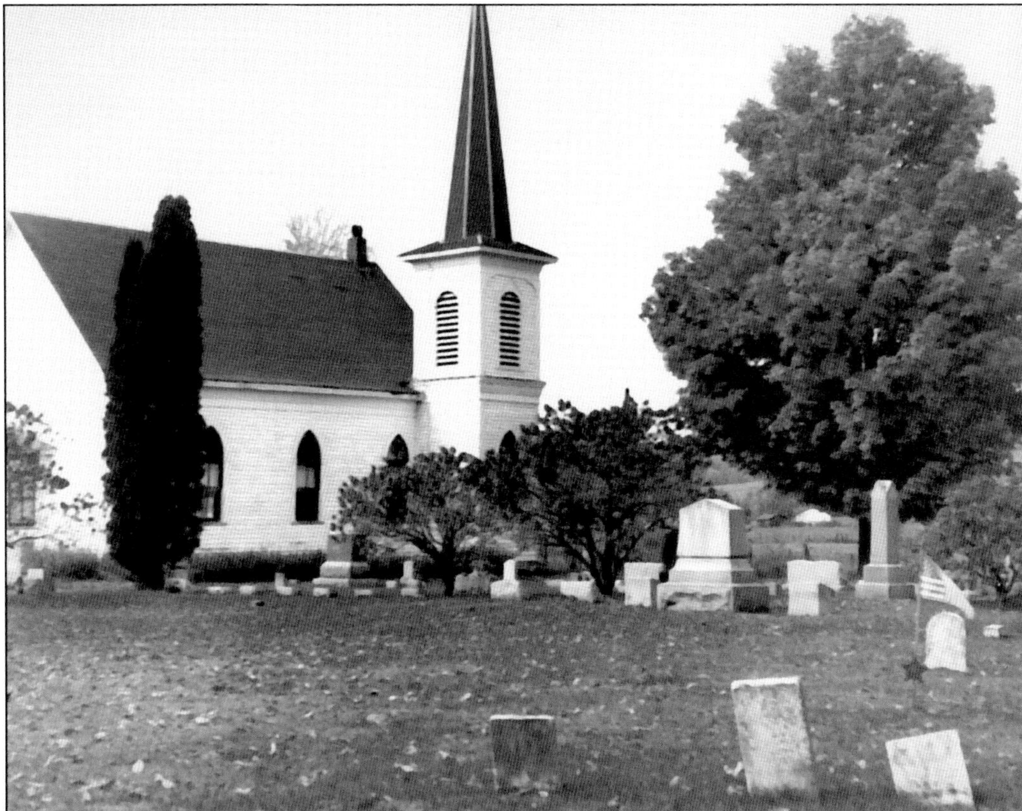

In 1797, Andrew Evers and Elijah Jackson built a log cabin in Spring Creek Township, and a new community began to grow. The first church was built in 1847 and was known as the Union Church. In 1875, the community built this church, West Spring Creek Congregational Church, on the western edge of the cemetery.

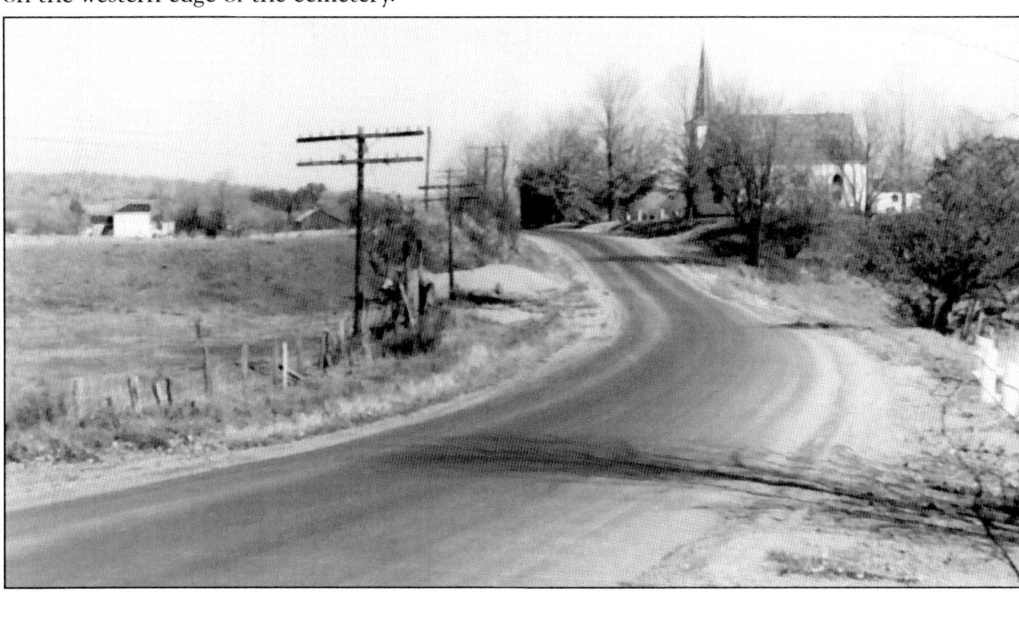

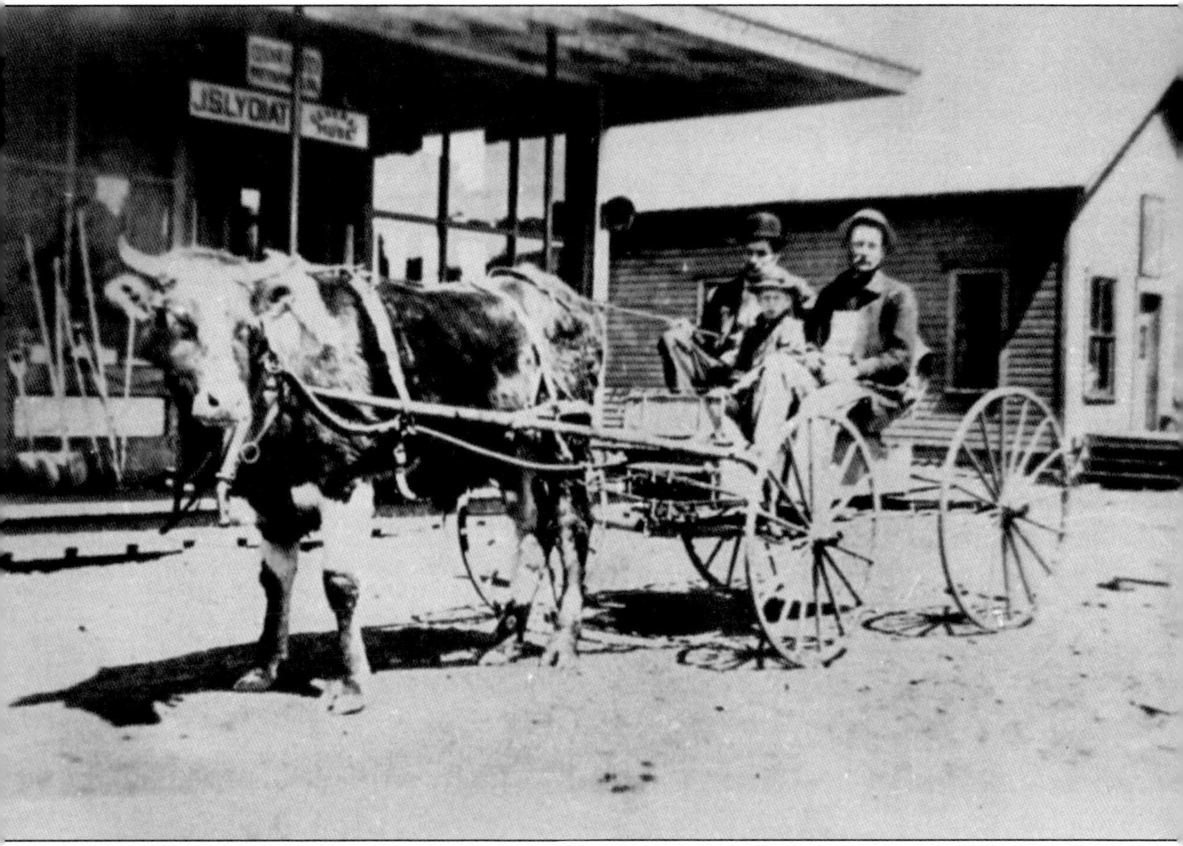

In Pittsfield Township, this 1912 postcard image is of the old post office with Perry Nicols's ox in front. According to Henry Danielson, sometime after 1826, James L. Acocks petitioned for a post office in Pittsfield (at that time the town was known as "Corners"). Acocks served as the postmaster for over 20 years.

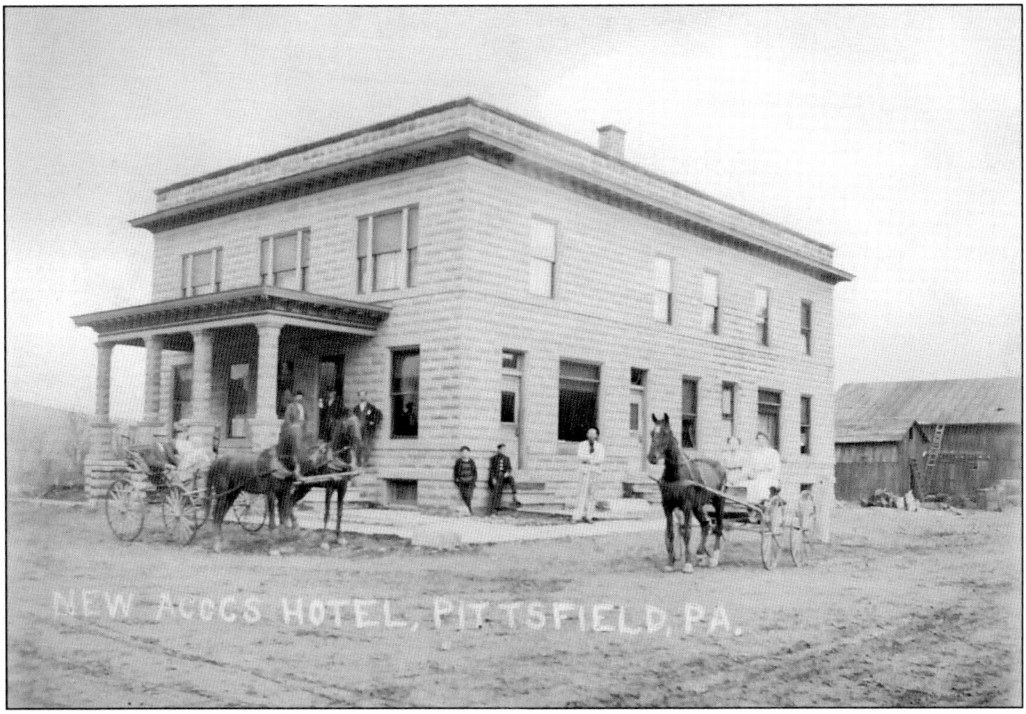

On January 20, 1846, James L. Acocks petitioned for a liquor license to operate the Acocks Tavern at the mouth of the Little Brokenstraw. The record references "adequate house, plenty of beds, bedding, and stabling." A hotel known as the Pittsfield Inn had been operated by Acocks's son-in-law Mark Dalrymple since 1832. The hotel burned down twice. The structure shown below burned to ashes on August 25, 1910.

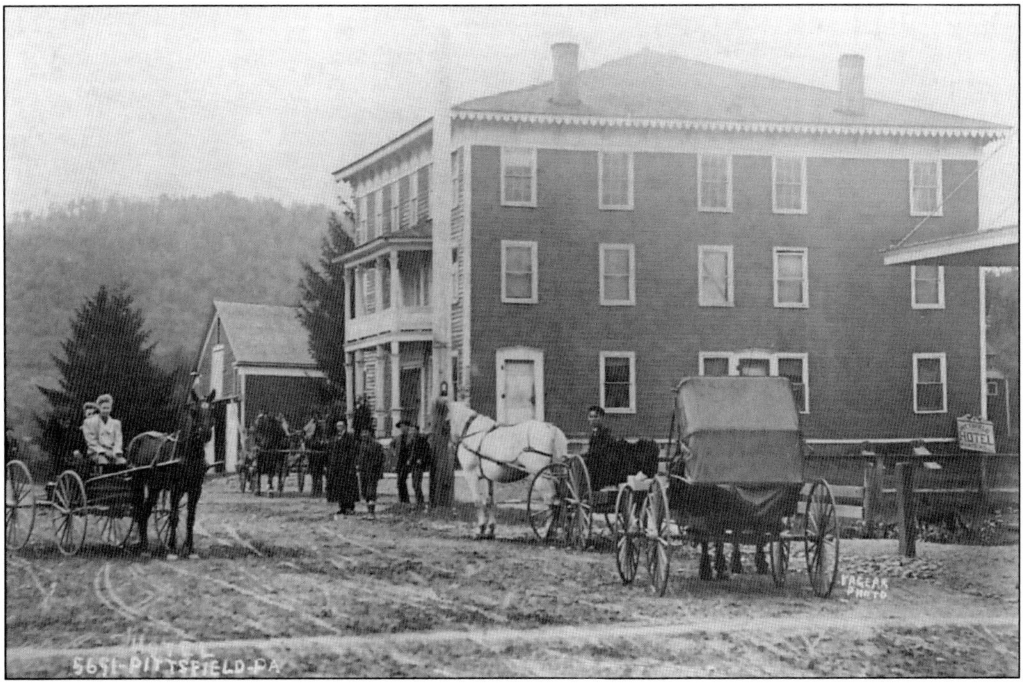

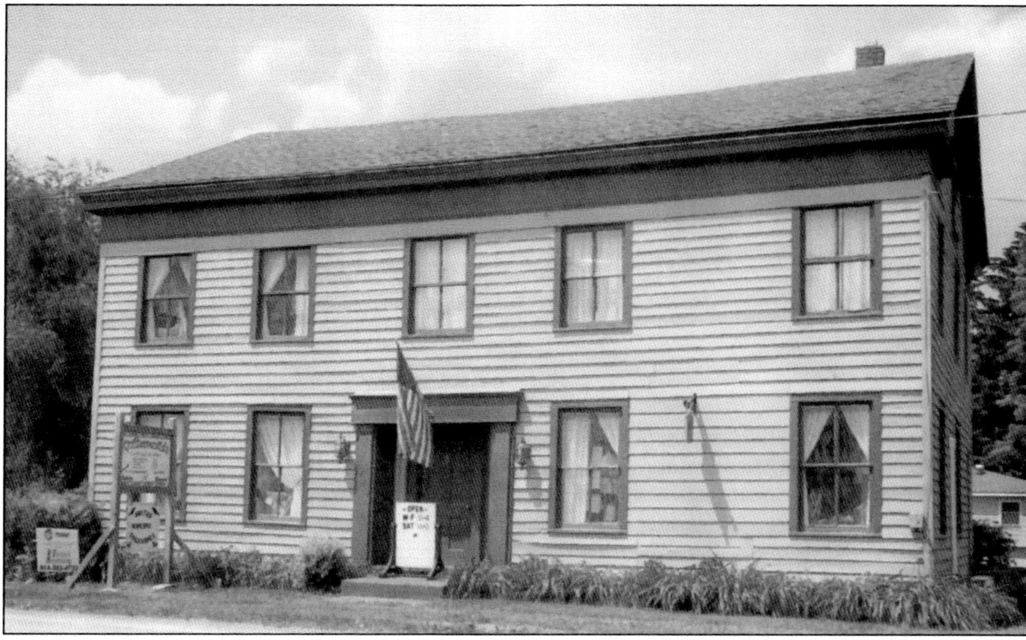

This 1810 house was originally built in 1790 by Robert Andrews. It began as an inn and had two front doors, one for women and one for men. The original water trough still exists under the pavement of Route 27. Col. Edwin Drake, the first man to strike oil, is said to have stayed here on August 13, 1859.

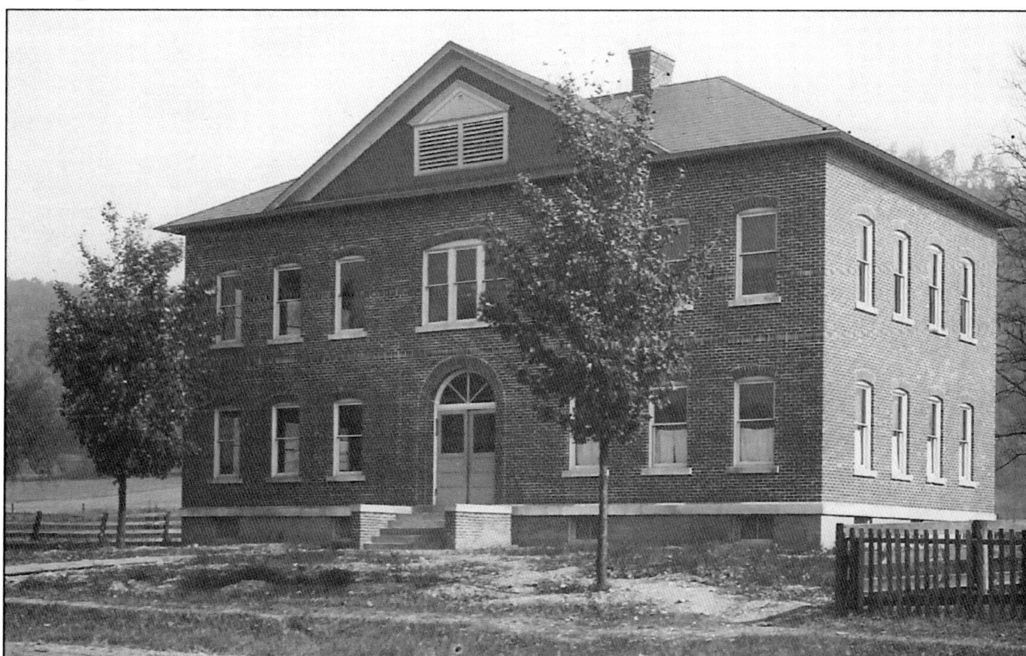

The Pittsfield schoolhouse is pictured about 1908. The building remains one of the few early brick schools still existing as a typical feature of the period. The message on this postcard reads, in part, "Dear Florence, this is where Esther will go this September. Tell Lily I will write her a card tomorrow. With a hug and a kiss. Good-by."

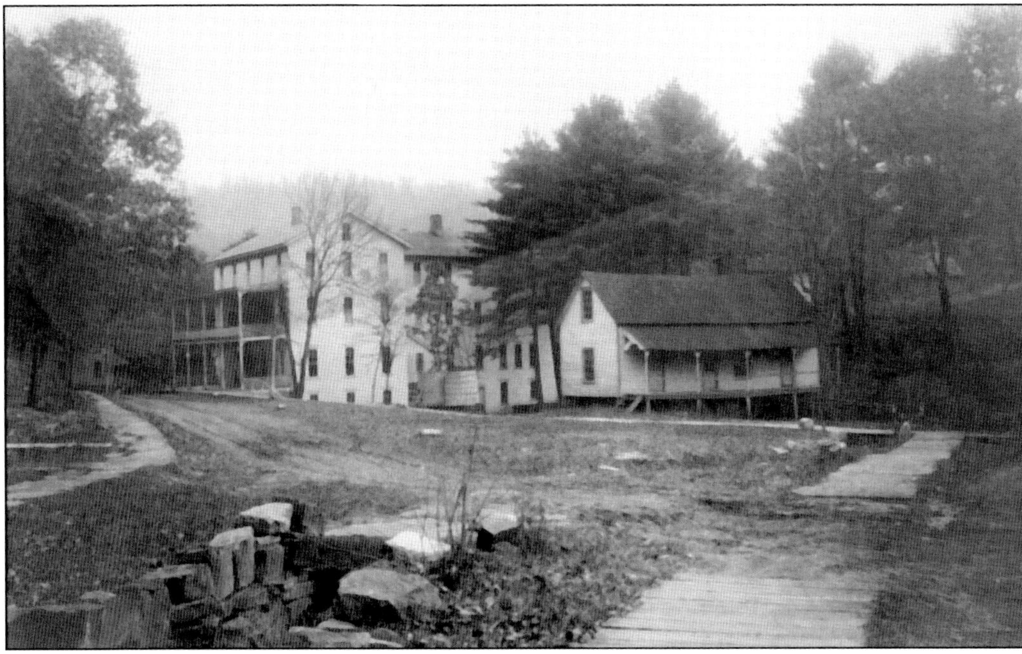

In Brokenstraw Township during the 1800s, foul-tasting substances were viewed as medicinal, and Dr. James Alexander of Youngsville hopped on the trend by giving sulfur-rich water from a spring near Irvine to sick patients, many of whom recovered. Word spread, and by 1879 Alexander's heir, William Culbertson, had founded Sulphur Springs Hotel, later christened the Allegheny Springs Hotel, shown here. The resort had a gazebo, bathhouse, cottages for guests, and a stagecoach.

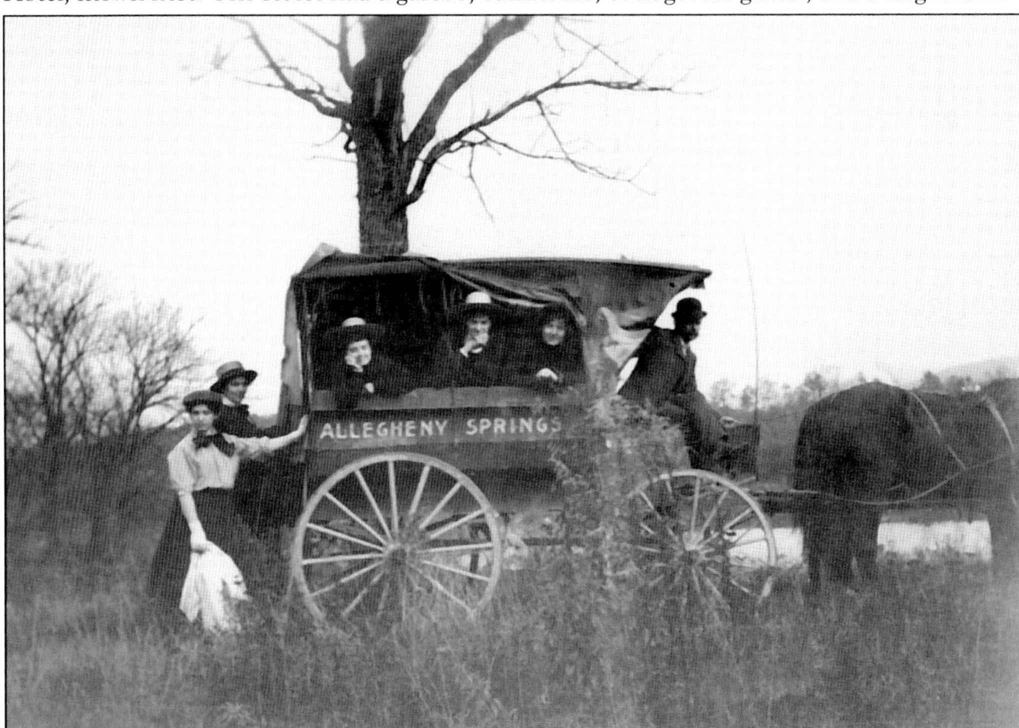

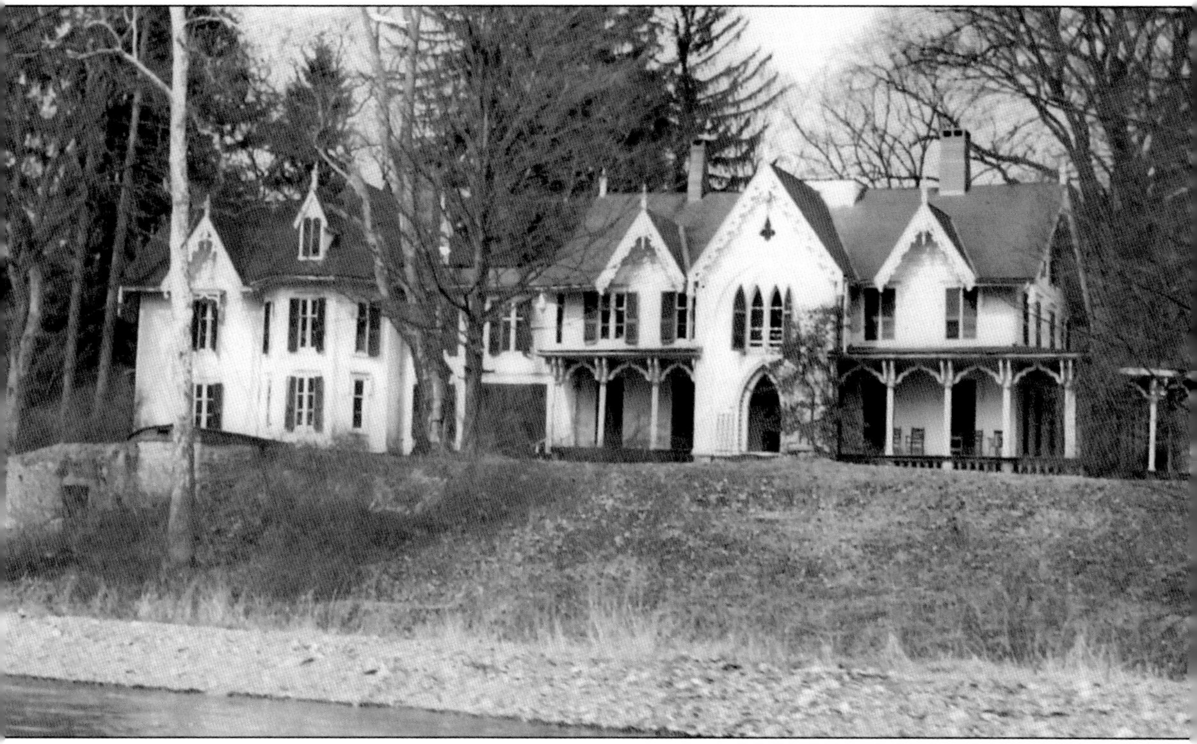

While Gen. William Irvine secured about 2,000 acres along the Brokenstraw Creek as early as 1792, it was his son Callendar who first developed a seasonal estate there, building a small home around 1822. In 1838, Callendar's son Dr. William A. Irvine moved permanently to the area and began expanding the house and grounds. The Gothic mansion seen here has a drive-through carriageway for bad weather.

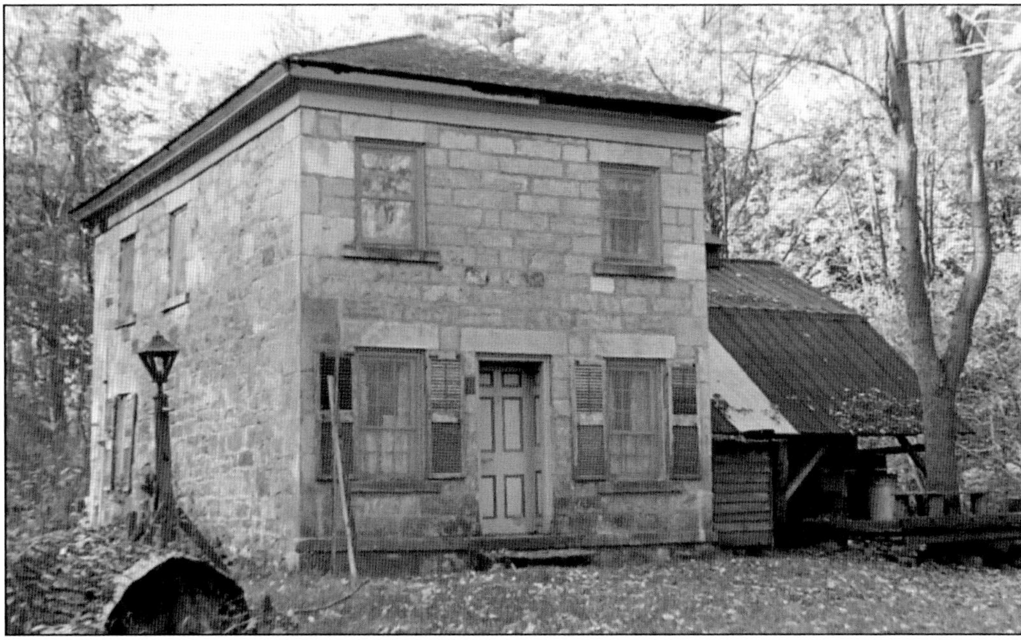

Dr. Irvine made many improvements to his estate. He and his workers developed pastureland; built a pond with an ornamental island; constructed a cut-stone retaining wall along the riverbank; and built gardens, greenhouses, barns, stables, and homes for the workers, including this one, the Little House in the Hollow. Dating from 1841, it still stands.

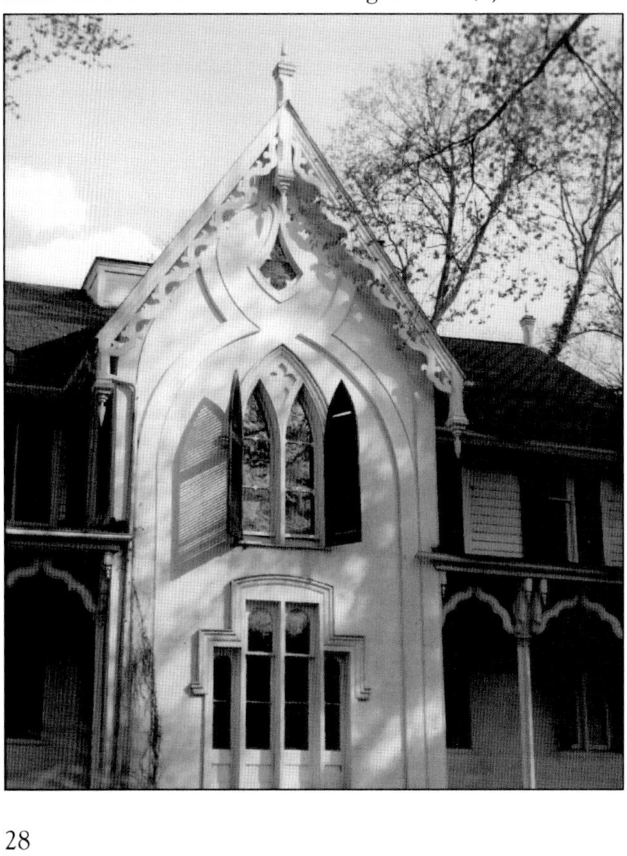

A gun-cleaning accident claimed Dr. Irvine's only son, Callendar, and his business endeavors fared so poorly that creditors split the estate between his two daughters, Margaret Biddle and Sarah Newbold. Sarah's four youngest daughters lived on in the mansion, and the last, Esther Newbold, died in 1963. This detail shows the north side of the house, which fell into disrepair and had to be torn down in 1973.

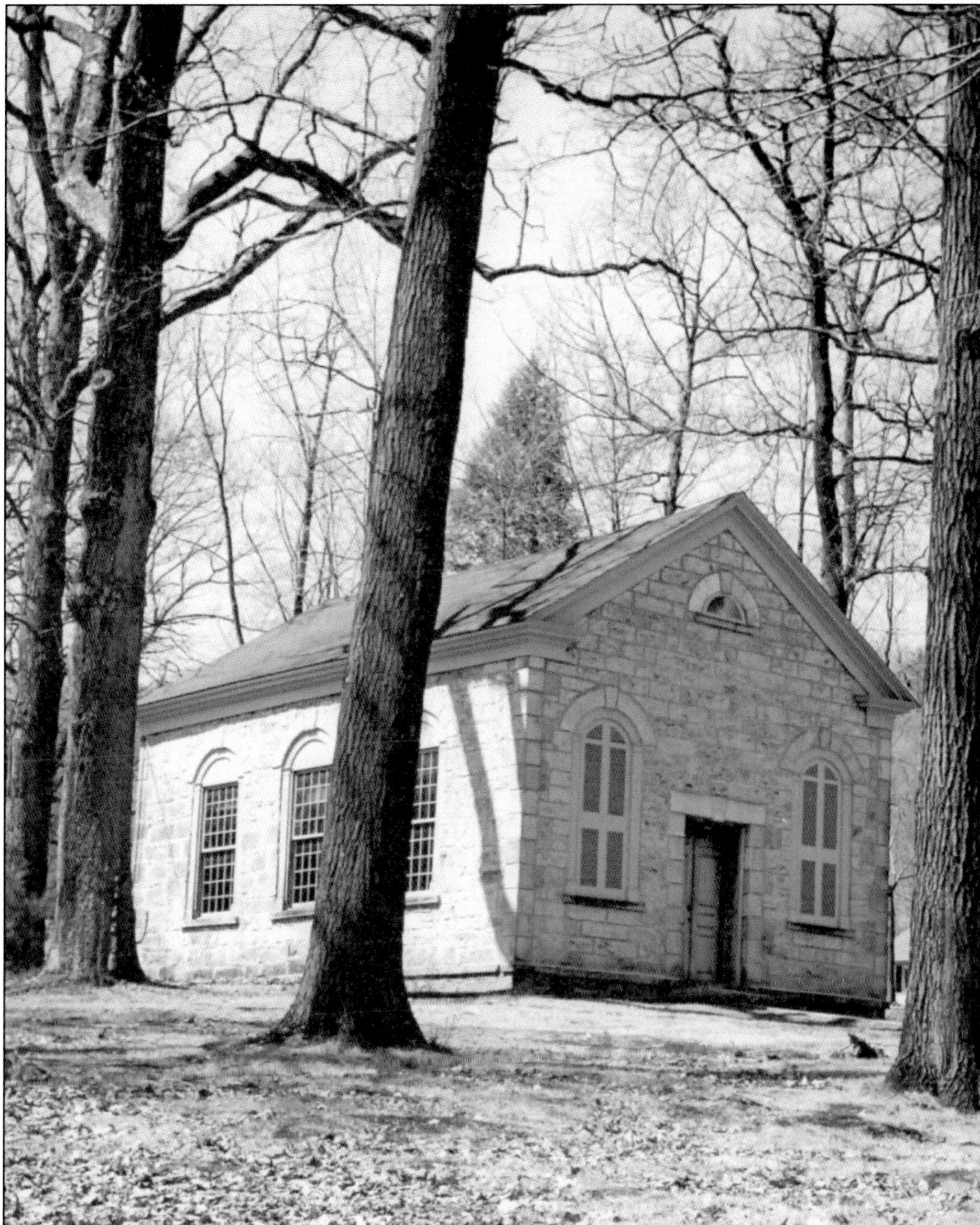

The Irvine Presbyterian Church, also known as the "Old Stone Church," was built by Scottish stonemason Robert Shortt at the behest of Sarah Duncan Irvine, wife of Dr. William A. Irvine. Sarah devoutly insisted that religion be brought to what was still a wilderness, and work began in 1838. Sadly, Sarah never saw the church's completion. The first service held in the tiny church was her funeral in 1839.

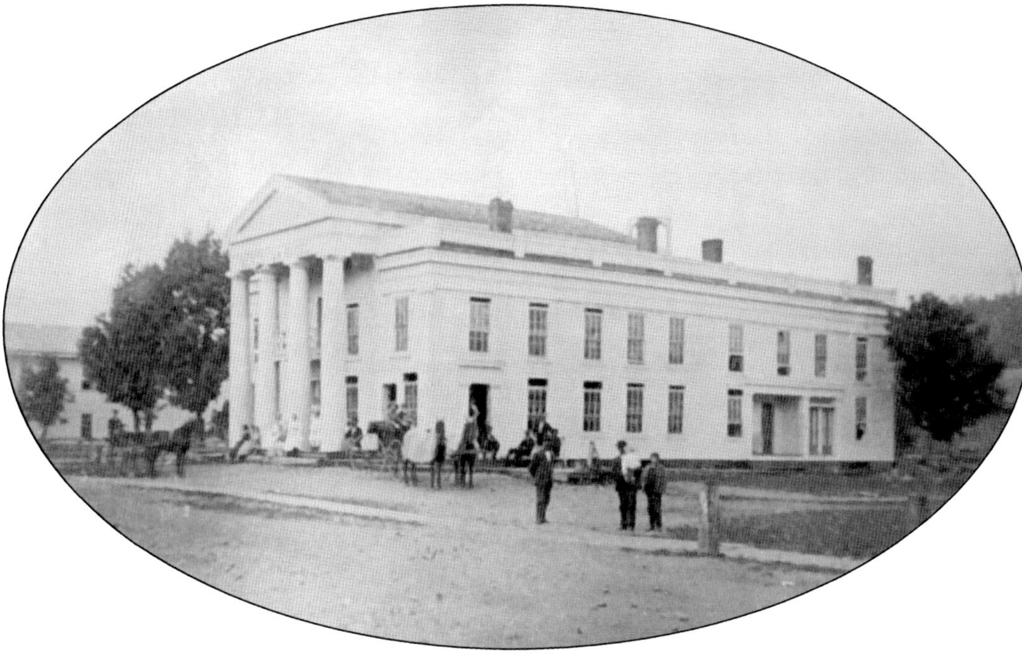

One of Warren County's early landmark buildings, the American Hotel in Youngsville stood at the corner of High Street and West Main Street. Built in 1850 by William Mead, this unique structure replaced another hotel building that had operated on the site since about 1827. The building was razed in about 1898.

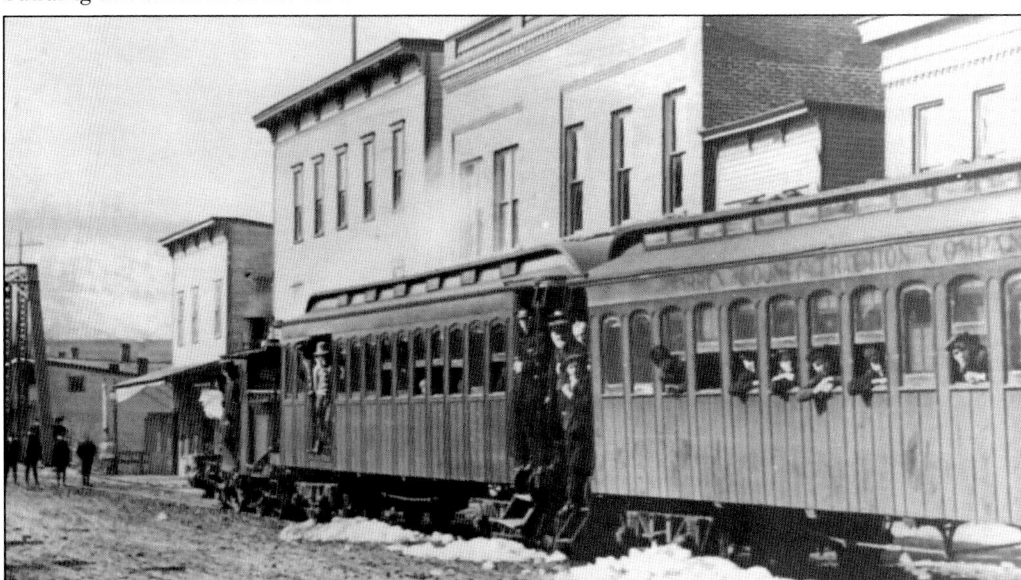

This small line connected Youngsville to Sugar Grove and was known variously as the Warren Traction Company, the Youngsville & Sugar Grove Street Railway Company, and John Day's "Dinky," after its founder. Lumbering across the 10-mile distance in about an hour, the small train reportedly consisted of former New York City elevated trains. It opened in 1903 and was in service until around 1920.

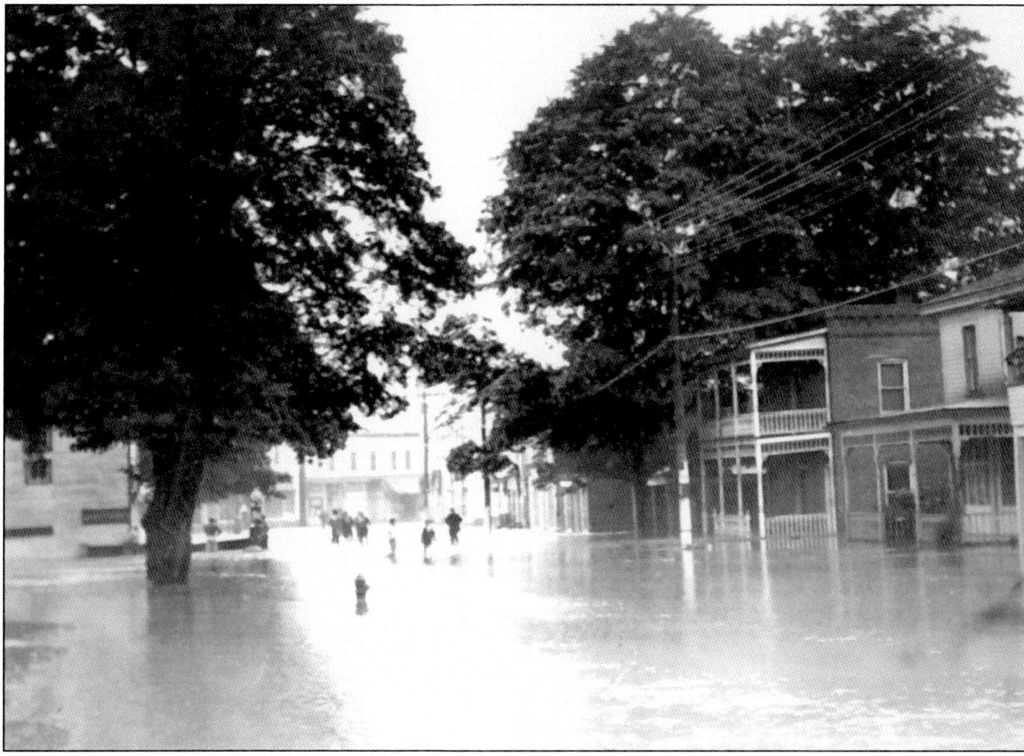

These two postcard scenes are from the June 1928 flood in Youngsville. Flooding is not uncommon in the Brokenstraw Valley, and one of the most famous floods to hit the area was the 1805 "Pumpkin Flood." That flood was so named because its high waters swept away crops, including pumpkins. That flood featured both high water and waterspouts.

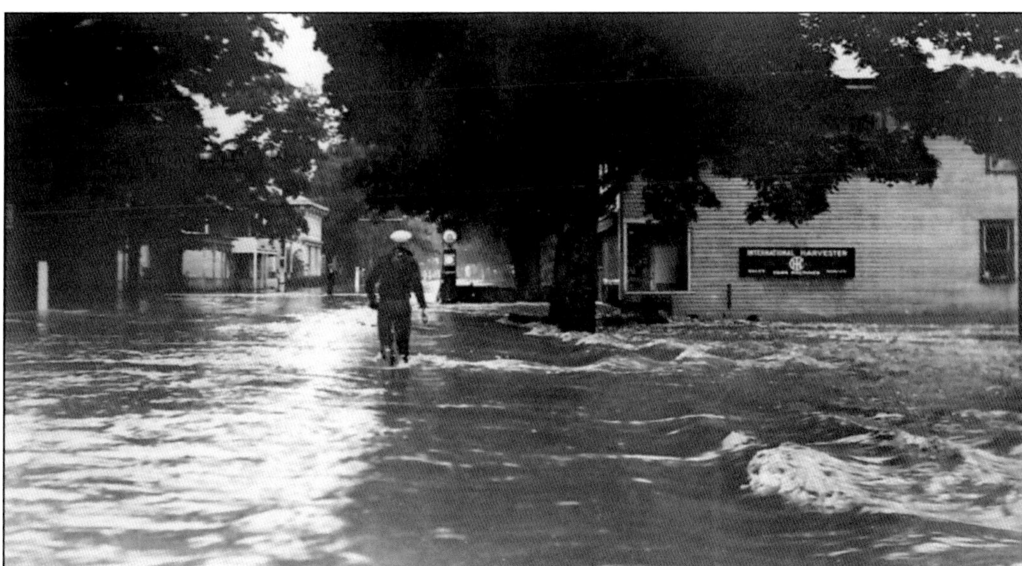

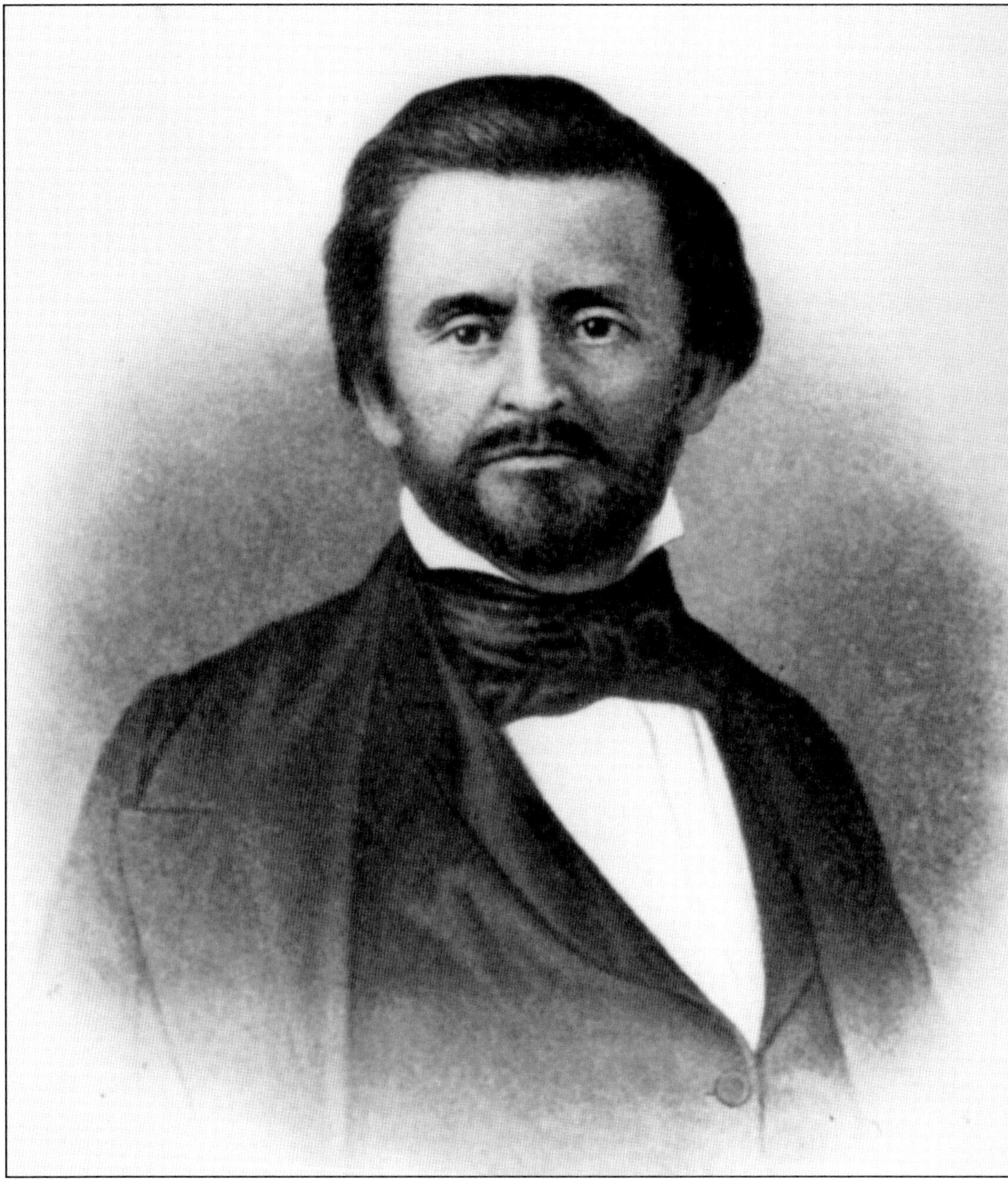

Henry Rouse came to Warren County from Mayville, New York. As a Tidioute schoolteacher, he accepted wooden shingles as payment and turned those shingles into a fortune in lumber, retail, and oil. In 1861, Rouse was severely burned in an oil explosion. On his deathbed, he dictated a will that gave money to the county to establish a home for the elderly and the indigent, now located in Brokenstraw Township.

Two

Northeast Warren County

Farmington, Pine Grove, Elk, Conewango, and Glade Townships

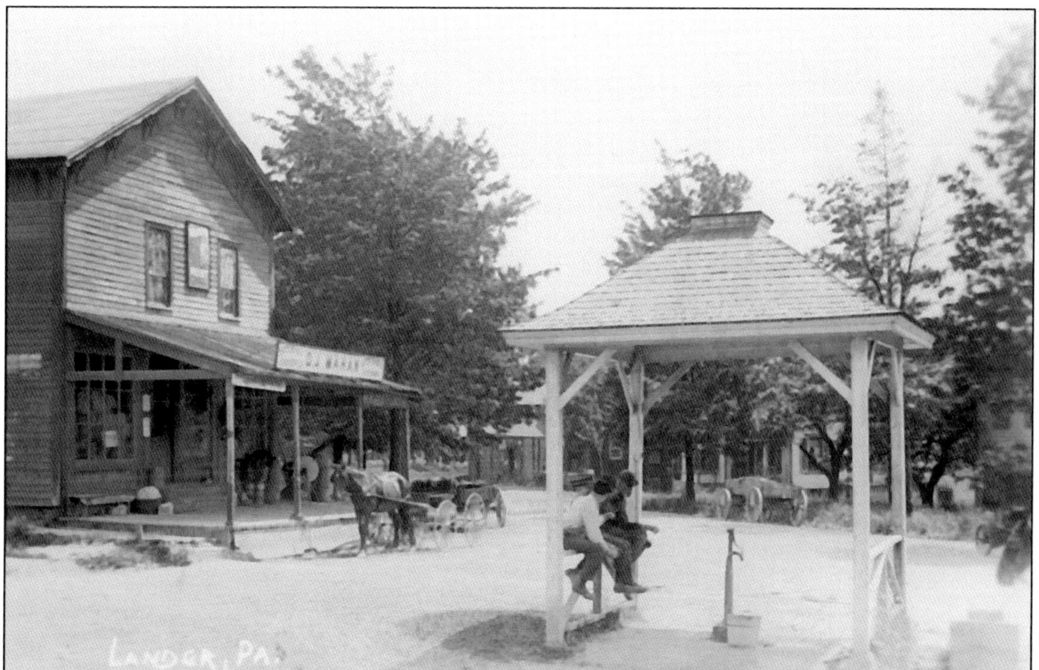

In 1946, the Lander town pump still dominated the Farmington Township crossroads, and the general store dispensed gasoline as well as groceries. But the proliferation of the automobile soon brought an end to many of these small-town amenities, except for the gas station. This store was first operated by R.E. Miller. The rear of the building housed the Lander Post Office. The business was subsequently operated by the Miller brothers and then Mahan. It functioned as a store from around 1865 to sometime in the late 1940s. The town pump proved to be a popular gathering place, as evidenced by this photograph taken around 1914. The pump remained a village icon until 1951, when it was removed. (Information provided by Rupert C. Loucks and Frank Burgett; Farmington Township photograph courtesy of Jeanette Walter.)

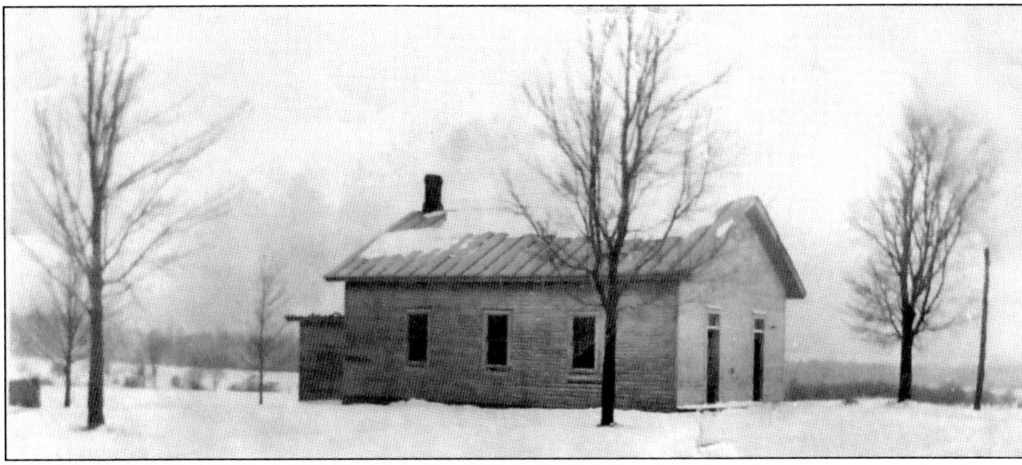

In 1805, John and Hugh Marsh built the first schoolhouse in what was then known as Marshtown. The school was built at the intersection of the Lander-Russell Road and Fairbanks Road. By 1900, there was a two-room school in Lander and eight other one-room school buildings scattered throughout the township. Between 1906 and 1907, the Lander White Wood School was moved to the Homer Preston farm and converted into a house. In 1907, a four-room brick school building, which became the Lander High School, was constructed. In 1925, a four-room addition was made to the school. This building was torn down in 1963 to make way for the new Lander Elementary School. In the meantime, construction had begun on the General Dwight D. Eisenhower High School, located near the site of the original Marshtown schoolhouse. The new high school was occupied on September 14, 1956, with the dedication ceremony taking place on April 9, 1957. (Both, Farmington Township photograph courtesy of Jeanette Walter.)

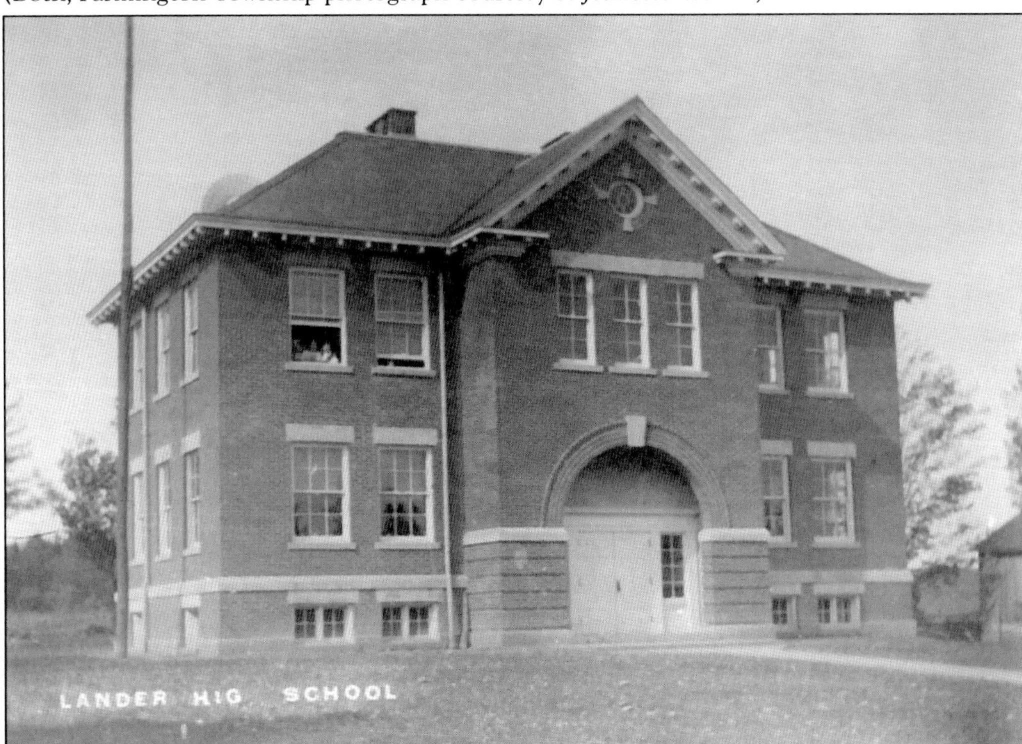

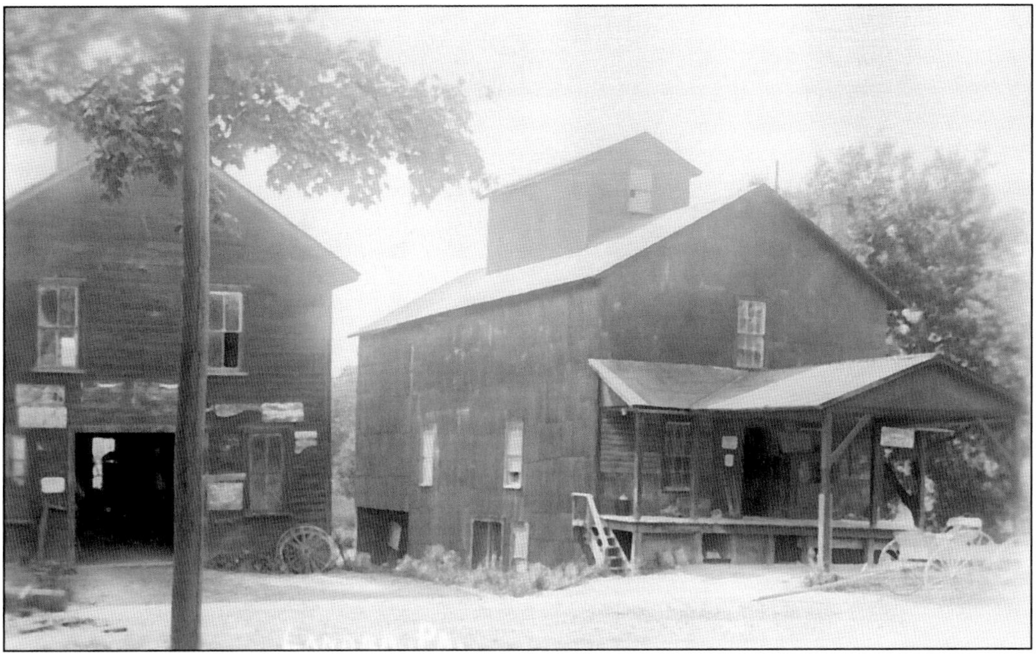

Both the blacksmith shop and gristmill were rebuilt in 1889 after a fire destroyed them on August 29, 1888. The fire started at A.R. Mix's steam sawmill and spread to Horace Mix's blacksmith shop. The fire consumed building after building, including a wagon shop and R.E. Miller's store. Hanse McKitrick rebuilt the blacksmith shop. The second floor was used for assembly and "exhibitions." The shop's last owner, Clair Putnam (who died in 1954), removed the second story. The gristmill was rebuilt by Ashbel R. Mix. The last owners-operators of the gristmill were Henry and Victor Lindell. The photograph was taken around 1917. (Information provided by Rupert C. Loucks and Frank Burgett; Farmington Township photograph courtesy of Jeanette Walter.)

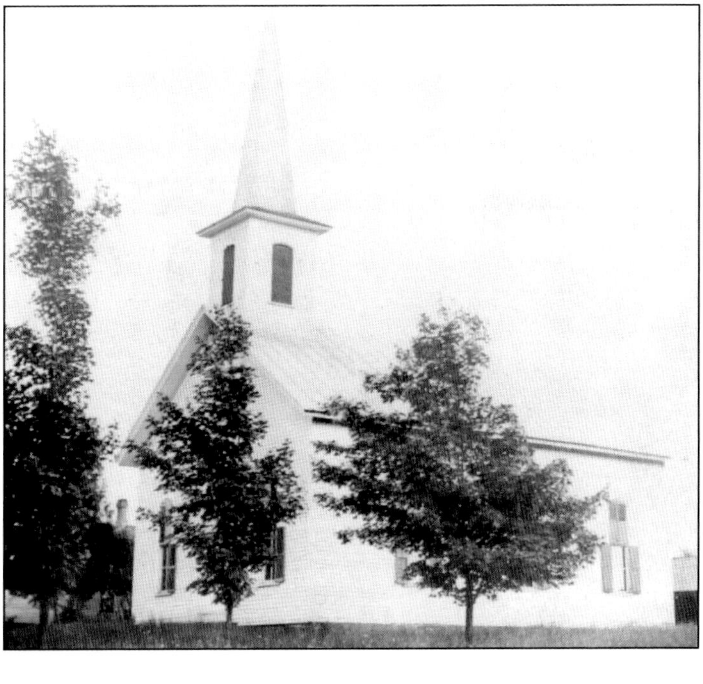

As told by Rupert C. Loucks and Frank Burgett, this church was built between 1881 and 1882 and replaced a structure that was located on the south side of Old State Road at Pond's Corners. Dedicated on June 20, 1882, the building burned in January 1909. Rather than rebuild, the congregants joined the Methodist church. The Farmington Congregational Church was located across the road from the current Lander United Methodist Church. (Farmington Township photograph courtesy of Jeanette Walter.)

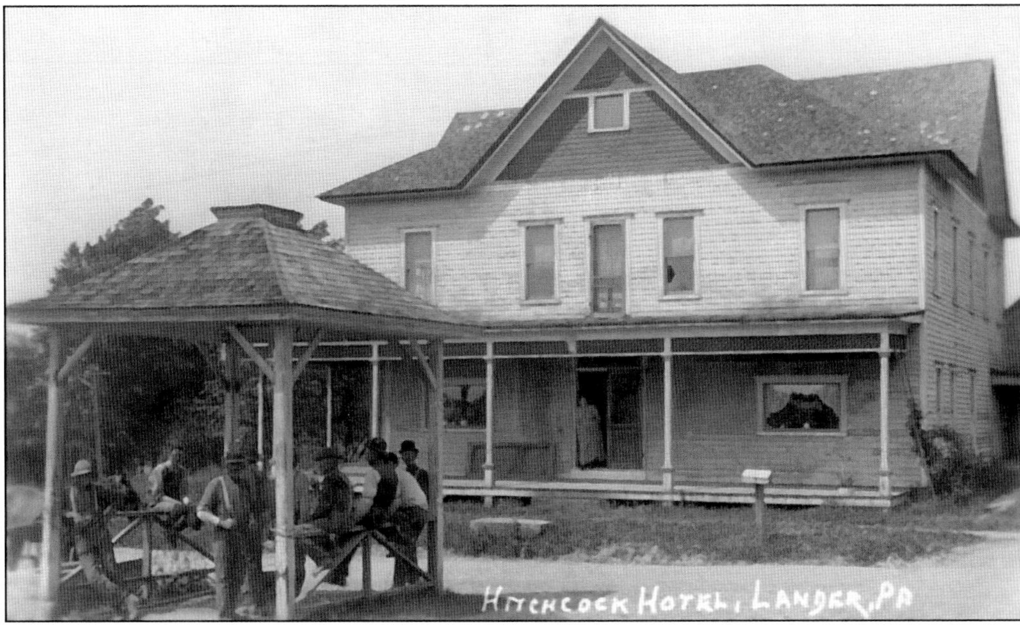

Built in about 1896, the landmark structure behind the town pump was referred to as "the hotel" throughout its life, though it functioned as such for a decade or less. It was constructed by Benjamin "Ben" Franklin and catered to travelers and transients alike. Drummers, or dry goods salesmen, were known to frequent the hotel. Card games, dinners, and a few dances were held on the premises, as well. In 1905, D.B. and Evaline Hitchcock became the owners. They used the building as a residence, taking in stray travelers when the occasion arose. The Hitchcocks' son, Stephen, eventually took over the hotel. He and his wife, Iva, installed an apartment on the west side of the building and rented the apartment out to tenants. (Farmington Township photograph courtesy of Jeanette Walter.)

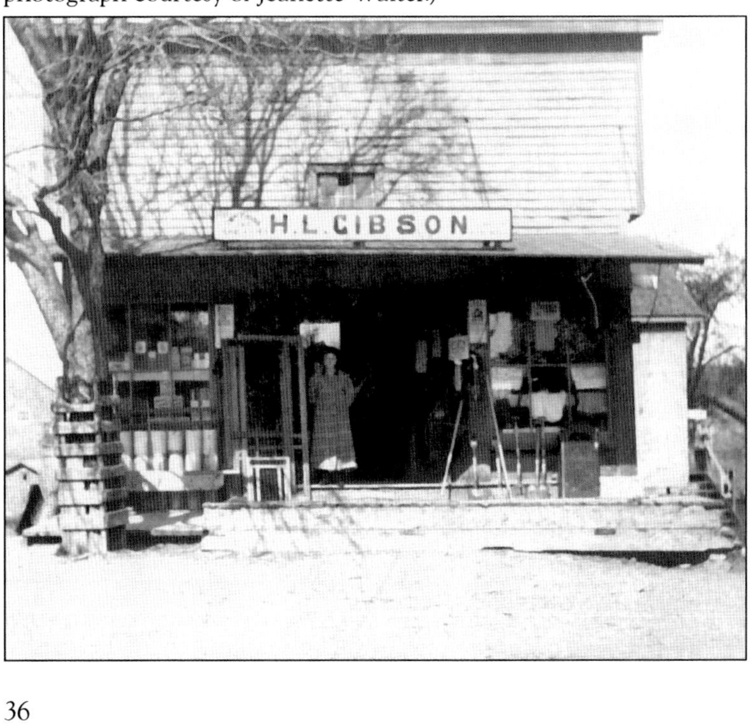

Across the street from the hotel, the H.L. Gibson Store sold dry goods and groceries to Lander residents. Previously owned by Melancthon Miles, the building burned down on September 11, 1910, when a 100-gallon oil tank in the store exploded. Shares were sold to rebuild it, and Maynard Sweeney owned it for a short time after it was rebuilt. This photograph dates from around 1911. (Farmington Township photograph courtesy of Jeanette Walter.)

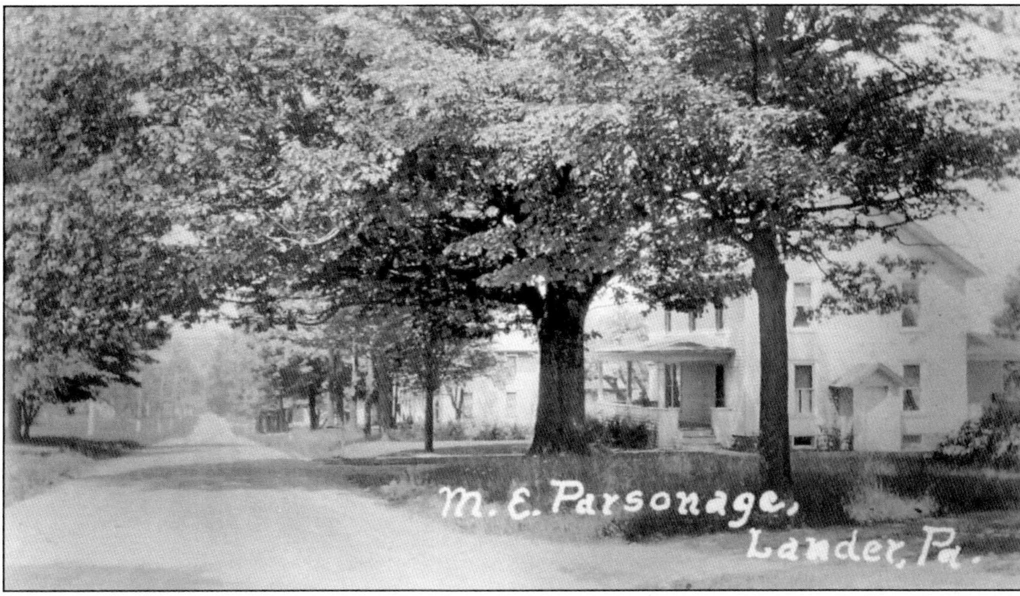

The Methodist Episcopal parsonage was originally located on North Miller Hill Road. In about 1915, the church purchased the house from E.M. Hodges for $1,250. The house was moved and rebuilt on its present location in 1926. Today, it remains the parsonage for the Lander United Methodist Church. (Information provided by Rupert C. Loucks and Frank Burgett; Farmington Township photograph courtesy of Jeanette Walter.)

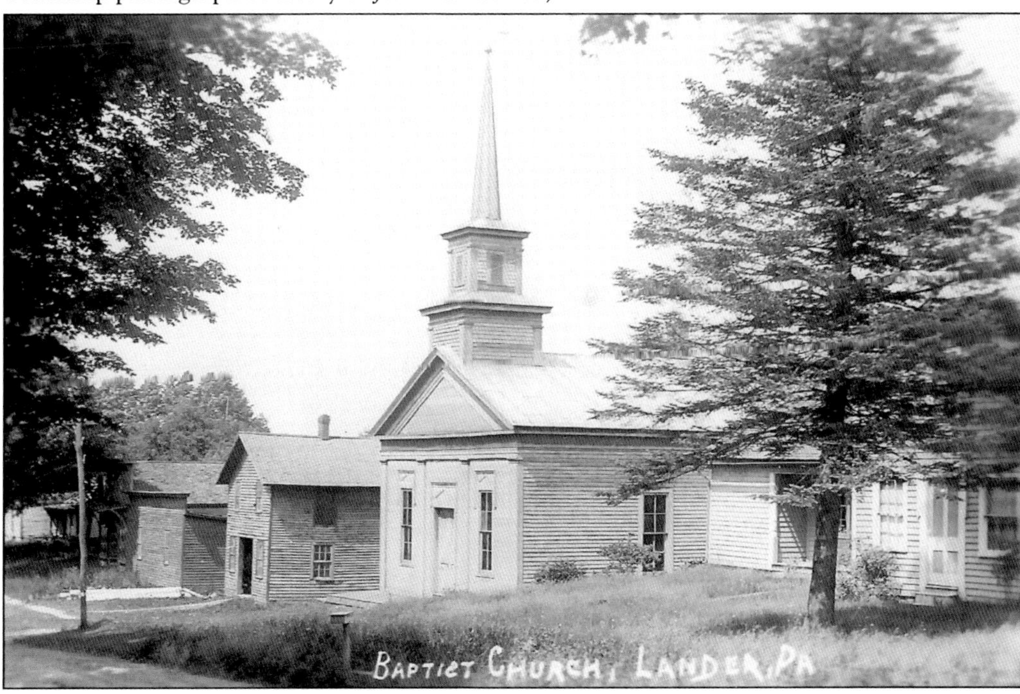

The church was originally located on Miller Hill Road. Services were discontinued sometime between 1924 and 1926. The building was then used for a school, housing second and third grades. This photograph was taken around 1917. (Farmington Township photograph courtesy of Jeanette Walter.)

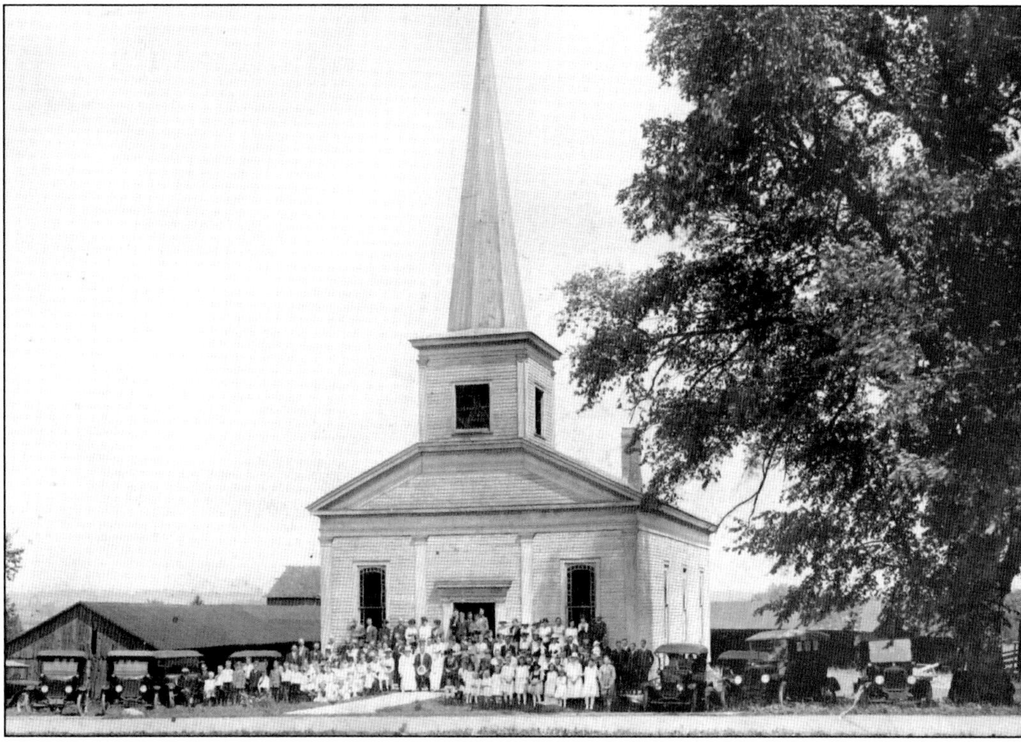

This photograph of the Methodist Episcopal church in Lander dates from around 1918. The church was built in 1861 and located on the north side of the Lander-Russell Road, in what was rapidly emerging as the recently formed Farmington Township's new economic-social center. The structure housed a new Methodist congregation formed by a merger of several older groups, most notably one on Old State Road to the east of Union Grove Cemetery. (Information provided by Rupert C. Loucks and Frank Burgett; Farmington Township photograph courtesy of Jeanette Walter.)

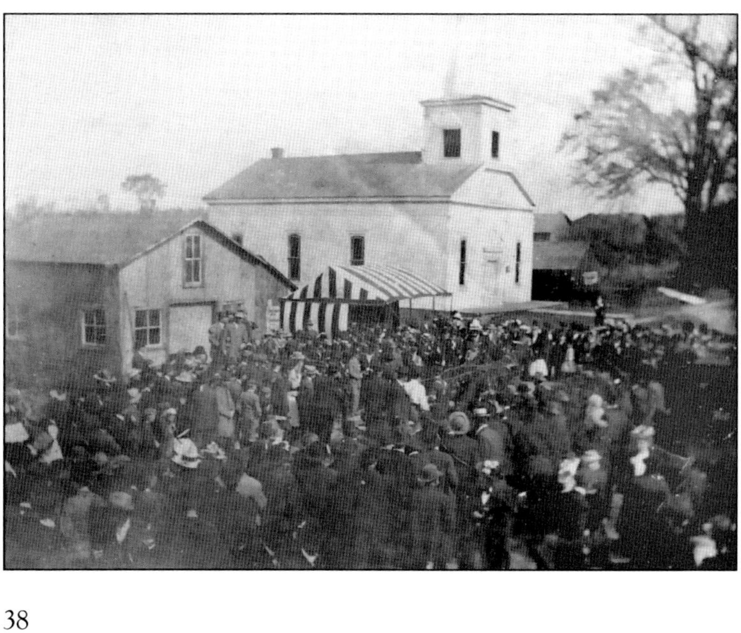

Agriculture has a deep-seated and widespread history in Farmington Township. It would naturally follow that, at some point, a fair would be held. Fairs were held in Farmington for many years as far back as 1859. In the 1930s, the attendance was the highest, with as many as 3,000 people coming. This photograph of the Lander Fair is dated 1904. (Farmington Township photograph courtesy of Jeanette Walter.)

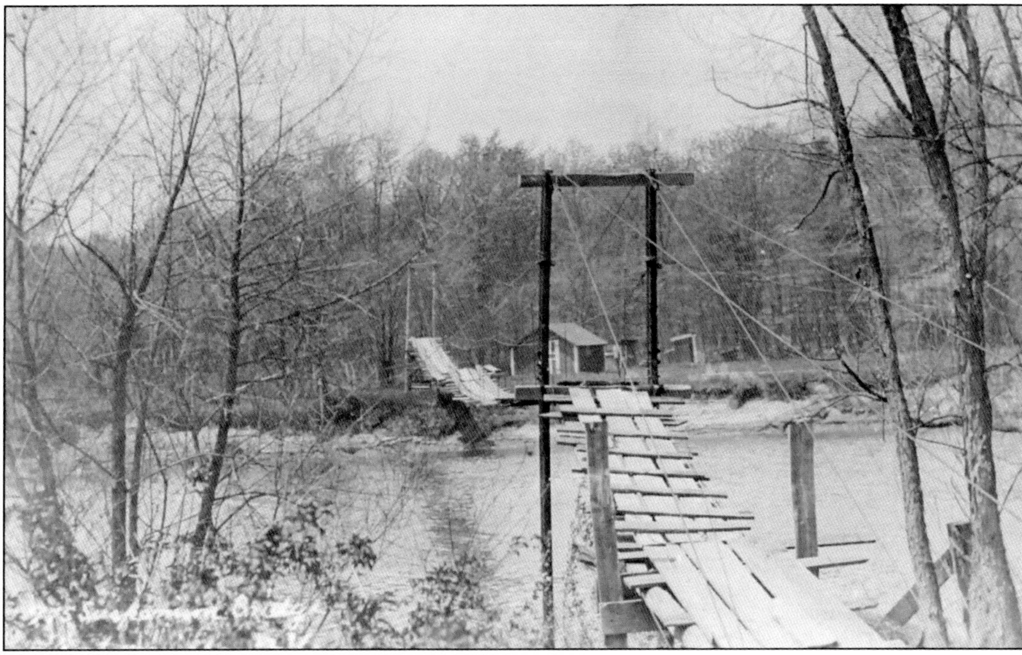

In Pine Grove Township, this swinging bridge crossed the Conewango Creek from Fentonville, New York, into Pennsylvania. Built after 1920, the bridge was used by Russell High School students and workmen going into New York until the spring of 1926, when ice and high water washed it away. It was never replaced. (Courtesy of Pine Grove Township.)

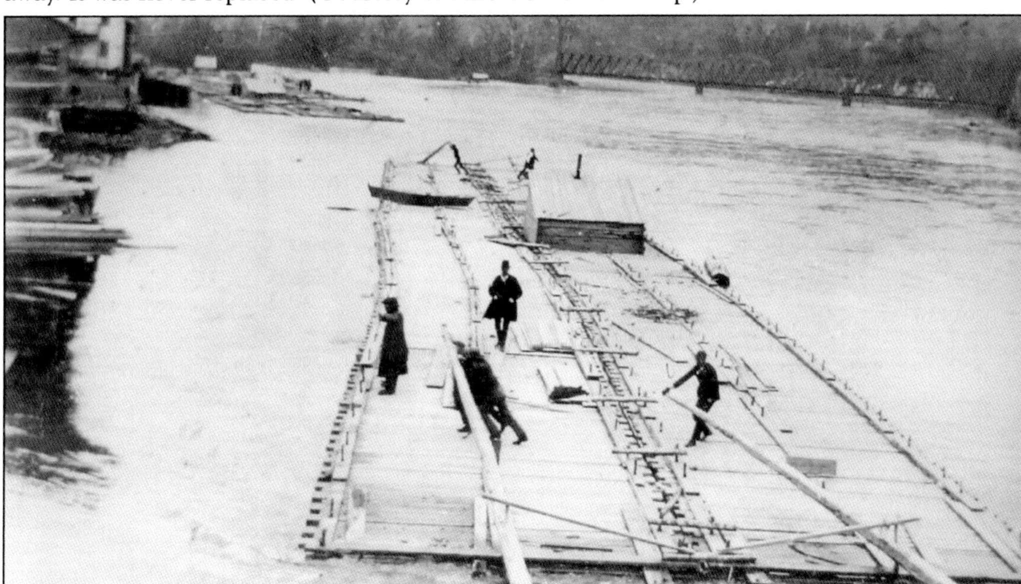

Lumbering thrived in Pine Grove Township, with much virgin white pine harvested. Cut in the fall and winter and skidded to the mills, the logs were sawed into boards and made into rafts. Rafting season in the spring made Russell a busy place. Rafts were often backed up two miles above Russell waiting their turn to go down the creek. The village was full of pilots and raft hands getting ready for the journey. The photograph depicts two Conewango rafts at Warren, where a third would be added to make up an Allegheny raft that would be sent on its way to Pittsburgh.

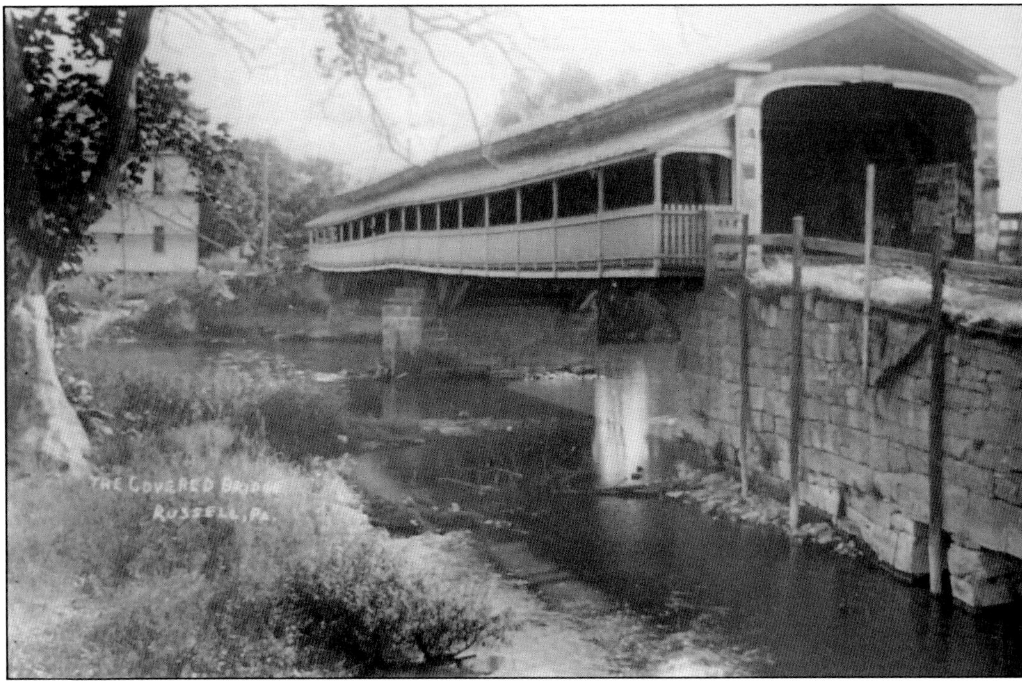

This covered bridge was built over the Conewango Creek in Russell by Ferdinand Perkins Sr. and his son in 1853. White pine timbers used in the arches and uprights, as well as other parts of the structure, were from trees that grew on the east side of the creek. The covered walkway on the north side of the bridge was added in 1900. The bridge was razed in 1937.

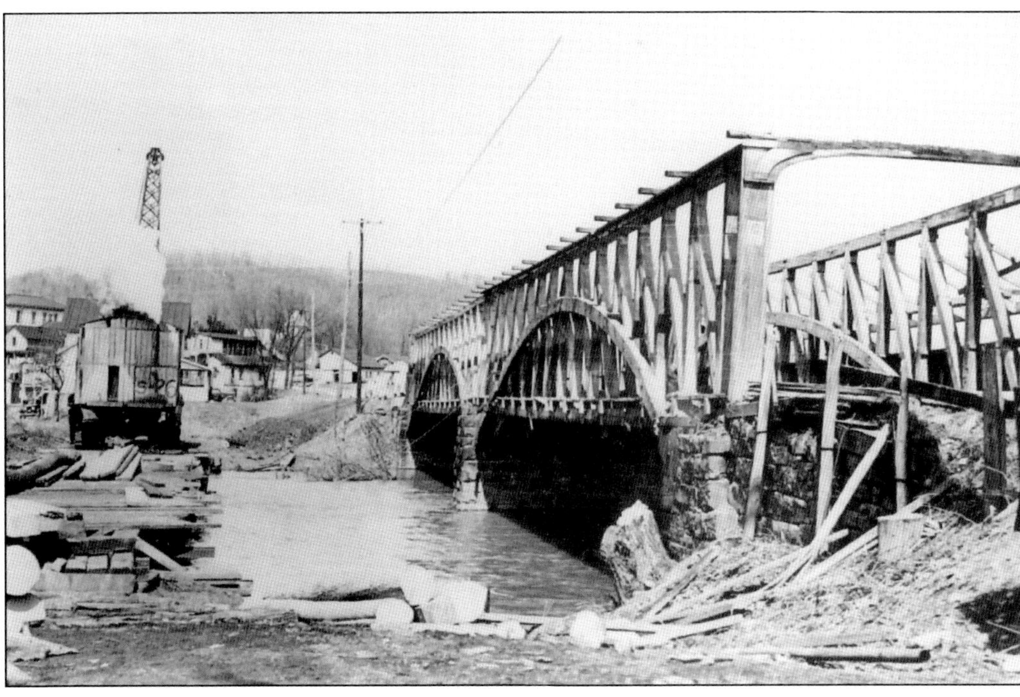

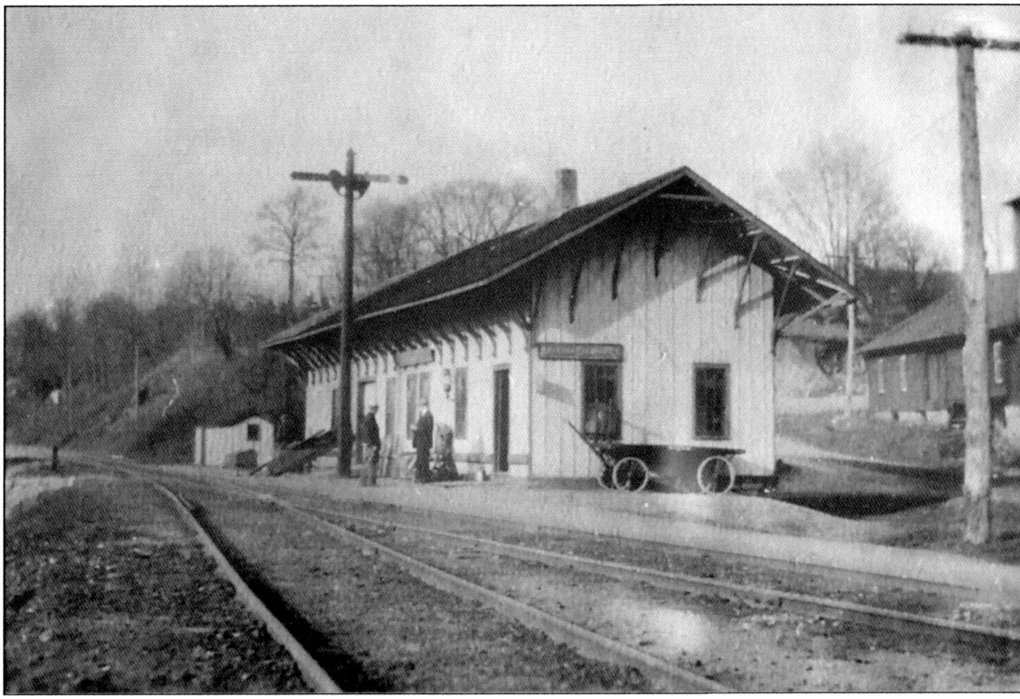

Russell's railroad station was built in the early 1870s by the Dunkirk, Allegheny Valley & Pittsburgh Railroad and razed about 1960. The last passenger train stopped in the village on July 12, 1937. Freight service continued for some years.

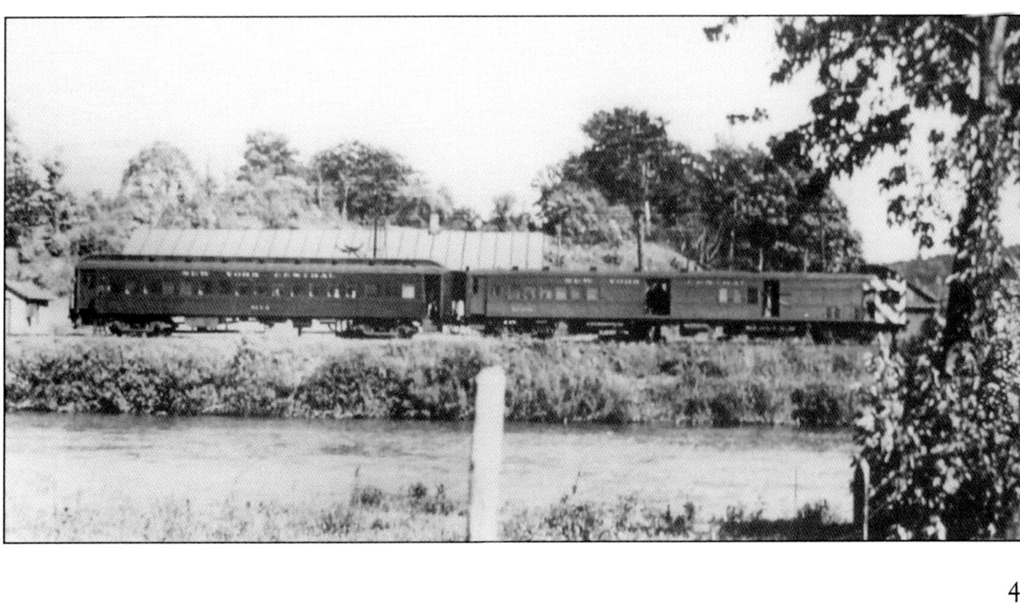

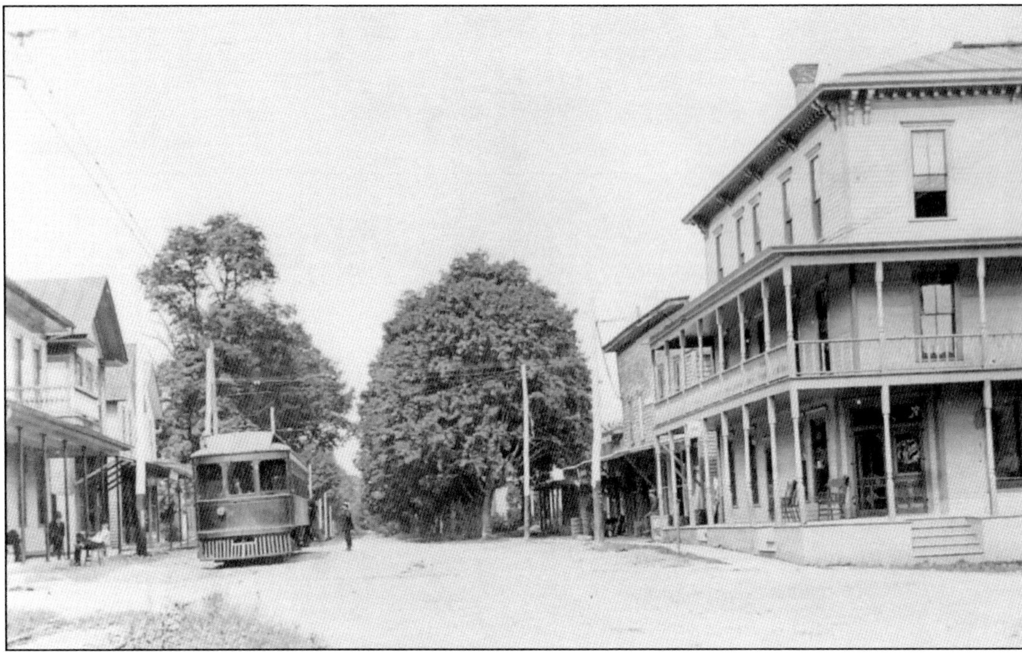

By 1905, a new form of transportation came to Pine Grove Township—the Warren & Jamestown Street Railway Co. The streetcar line went from Warren through North Warren, Russell, Akeley, Fentonville, and Frewsburg, New York, and on to Jamestown, with 53 designated stops along the way. The cars traveled along the west side of the Conewango Creek up through Russell's Main Street. Going north, the line made a right turn and crossed the bridge toward Akeley and then turned left to head into New York. Cars carried passengers and freight. A complete run from Warren to Jamestown with no stops took 47 minutes. Cars could travel up to 50 miles per hour.

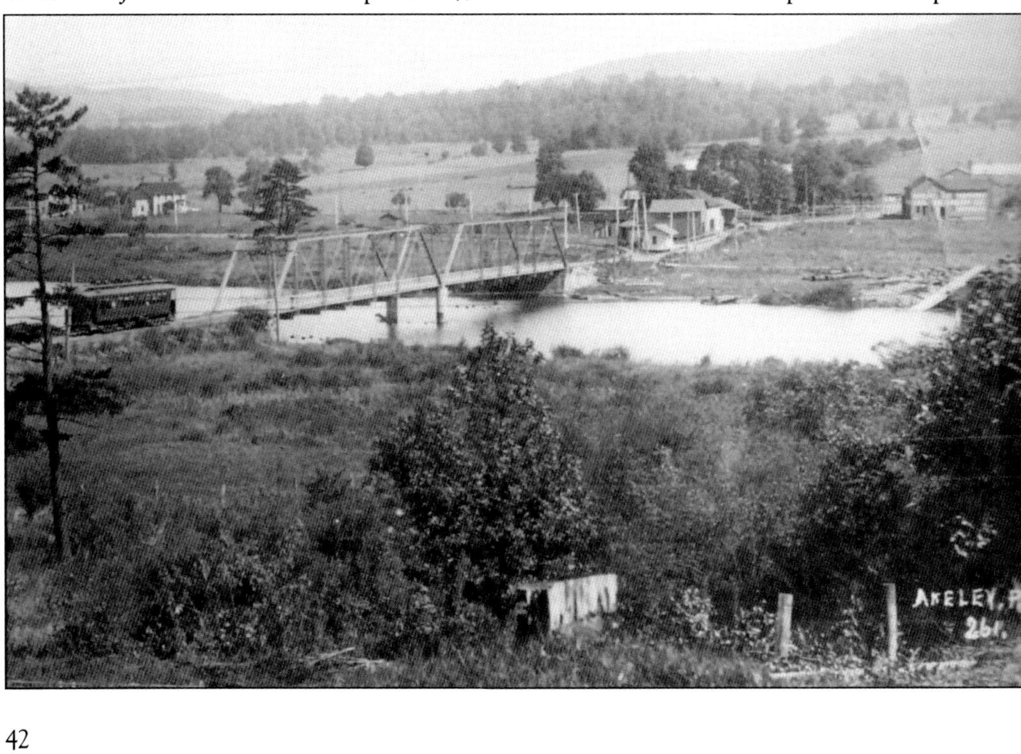

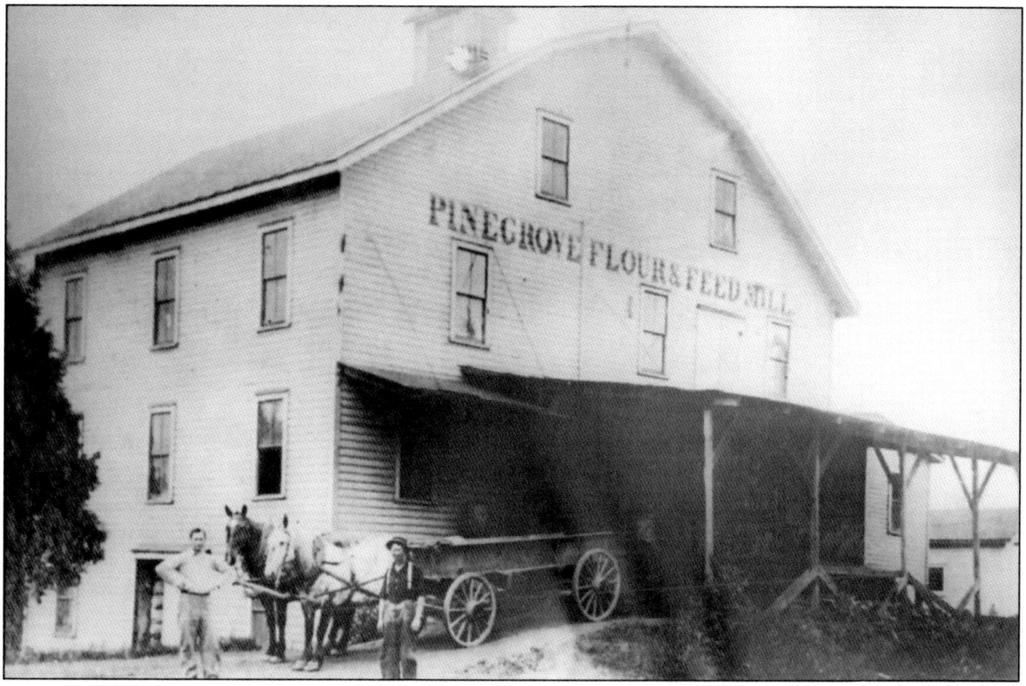

The townships had gristmills to grind farmers' grain into flour and feed. The Pine Grove Flour & Feed Mill was owned and operated by the Fred Thompson family. This four-story mill operated from 1907 to 1937.

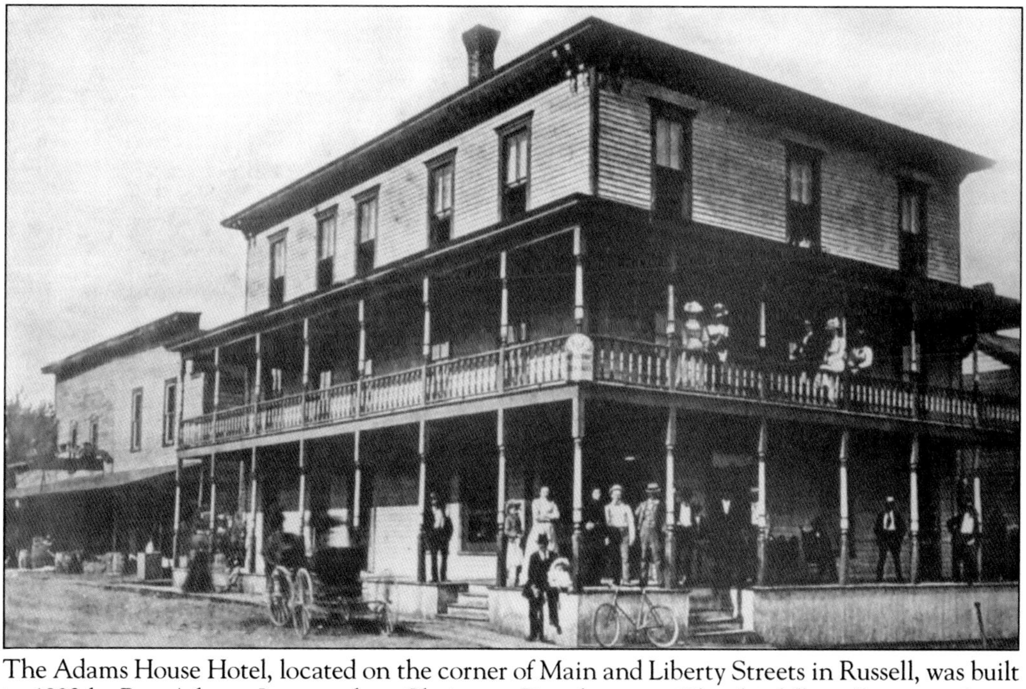
The Adams House Hotel, located on the corner of Main and Liberty Streets in Russell, was built in 1893 by Roy Adams. It opened on Christmas Day that year. The third floor (later gone) was where the Russell chapter of the Independent Order of Odd Fellows (IOOF) would gather. The first-floor spaces housed many grocery stores until the spaces joined to form a hardware store.

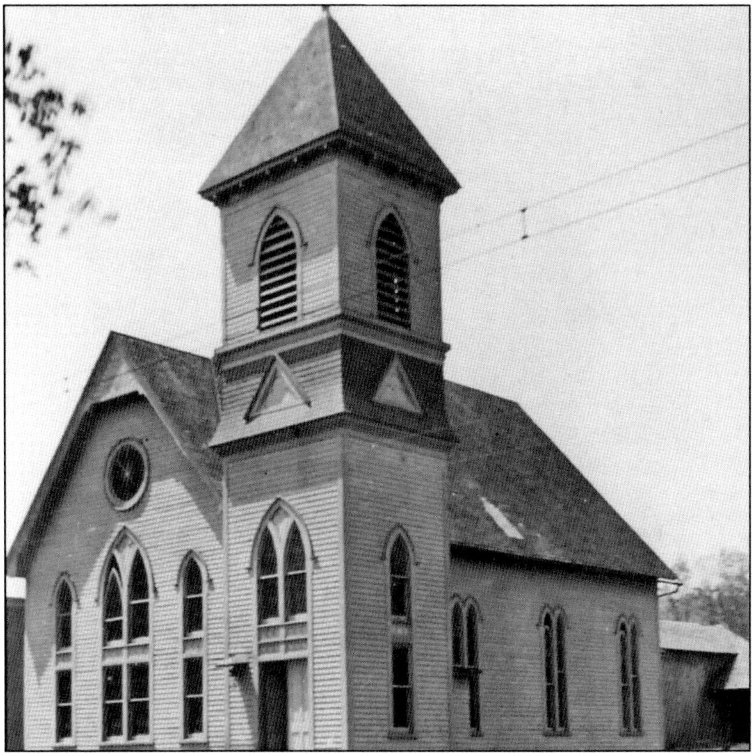

Russell Methodist Episcopal Church on Main Street was built in 1854. This structure was initially called the Russell Union Church as several denominations used it for services. Extensive remodeling had begun in 1903, including the erection of the steeple shown here.

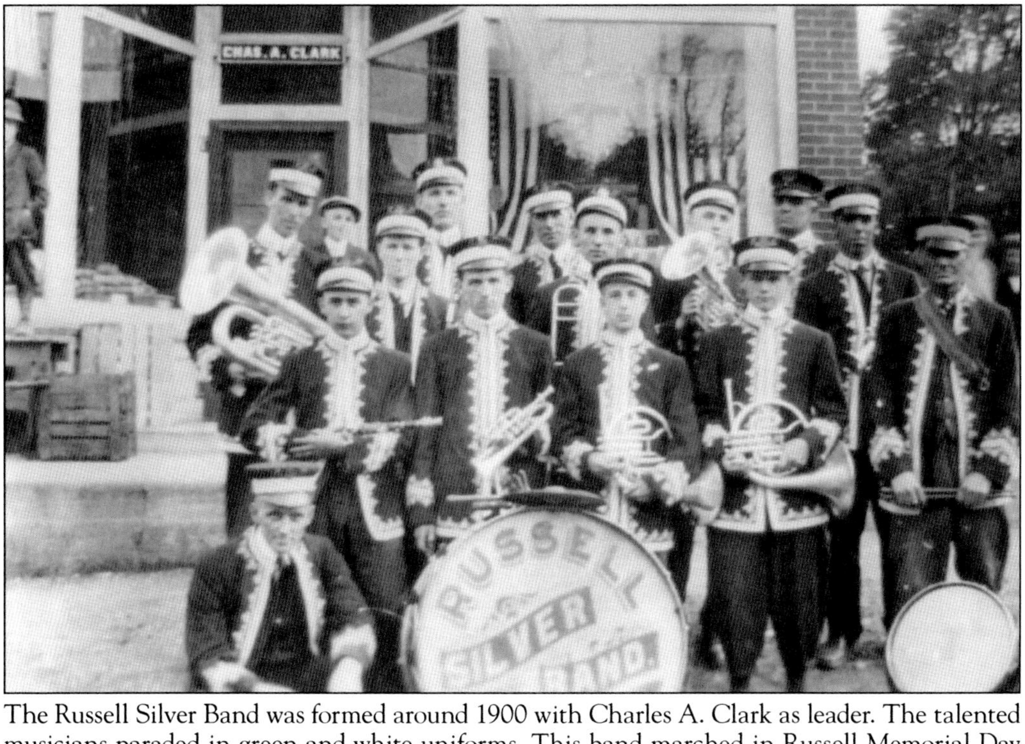

The Russell Silver Band was formed around 1900 with Charles A. Clark as leader. The talented musicians paraded in green-and-white uniforms. This band marched in Russell Memorial Day parades and special occasions into the 1930s.

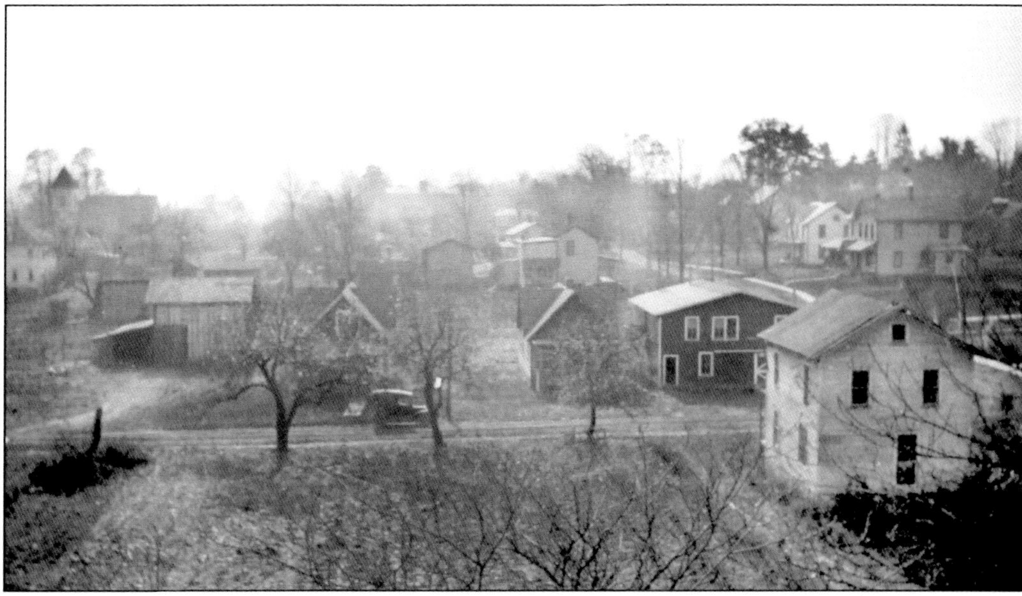

In this c. 1915 view of Russell looking south, State Street is in the foreground, Pine Street is on the right, and Main Street is located on the far left. Note the steeple added to the Methodist church in 1903. (Courtesy of the Harold C. Putnam collection.)

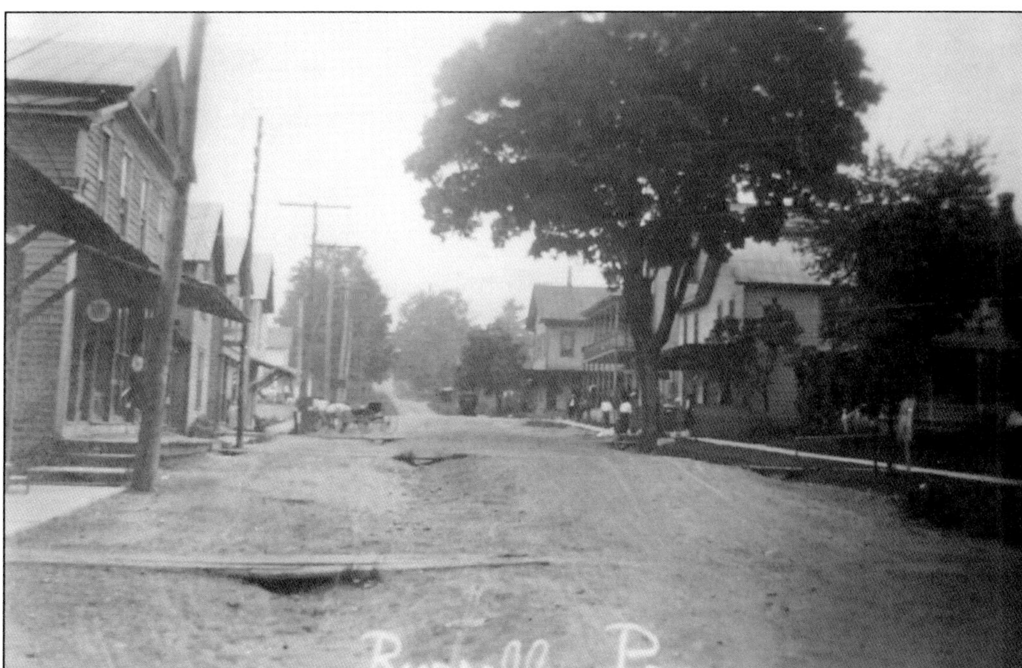

This is a postcard image with a view looking north on Liberty Street in Russell.

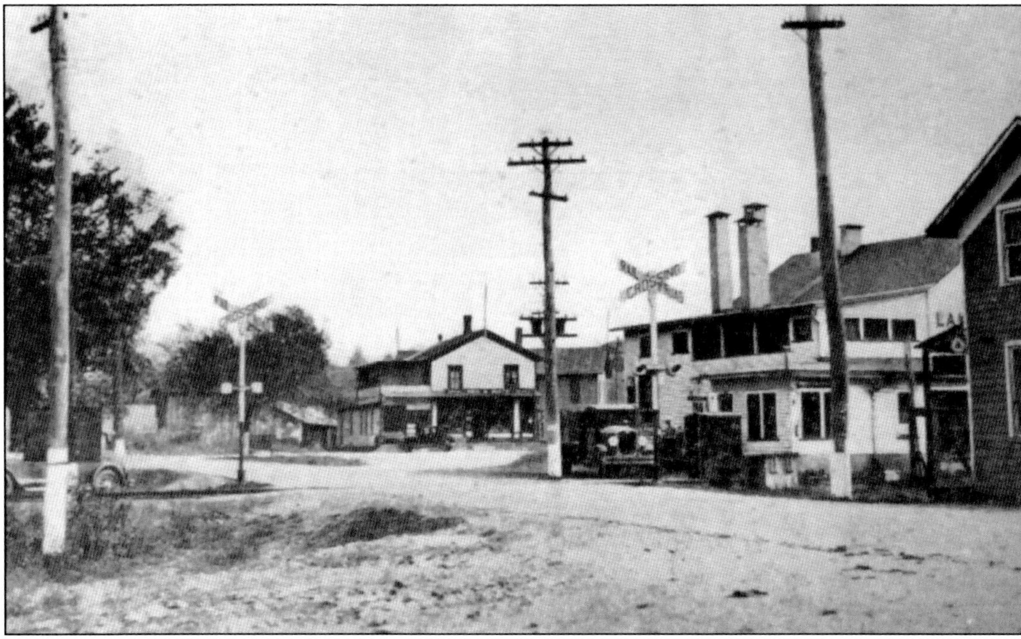

This photograph of Akeley was taken about 1928. Pictured, beginning from the left, are the Hale grocery, the Lake Shore Creamery, and the Akeley Post Office. The Lake Shore Creamery in downtown Akeley was owned by the Randalls from 1910 to 1945.

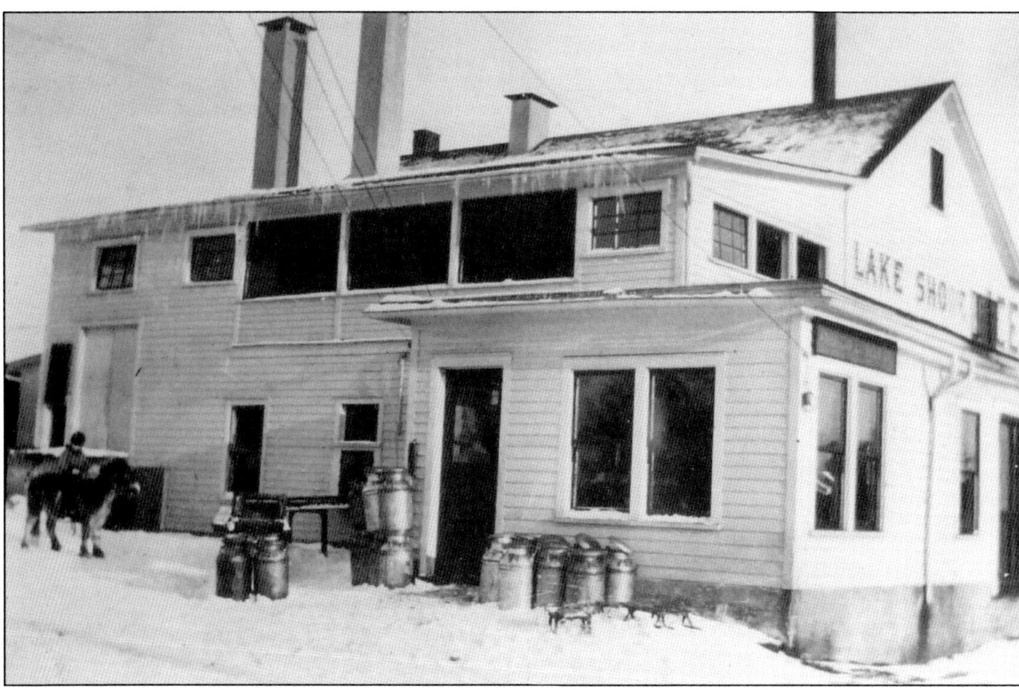

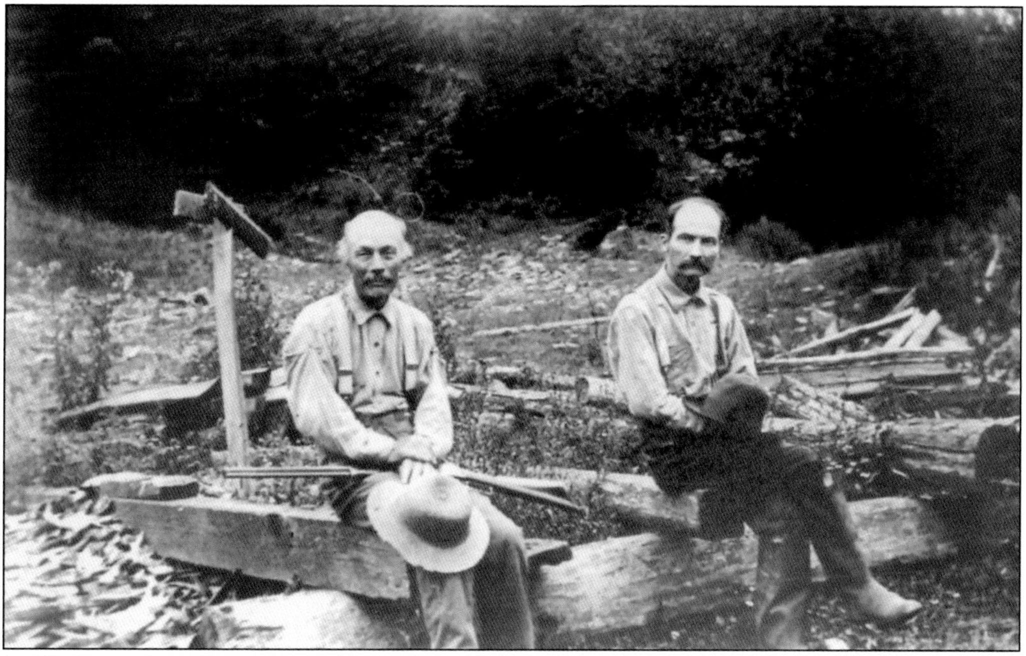

In Elk Township, Philemon (left) and John Robert Grannis, sons of William and Almyra, lived near the State Line Run area in the northern part of the township in the late 1800s and early 1900s. They were lumbermen and farmers.

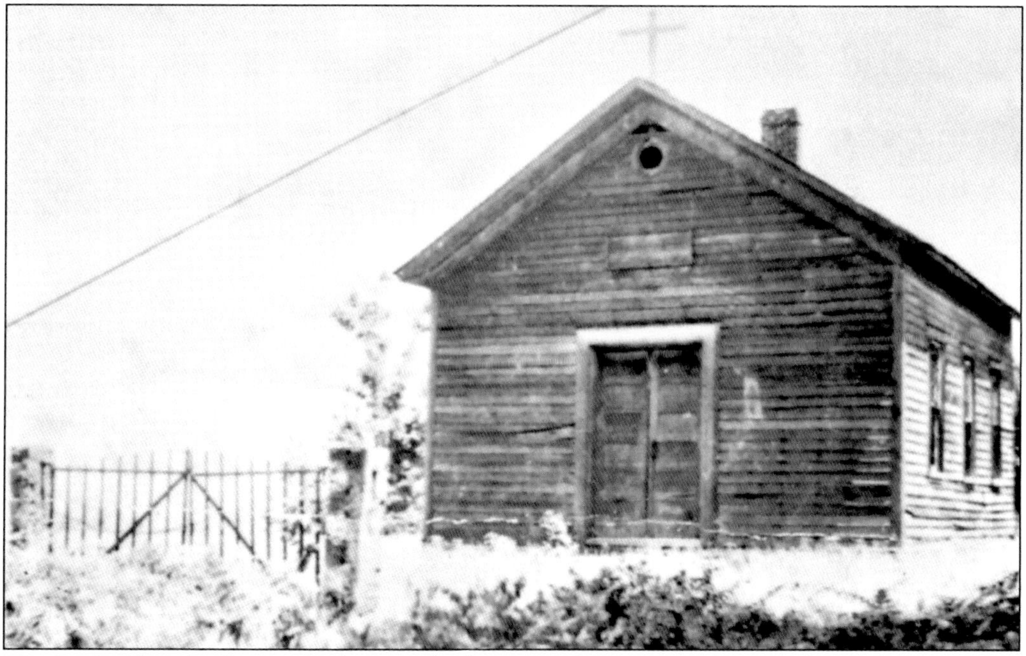

The Little Church of Seven Dolors was built in 1874 by Swan Erickson and torn down in 1941. It was the first Catholic church established outside Warren city limits. The salvageable lumber was taken to Bradford to build a private home. The Irish Catholic families who came to Quaker Hill were patrons of the church and were buried near it, where their tombstones are now visible, surrounded by the stone posts around the cemetery.

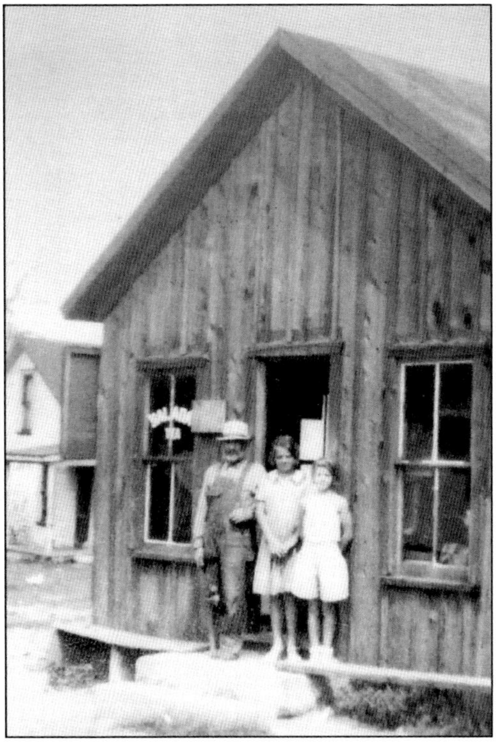

The Dodge School building was built near the Allegheny River in 1834 and closed around 1904. It was rebuilt by Charles Martin and Jim Lounsbury in the 1870s. Sometime around 1920, John Chinberg moved the school to Peterson Road and used it as a grocery store and harness shop. The picture shows John Chinberg (left), Marie Mack (center), and Gerissa Westfall standing in front of the building.

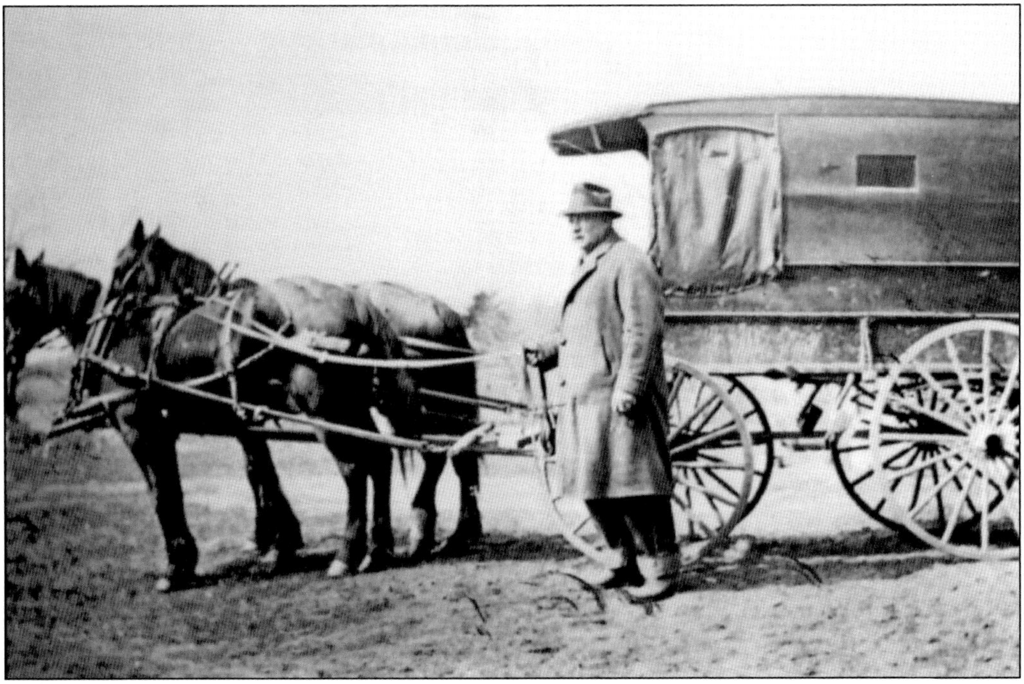

Mack Brainard was one of the drivers who drove the school "bus" to transport the children to the Friendship School. The wheels were replaced with sleds during the winter to enable the team to pull it through the snow. Lanterns were used to keep the children warm, and blankets were placed over their knees.

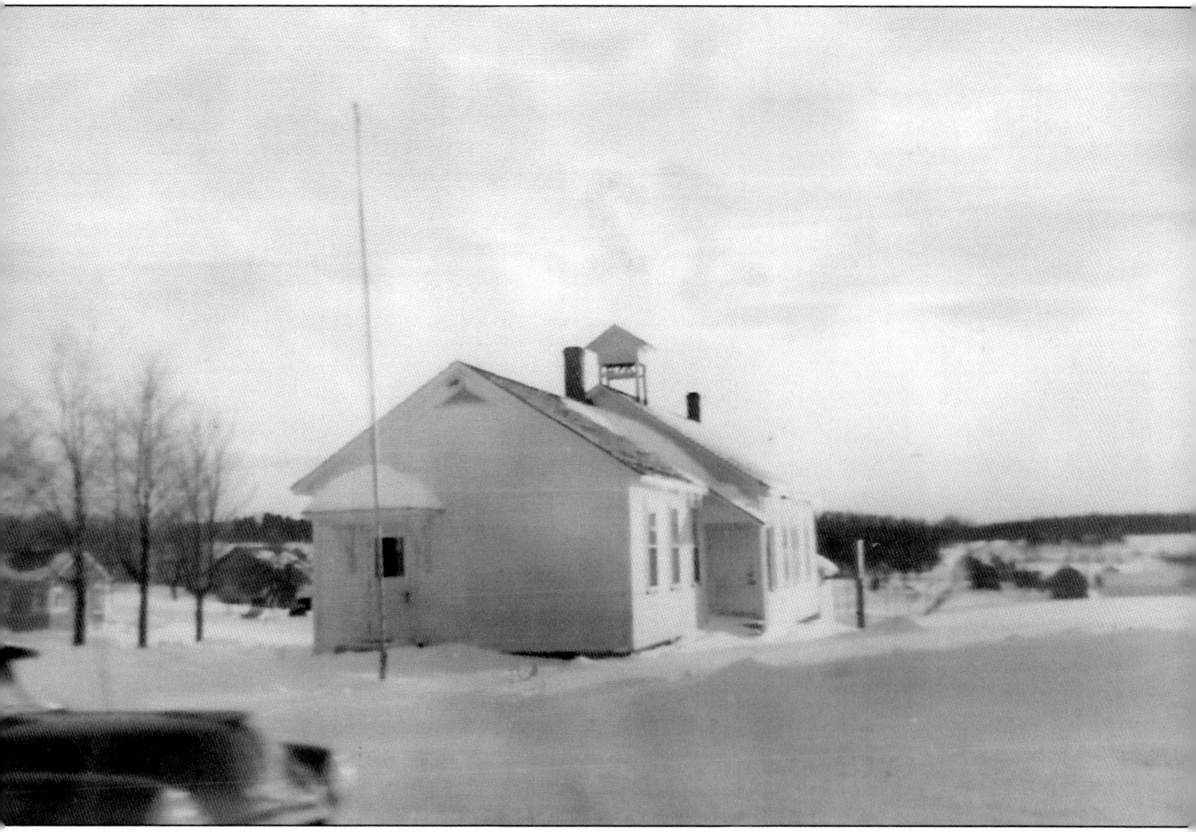

The school at Scandia Corners was opened in the late 1870s and operated continuously until 2000, serving residents of Elk Township for over a century. It is one of 12 one-room schools that were once located in Elk Township. One can see the school bell in the cupola, the chimney of the wood-burning stove, and the outhouse. Today, the original one-room school has been restored to its original appearance by volunteers from the Elk Township Historical Society.

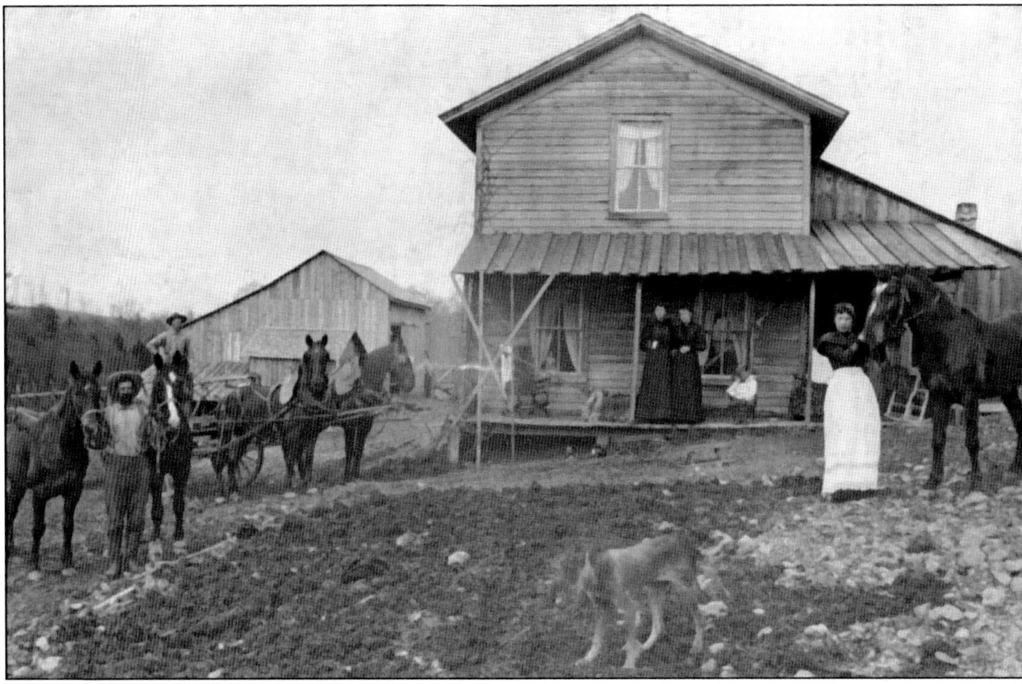

The Roper family farm was located on the banks of the Allegheny River in Elk Township. The Ropers settled here in 1832, and their descendants lived here for over a century, keeping the farm in production until it was inundated by the rising water of Kinzua Lake, when the dam was built in the 1960s. The woman holding the horse rein on the right is Tillie Carlson, the man on the left is Andrew Bennett, and the child is George Manley Bennett, born in 1889.

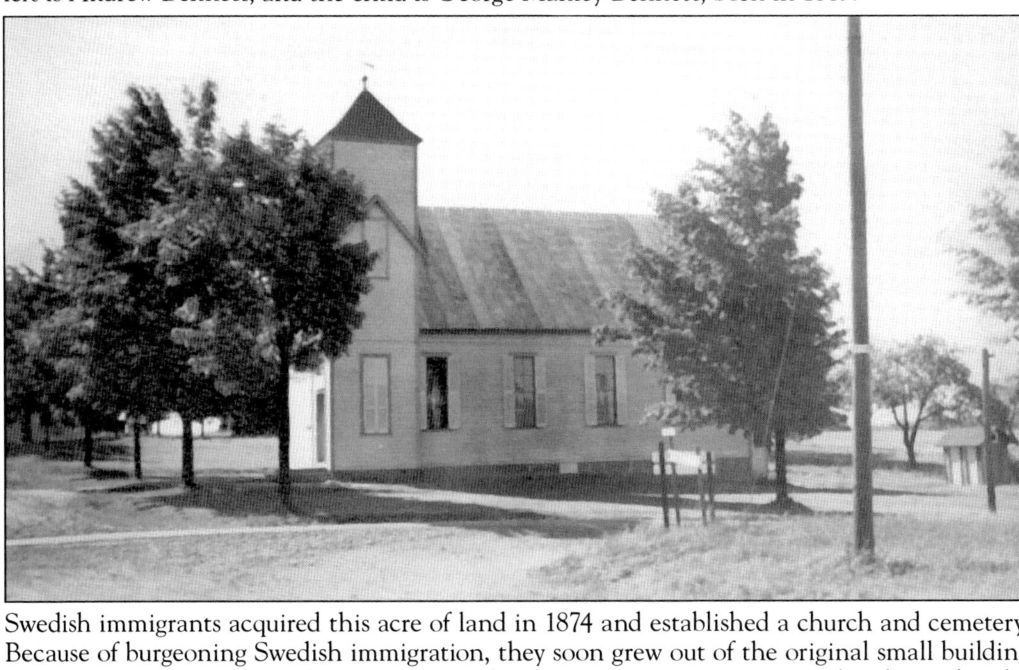

Swedish immigrants acquired this acre of land in 1874 and established a church and cemetery. Because of burgeoning Swedish immigration, they soon grew out of the original small building and built this sanctuary in the late 1870s. It has been in continuous use to this day and is the oldest sanctuary in the Covenant denomination.

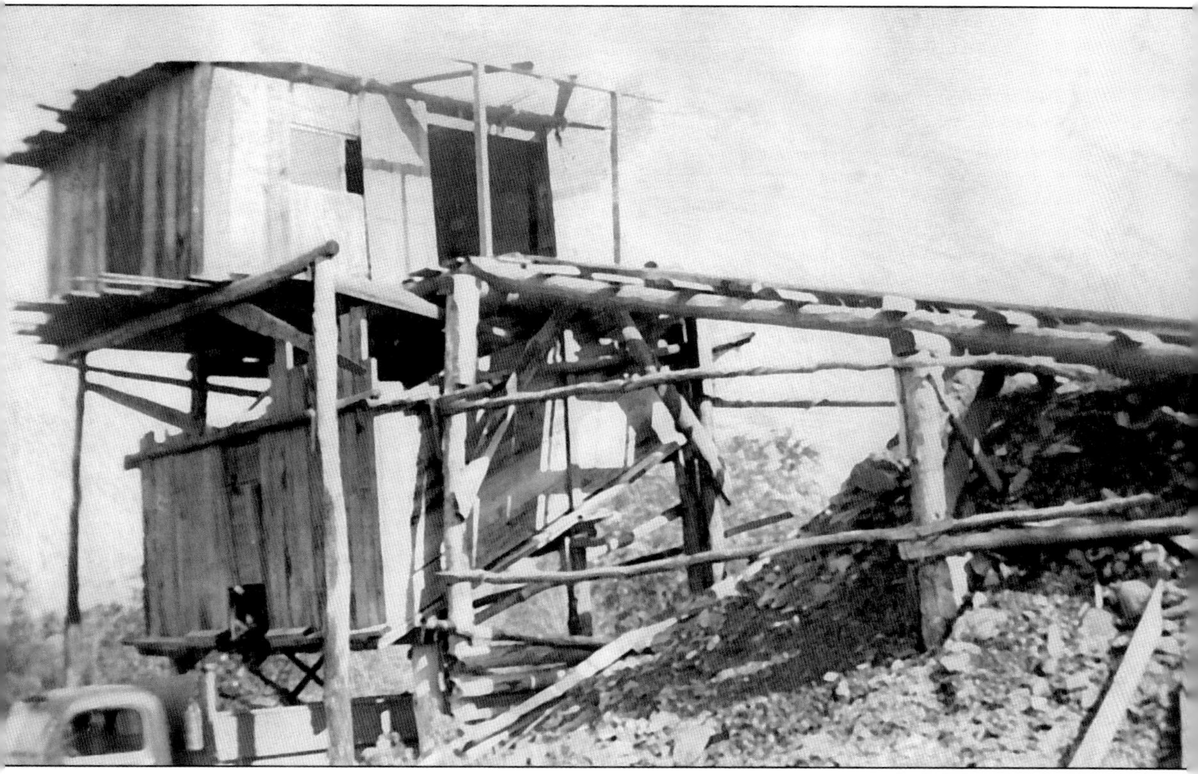

In 1834, Pond Curtis discovered coal as he was digging a well near what is now known as Coalbed Road in Scandia. The mine operated for about 100 years, with its longest proprietors being members of the Dinsmoor family, David and his son Silas. As the veins are near the surface, the mineshafts were fairly shallow. The quality of the coal was quite soft and produced a lot of smoke. The mine ceased to operate after the 1940s. (Courtesy of Ernest Hoag Jr.)

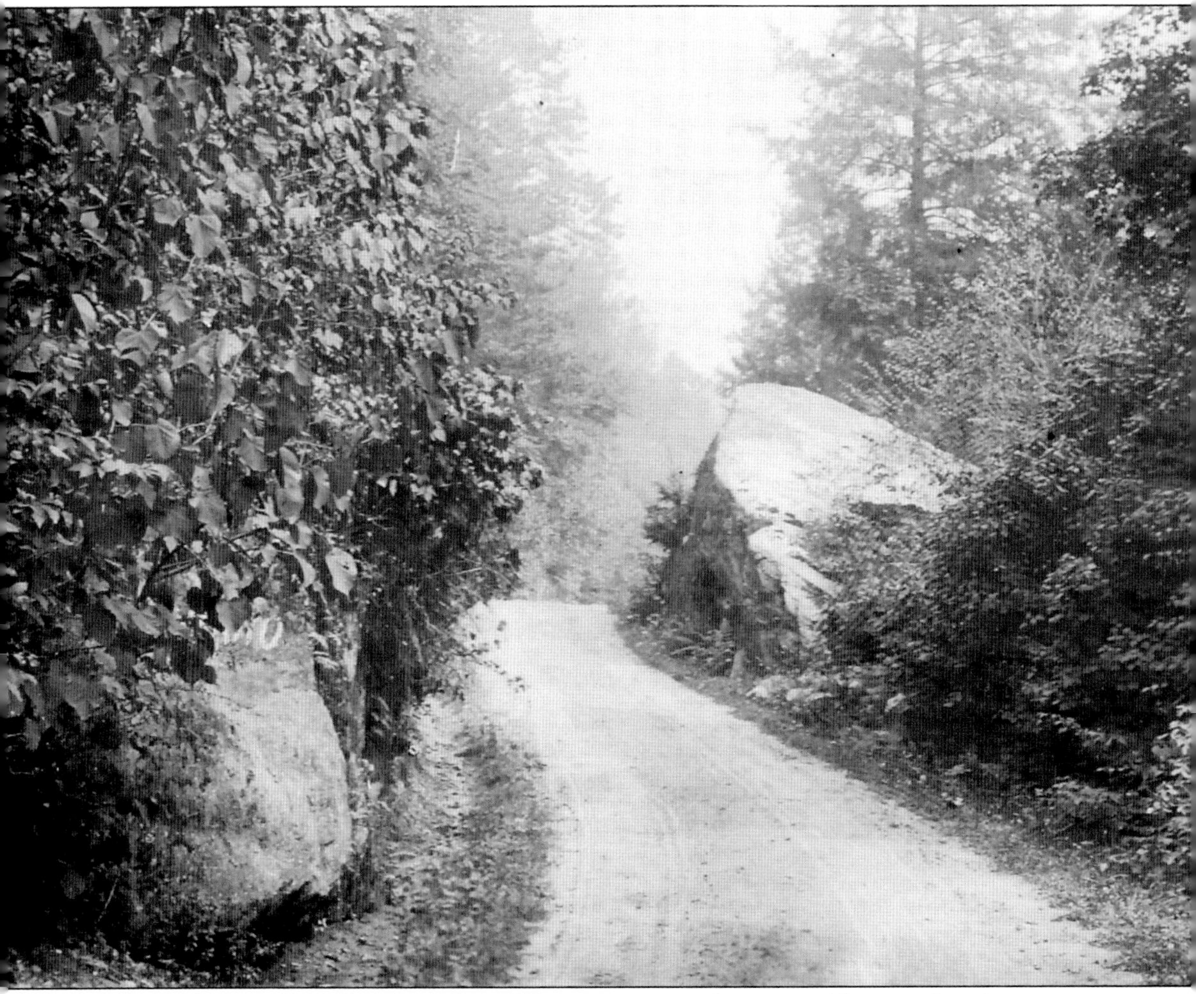

The earliest roadbed from Scandia to Warren penetrated a group of huge rocks, about a quarter mile from the junction of Hatch Run Road. A narrow passage was cut directly through the rocks, just wide enough for one buggy or car. As the passage was slightly curved, the motorist had to stop before entering to honk the horn, warning anyone coming in the opposite direction. Years later, the passage was widened, but eventually the road was rerouted to bypass the rocks completely. Clyde and Olga Miller operated the Wigwam hot dog stand there that attracted a steady stream of customers from miles around in the mid-20th century.

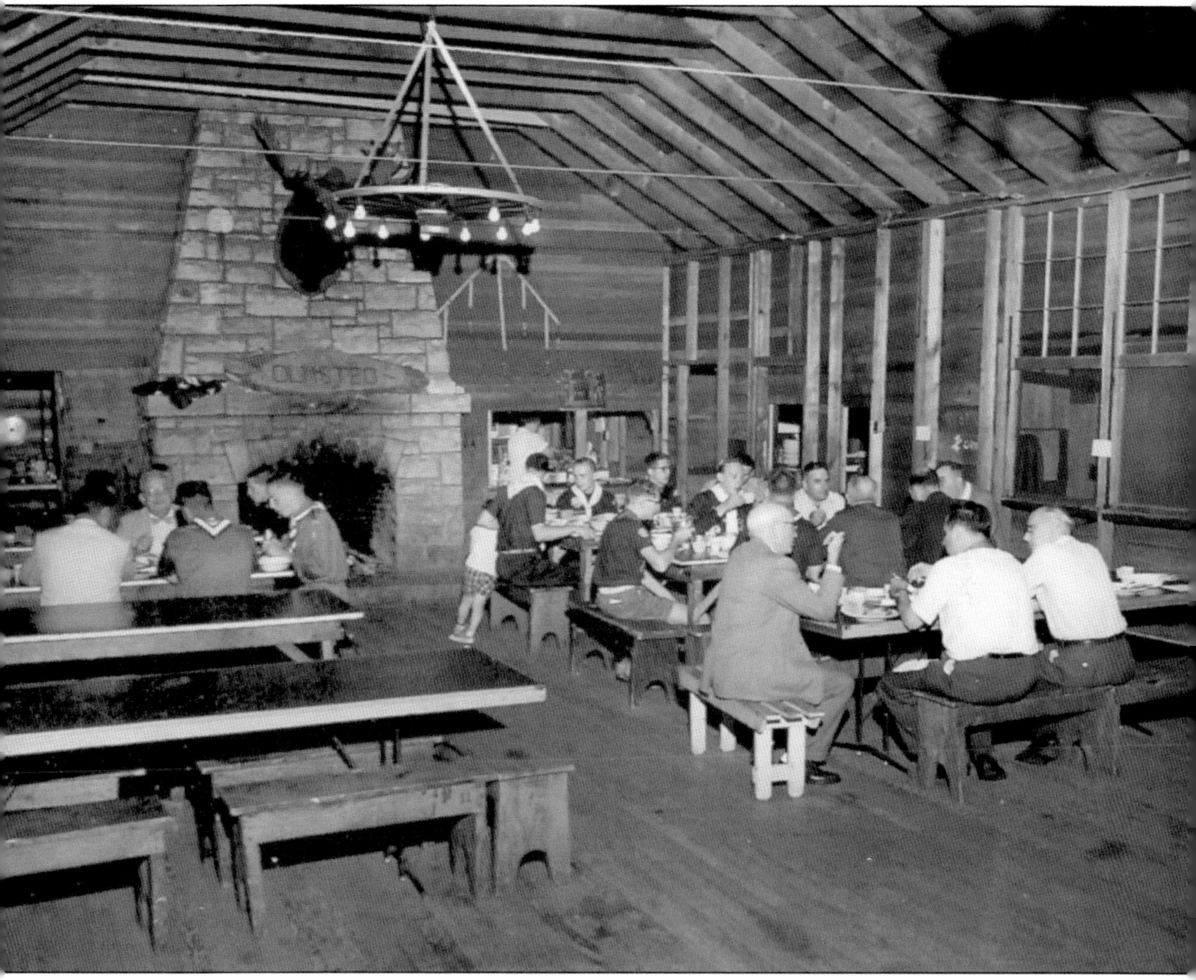

Camp Olmsted, located off Roper Hollow Road and situated along the Allegheny Reservoir, is operated by the Chief Cornplanter Council of the Boy Scouts of America. The camp was founded in 1927 by George Olmsted of Ludlow, Pennsylvania. In 1964 and 1965, most of the camp was relocated to a higher point above the rising waters of the reservoir. This is an interior photograph of the camp from 1960.

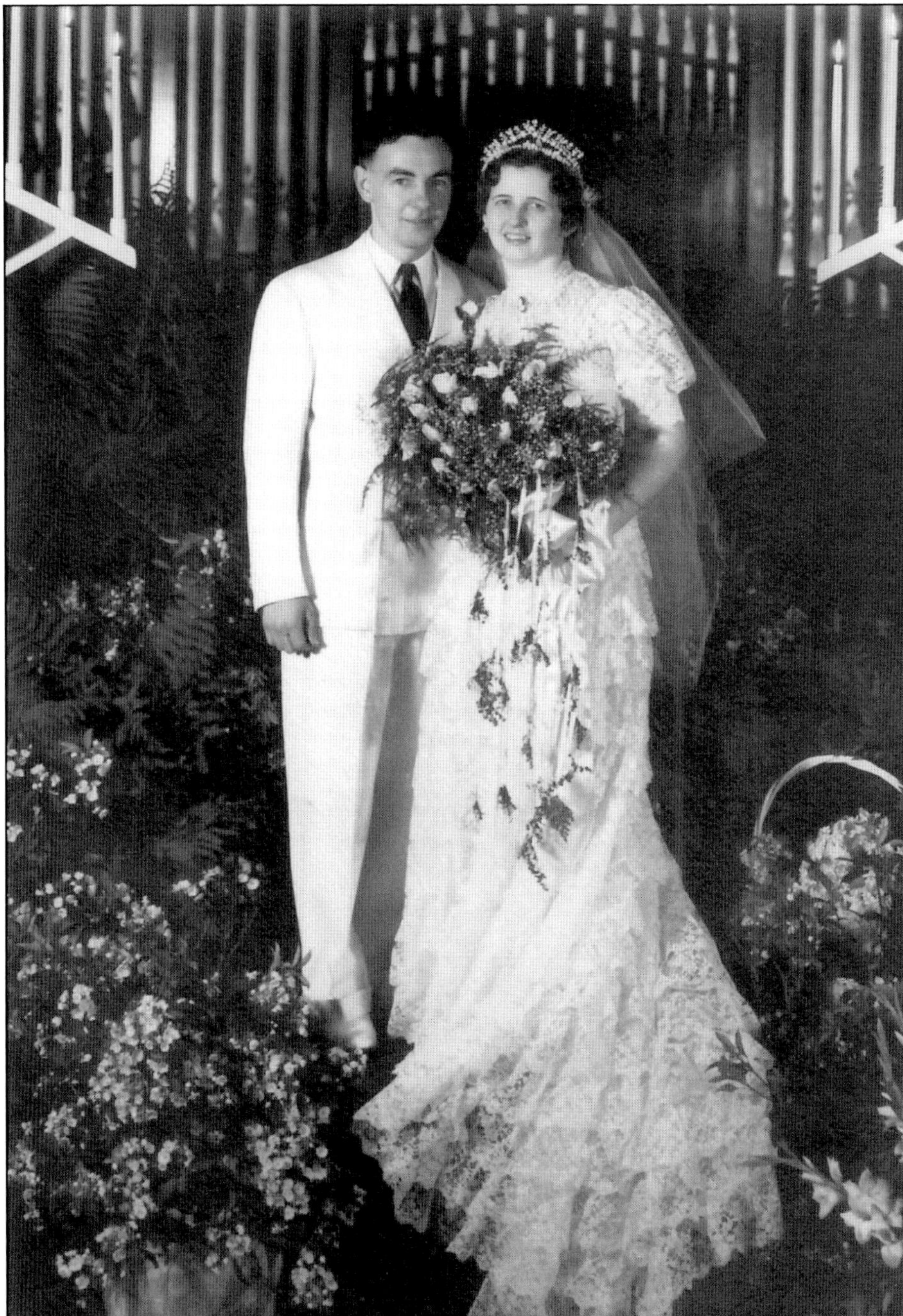

In Conewango Township, photographer Everett Stoke and Charlotte Bloomquist were married in North Warren Presbyterian Church on June 29, 1938. Their reception was the first event held in the new Community House. Since Charlotte worked with Everett, their business was named Stokes Studio. Everett was an artist with a camera. His work included portraits, weddings, school groups, community events, businesses, and industries. Stokes Studio left its mark in Warren County. (Courtesy of Mary Putnam.)

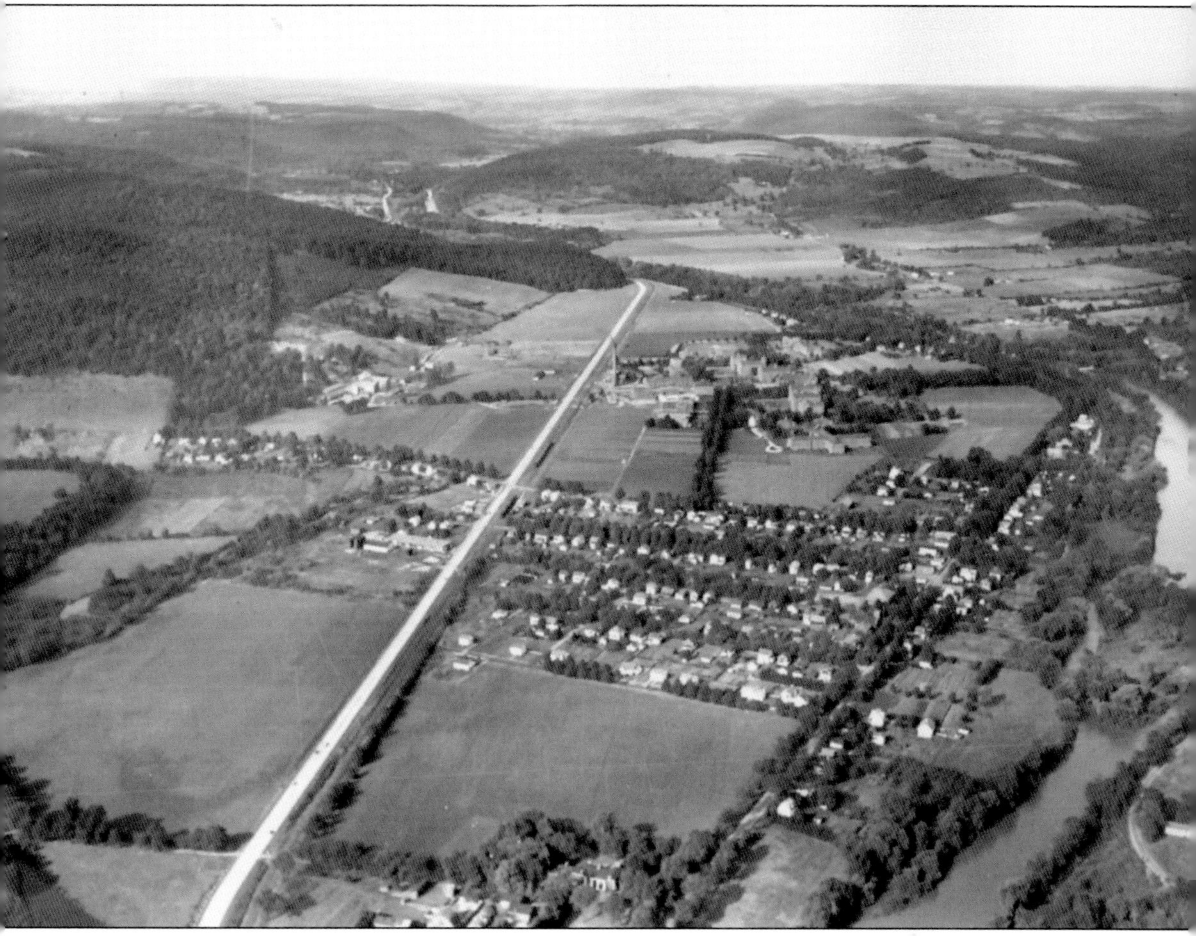

From his small plane, Everett Stoke took numerous aerial photographs of Conewango Township and beyond. This 1945 view is a reminder of the community's origins with Daniel Jackson, the Berrys, and the Wetmores. Timberland became farmland in the hills and valleys. The railroad, state hospital, and farm brought construction and business. The 1940 three-lane highway led to further development. The Wetmore home and farm are in the foreground. (Courtesy of the Everett Stoke aerial collection.)

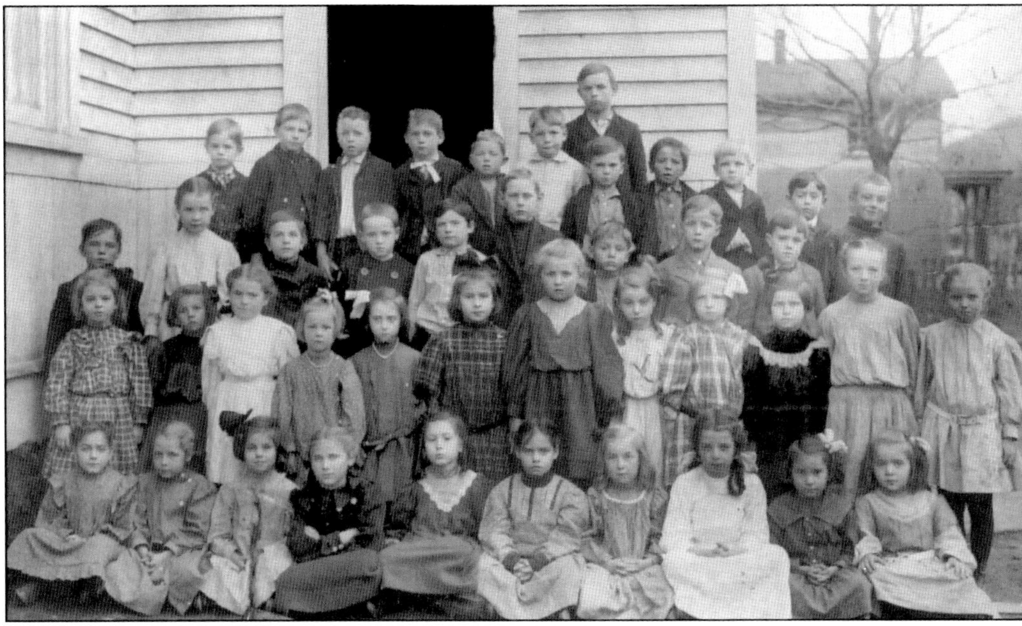

These North Warren School children were photographed about 1910. Their teachers usually boarded with local families. This two-story frame school was built in the late 1880s after the second school burned on School Street. The first village school stood on property owned by the Berry family. Later, it was converted to a home that became 411 South State Street. Numerous one-room schools dotted the township. (Courtesy of Mary Putnam.)

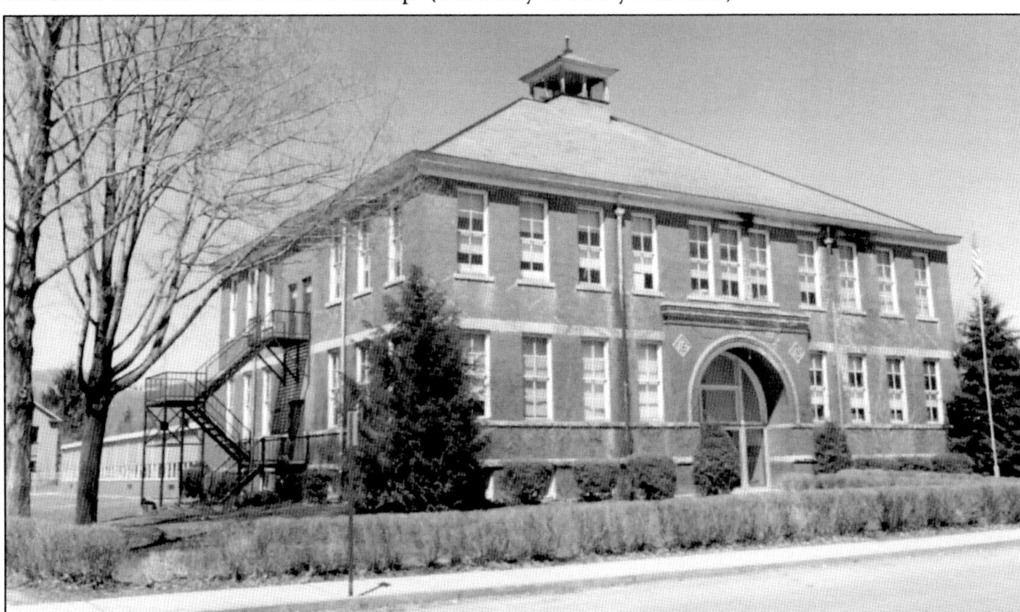

The brick school was built in 1913 and graduated its first high school class in 1915. Seventh and eighth graders moved to Beaty in 1949. The modern 1957 addition provided needed elementary space. Closed in 2005, the fine North Warren School was razed in 2007. A generous local couple donated the property to the North Warren Presbyterian Church for the Community Park where the school bell is mounted. This image was taken in 1975. (Photograph by Carl E. Wolf.)

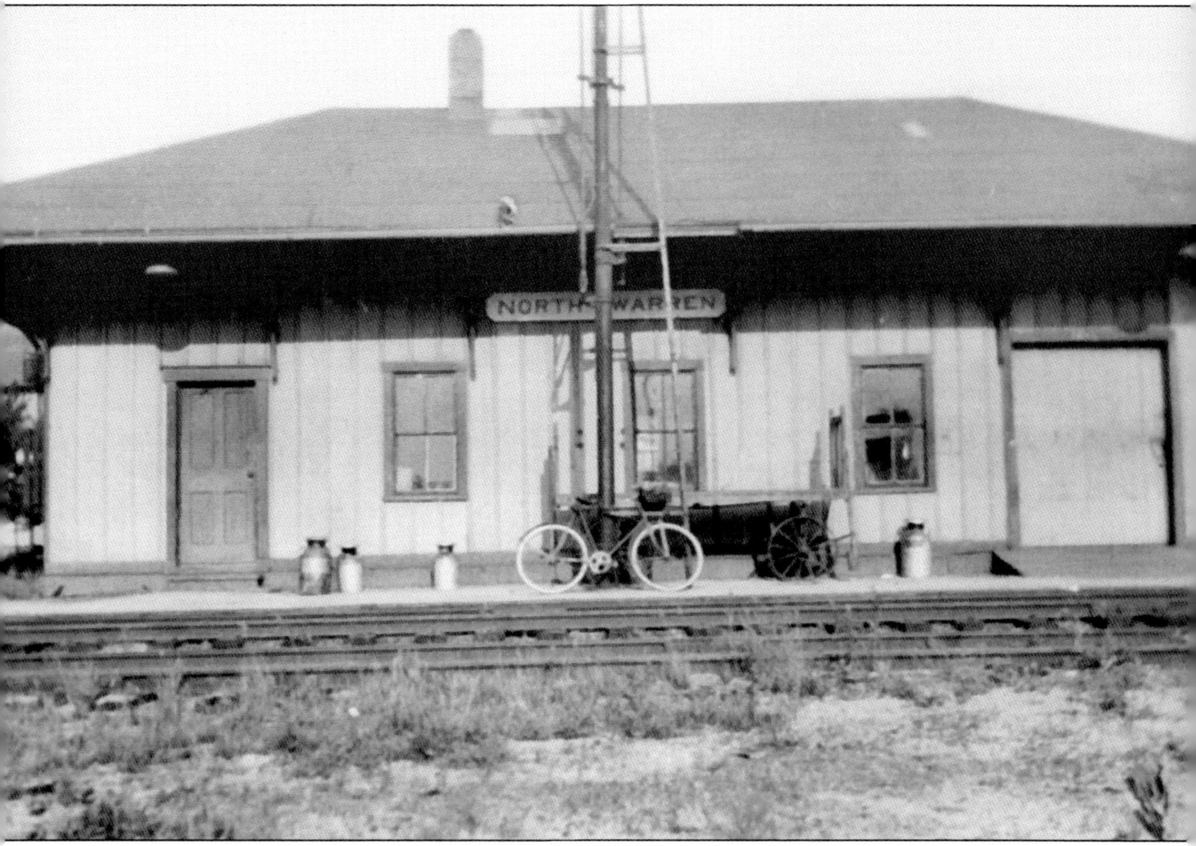

When the railroad came, the name of the village was changed from Berry's Corners to North Warren. The new depot for the Dunkirk, Allegheny Valley & Pittsburgh Railroad was built in 1874. The New York Central Railroad came later. The depot deteriorated after train service ended. Subsequent owners brought renovations and new uses. The Train Station has been a popular restaurant for many years. This print was made by Ronald Snyder from a 1940 photograph by August Johnson.

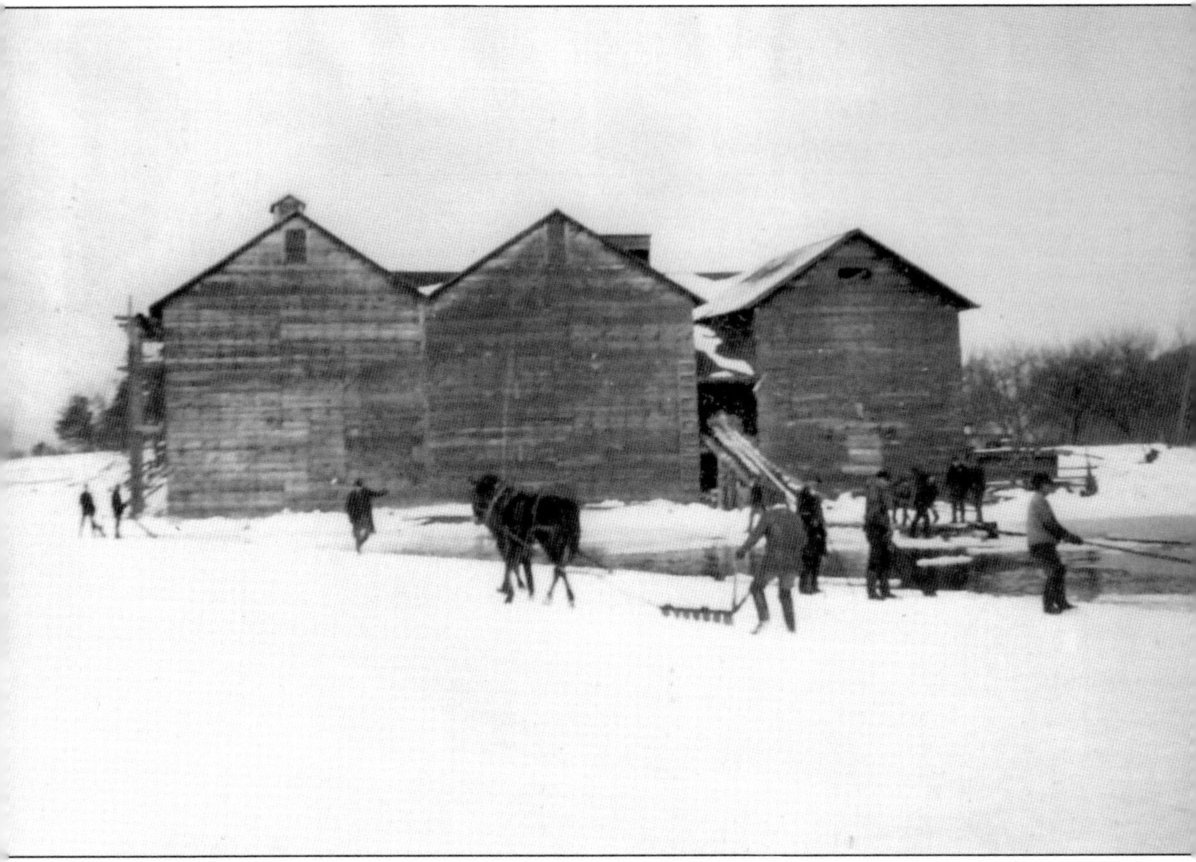

By 1900, John F. Phillips and Son (Wendell) were selling pure springwater ice. Ice barns stood adjacent to the ponds on the east and west sides of the railroad tracks in Venturetown. After being cut by horse-drawn saws, the ice blocks were loaded into the barns and stored in sawdust. Ice-skating was permitted when the ponds refroze. Wendell closed the business in 1935. The horse and wagon barns survived. (Courtesy of Mary Putnam.)

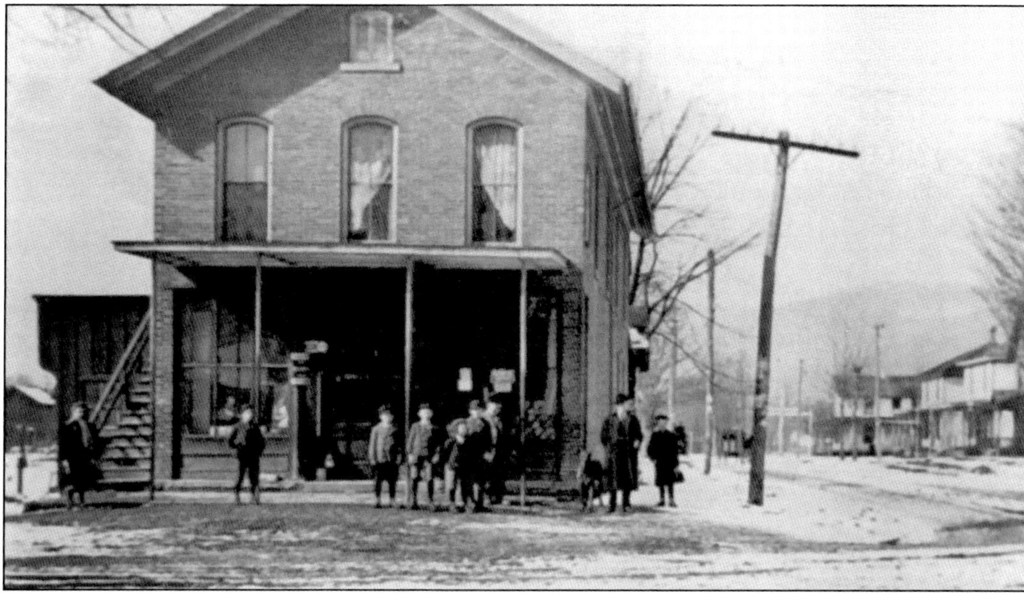

John Buck built his grocery store in 1880 near his home on State Street. His friend Dr. Ernest Cowden had an office in the rear of the building and practiced from 1882 to 1932. By 1912, clerk Martin Sanden became the owner and operated the store with his sons, Boyd and Elvis. Other businesses and the fire department lined the block to the south. The post office served the village at Jackson and Berry Streets. (Courtesy of Mary Putnam.)

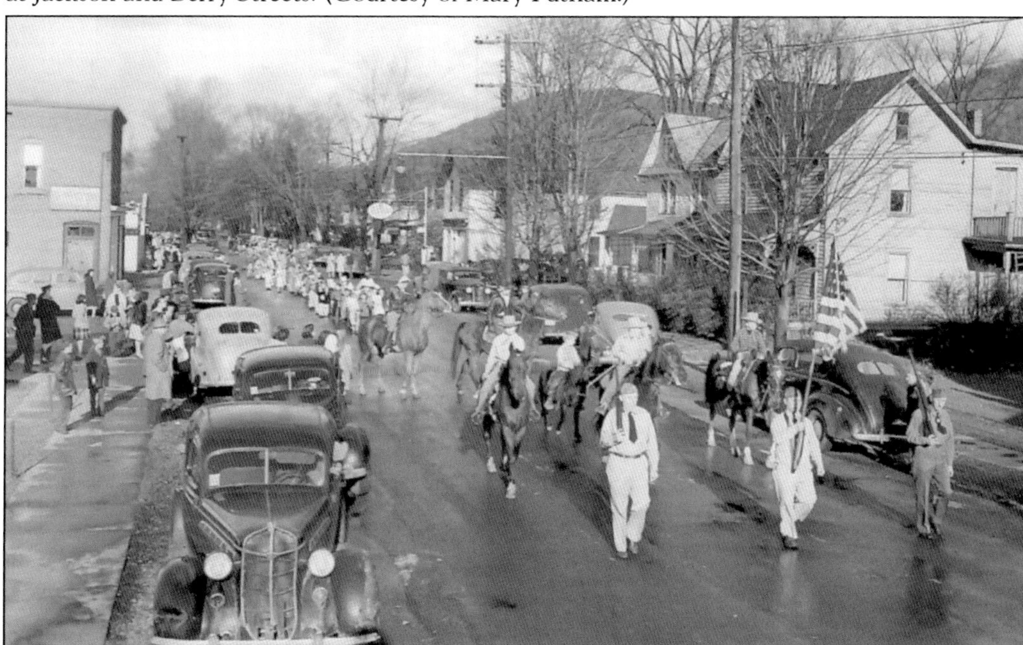

The annual Halloween parade attracted much attention. Participants gathered on the Warren State Hospital grounds and proceeded down Jackson Street and along South State Street to the Community House. Costume judging, prizes, and refreshments followed. North Warren School celebrated with costumes, parades, and parties. The Halloween Carnival at the Community House brought crowds. (Courtesy of Mary Putnam.)

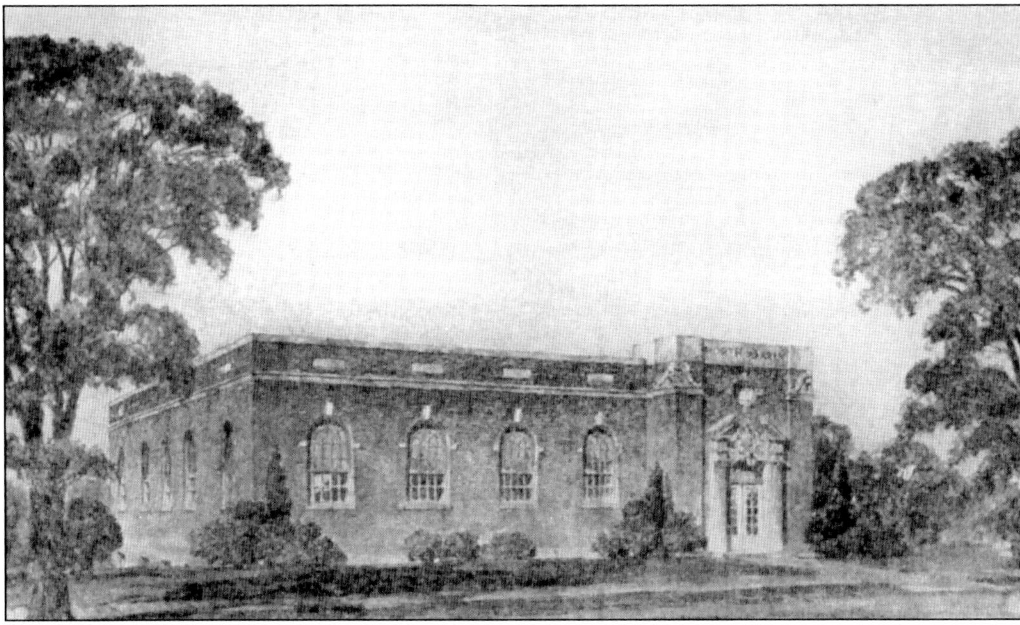

Organized in 1923, the North Warren Civic Club worked to make the village a better place to live. Realizing the need for an activity center, the club pursued the construction of the Community House in the 1930s. Funds were raised for the multiuse structure that cost $36,000. Bingo and special events produced income. Since its dedication in April 1938, groups of all ages have used this unique place. (Drawing from the 1938 dedication program.)

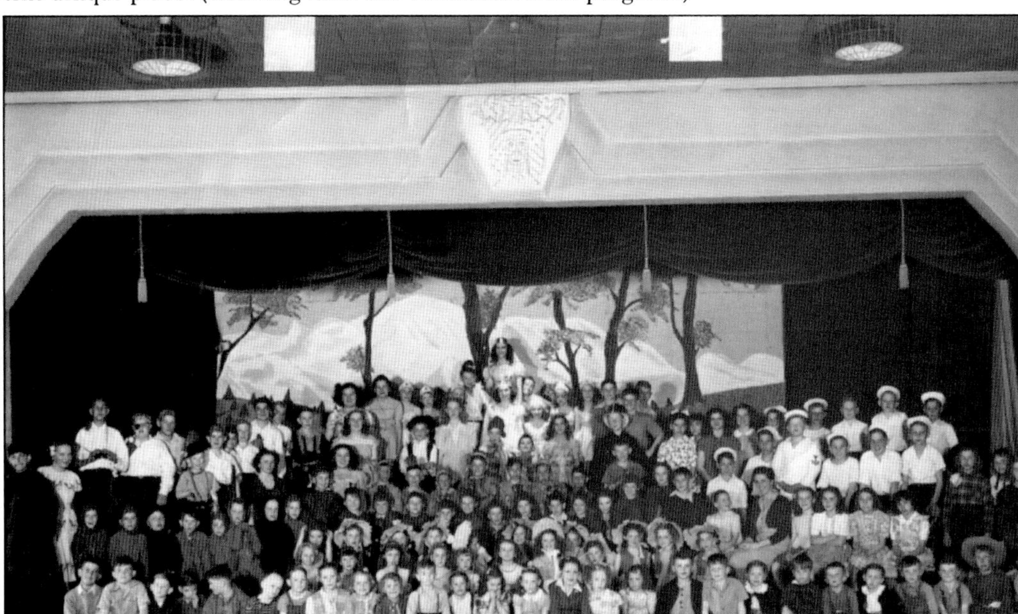

A highlight of the spring was the North Warren School operetta on the Community House stage, seen here in May 1946. In 1946, *Dream Boat* built memories with its sets, cast, costumes, and music. The gym has brought a variety of activities over the years, with basketball being the most popular. The school district leased the building from the 1950s until 1980 for class space. Head Start and North Warren Presbyterian Day Care followed. (Photograph from Stokes Studio.)

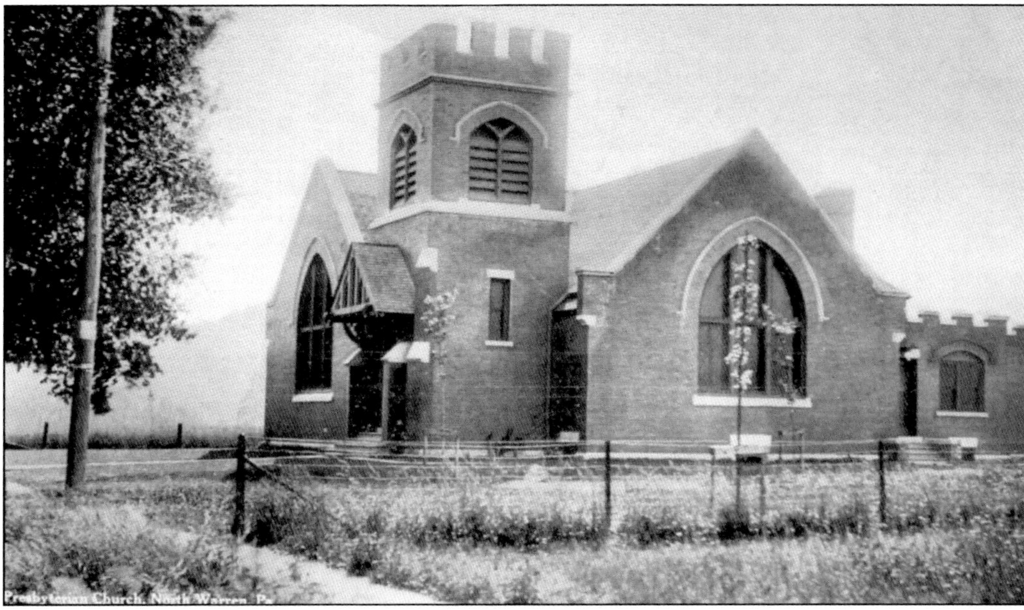

The North Warren Presbyterian Church was organized in 1894 by members who met at the Sabbath School Chapel next to the North Warren School. The Wetmore family gave property for the 1878 chapel and the new brick church that was dedicated in February 1905. New additions occurred in 1961 and 1998. The sanctuary was remodeled between 1966 and 1967. The church accepted ownership of the Community House in 1982. This 1905 image was printed from a postcard by Stokes Studio.

The North Warren Volunteer Fire Department was incorporated in 1942, but the first firehouse was built in 1917. It was a small building on Jackson Street with a large brass bell mounted on the roof. The department had moved to a vacant structure on South State Street before the new three-bay building was constructed there in 1954. In 1974, the present structure was built around and above the one from 1954. (Courtesy of Carl E. Wolf.)

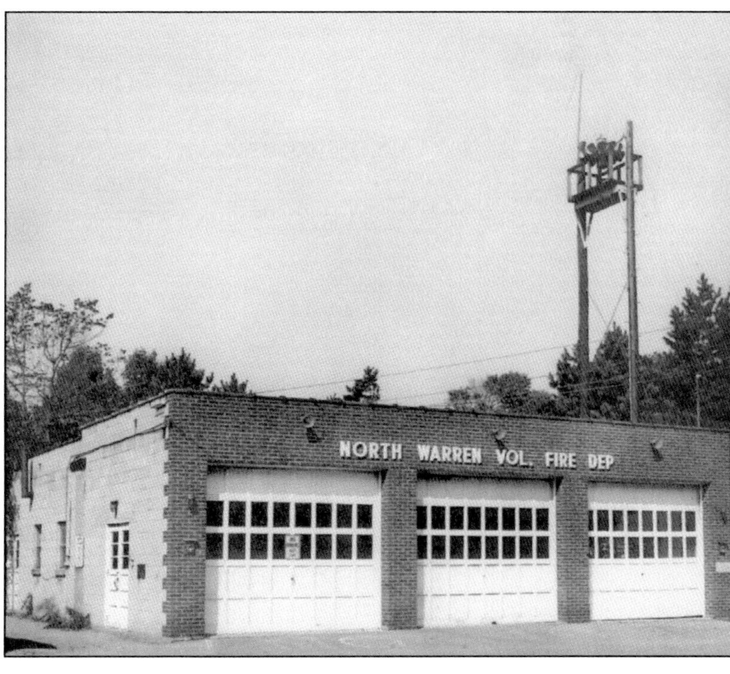

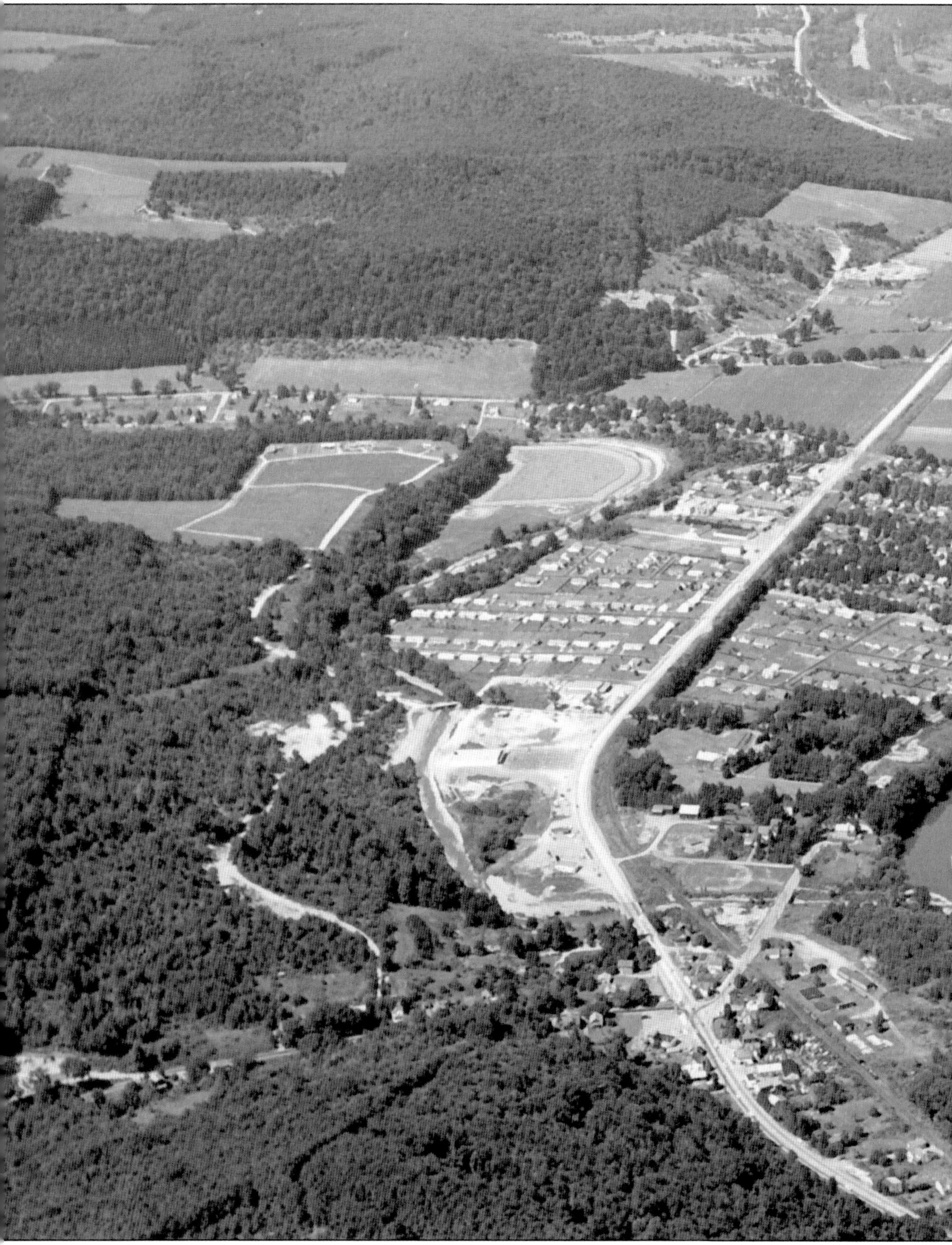

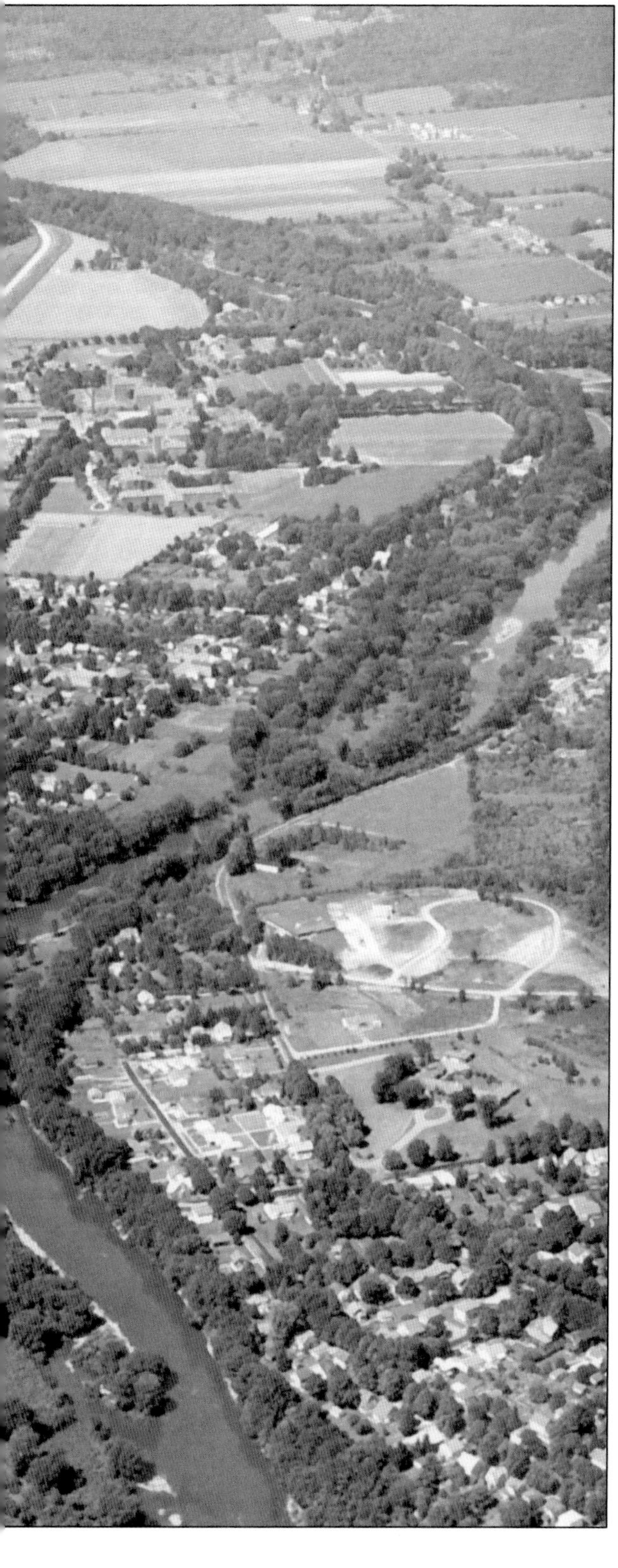

The North Warren region, including Yankee Bush, is a story of growth and change. By 1959, when this image was taken, farmland was being consumed for new homes and streets. Jackson Run was pushed along the hillside to allow for commercial development that included Quality Market. Venturetown, which was named by oilmen with refineries, is in the foreground. The structures vanished due to construction of the four-lane highway in the early 1970s. (Courtesy of the Everett Stoke aerial collection.)

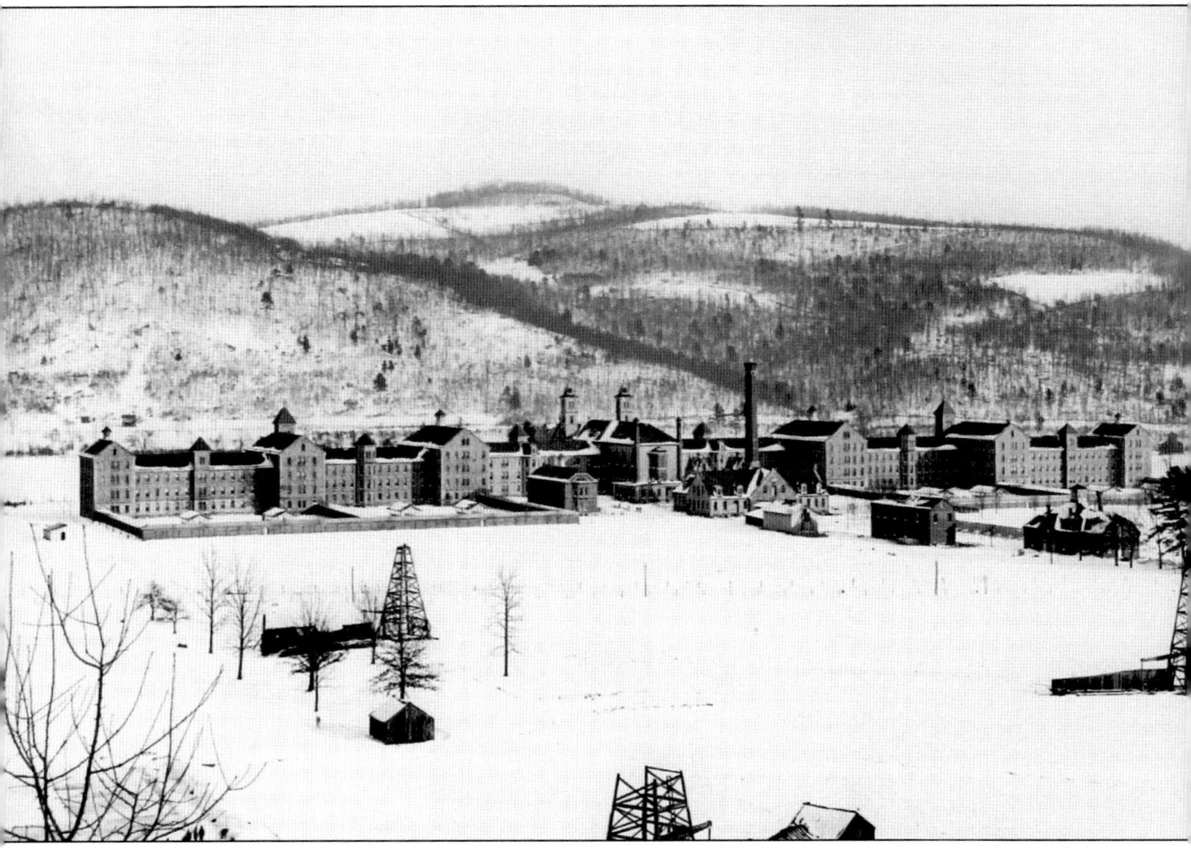

The Warren State Hospital, located in North Warren, was built in 1873 when the Pennsylvania Legislature decided to build a new mental institution. The hospital was to serve Erie, Crawford, Mercer, Venango, Warren, McKean, Elk, Forest, Cameron, and Clarion Counties. John Curwen, MD, was the first superintendent and began accepting patients in 1880. The hospital's original plan called for four stories to accommodate 750 patients. However, patient numbers have significantly declined over the last several years.

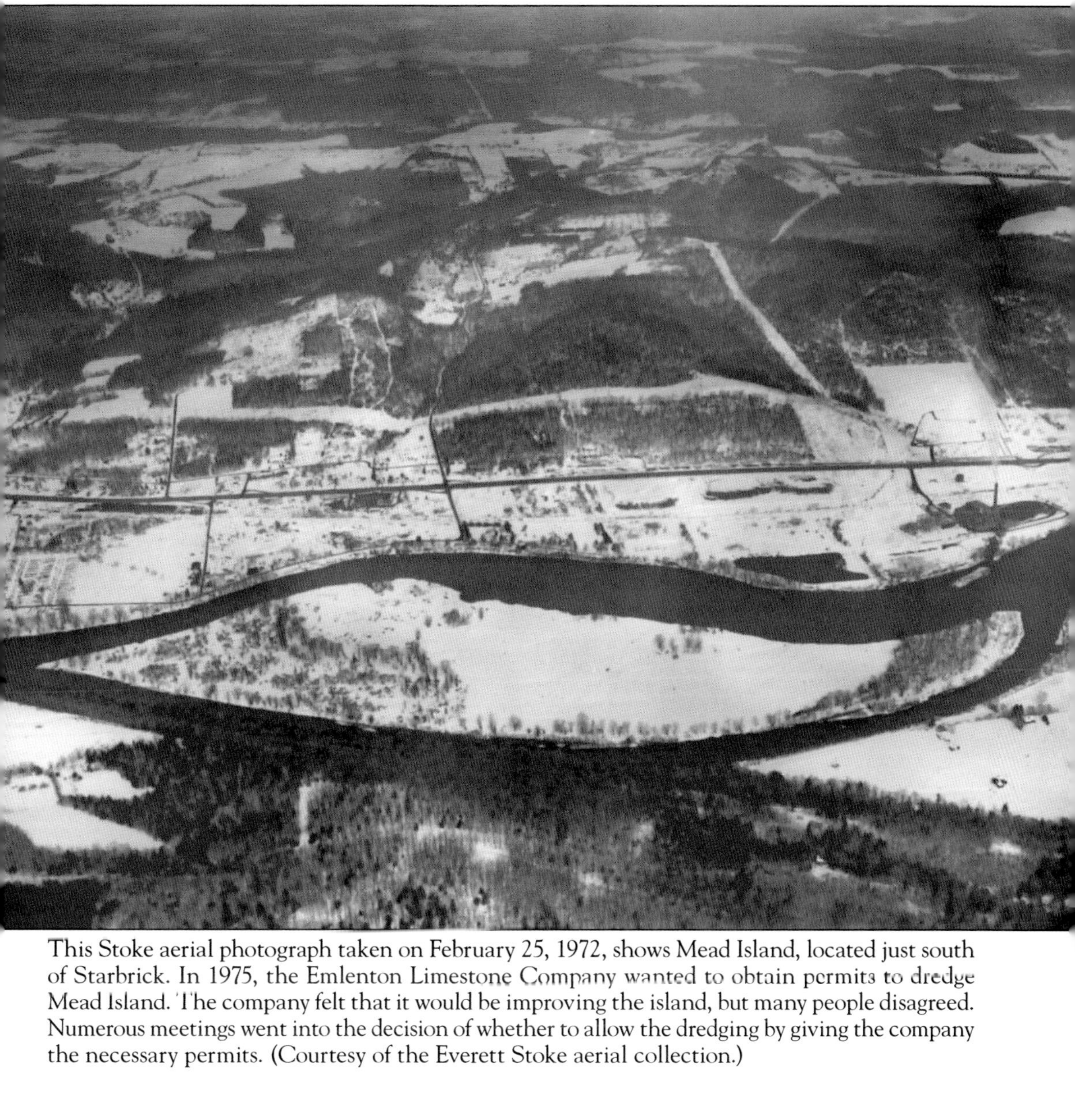

This Stoke aerial photograph taken on February 25, 1972, shows Mead Island, located just south of Starbrick. In 1975, the Emlenton Limestone Company wanted to obtain permits to dredge Mead Island. The company felt that it would be improving the island, but many people disagreed. Numerous meetings went into the decision of whether to allow the dredging by giving the company the necessary permits. (Courtesy of the Everett Stoke aerial collection.)

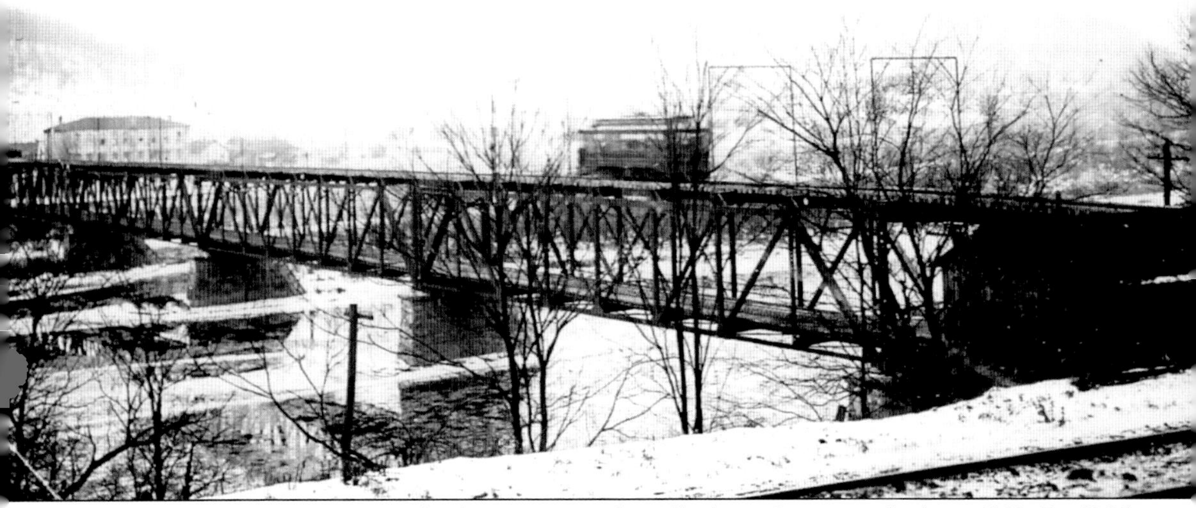

In Glade Township, an iron bridge spanning the Allegheny River was built in 1892. By 1905, the Sheffield streetcar tracks were placed as an upper deck on the Glade Bridge. For a period of time, streetcars would run from Warren to Sheffield on an hourly basis. The streetcars were discontinued in 1928.

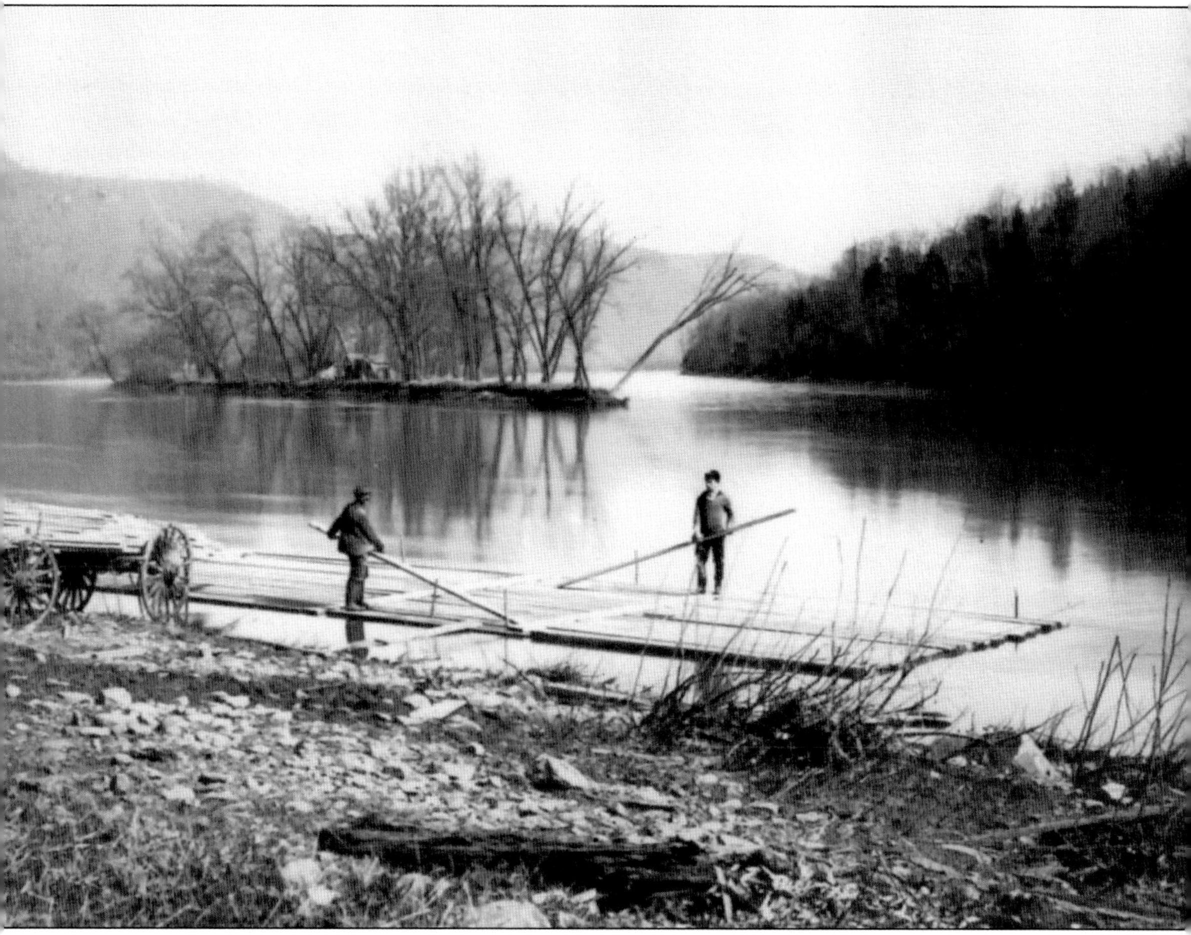

Hemlock is a small settlement strung along the Allegheny River east of Warren. It was named because of the heavy growth of hemlock trees in the vicinity. Local streams and the Allegheny River were instrumental in moving lumber to a market downstream. Pittsburgh was the destination for most, but some went as far as New Orleans. Most rafting was done in the spring, when water levels were high.

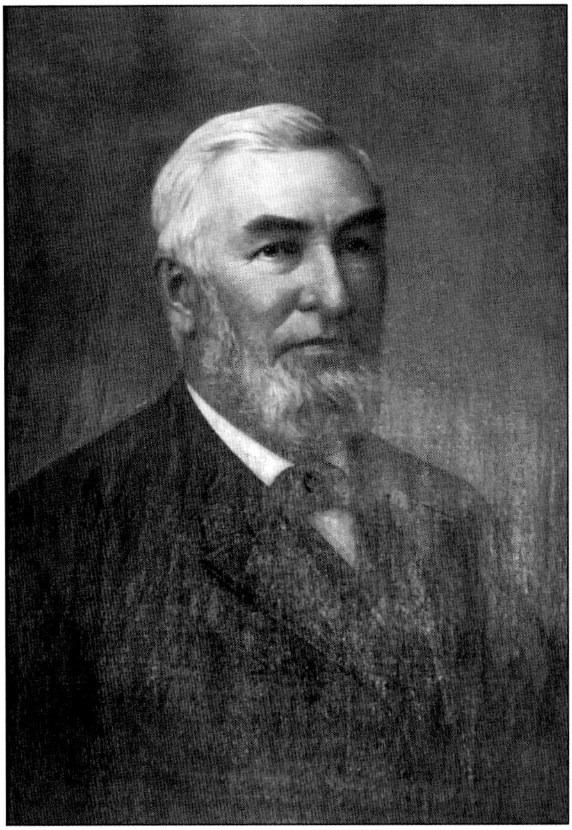

David Beaty (1811–1889) left his home in Beaver County with $1.75 in cash and a young ox that his father had given him. Beaty made a name for himself, first in lumber and then in the oil boom of the area. His mansion in Glade Township was built in 1873. He was the father of three sons—Orris W., David W., and Albert B., who passed away in 1851 at the age of three years.

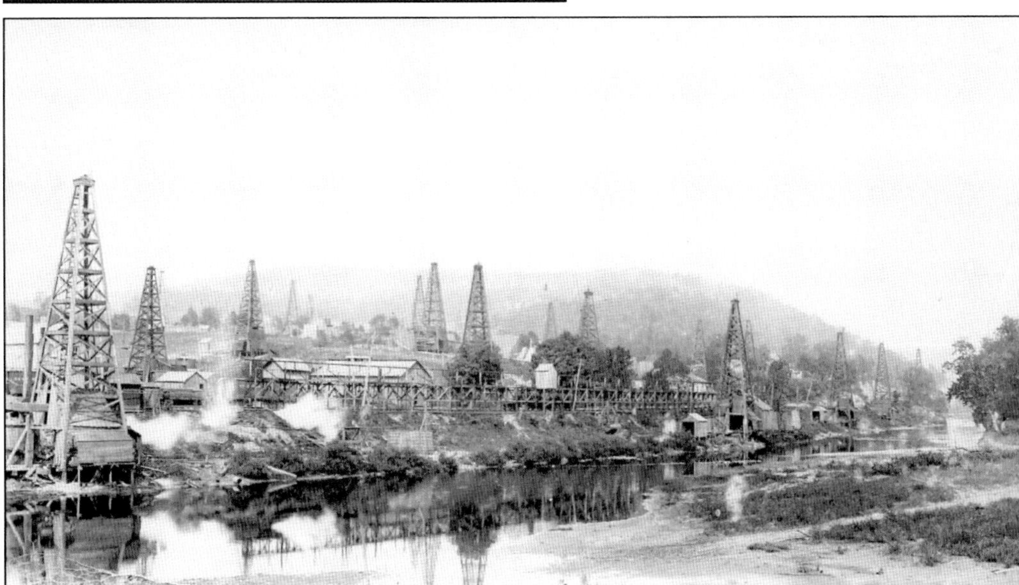

This photograph was taken around 1885 and shows the Glade oil field and oil loading racks just above Glade Bridge at the Western New York & Pennsylvania Railroad siding. The 1880s were the heyday of the township when the Garland sand oil pool along the Allegheny above Glade Run was developed.

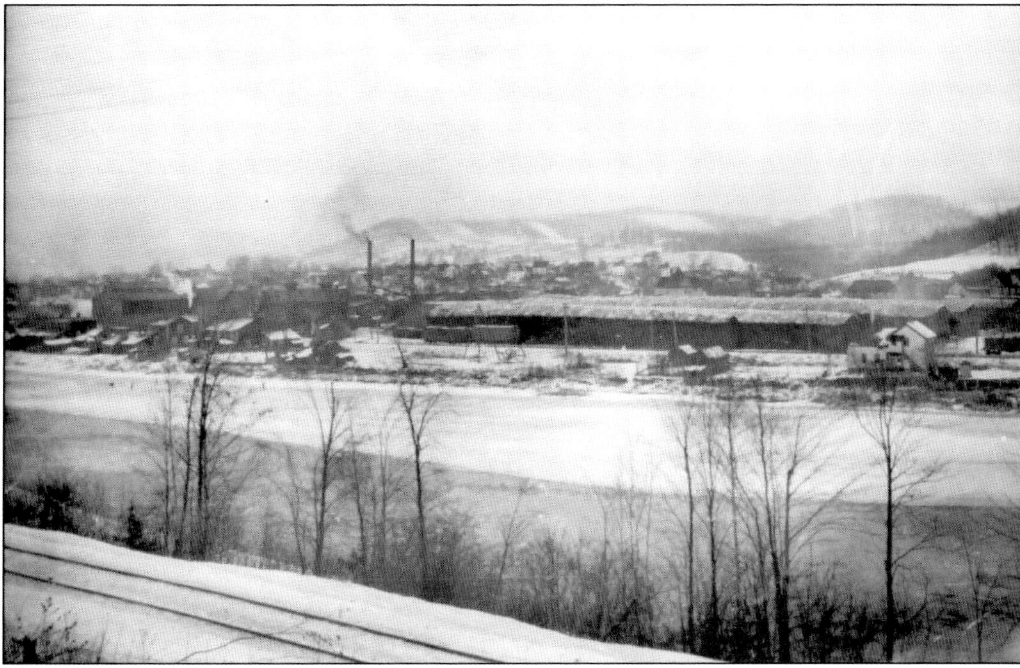

One of Warren County's important early industries was the tanning of leather. Tanneries built up near the source of hemlock bark, which was used in the tanning process. Hemlock timber was in abundance here at that time. These images capture Glade Run Tannery and its employees around 1900. The tannery burned to the ground on August 13, 1923.

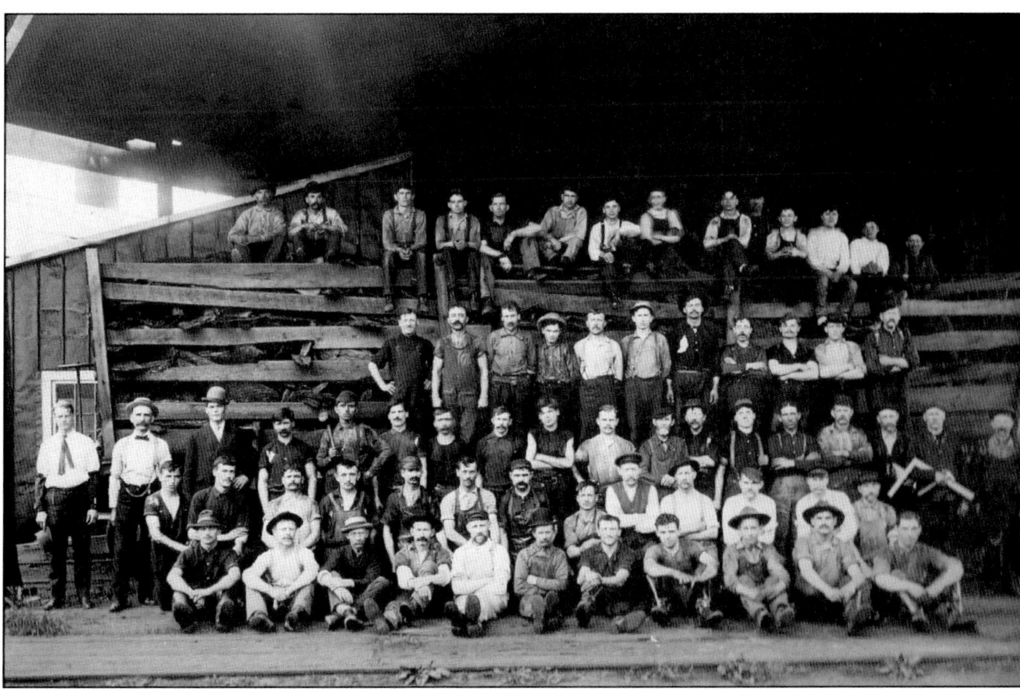

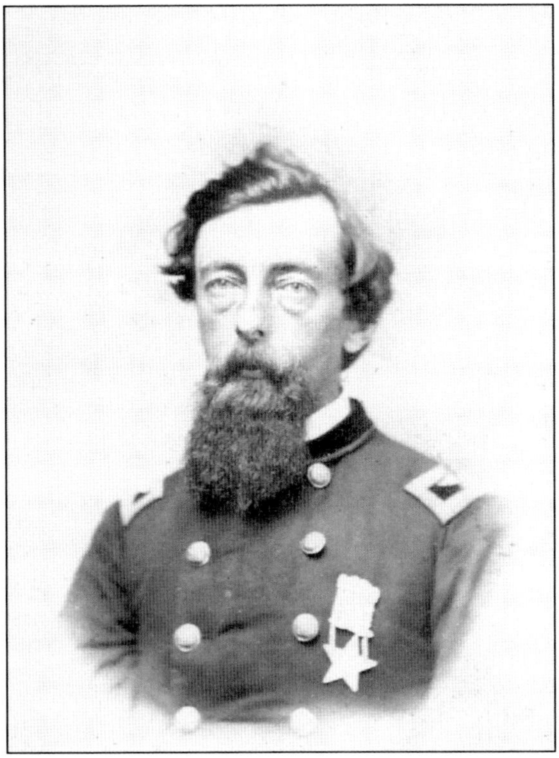

George A. Cobham was the second son of Henry Cobham, a barrister from Liverpool, England. Born on December 5, 1825, George came to this country in 1834. He was a natural leader, saver, and planner. In 1861, he went into service for his new country and ended up giving his life on the battlefield at Peach Tree Creek, Georgia, on August 20, 1864.

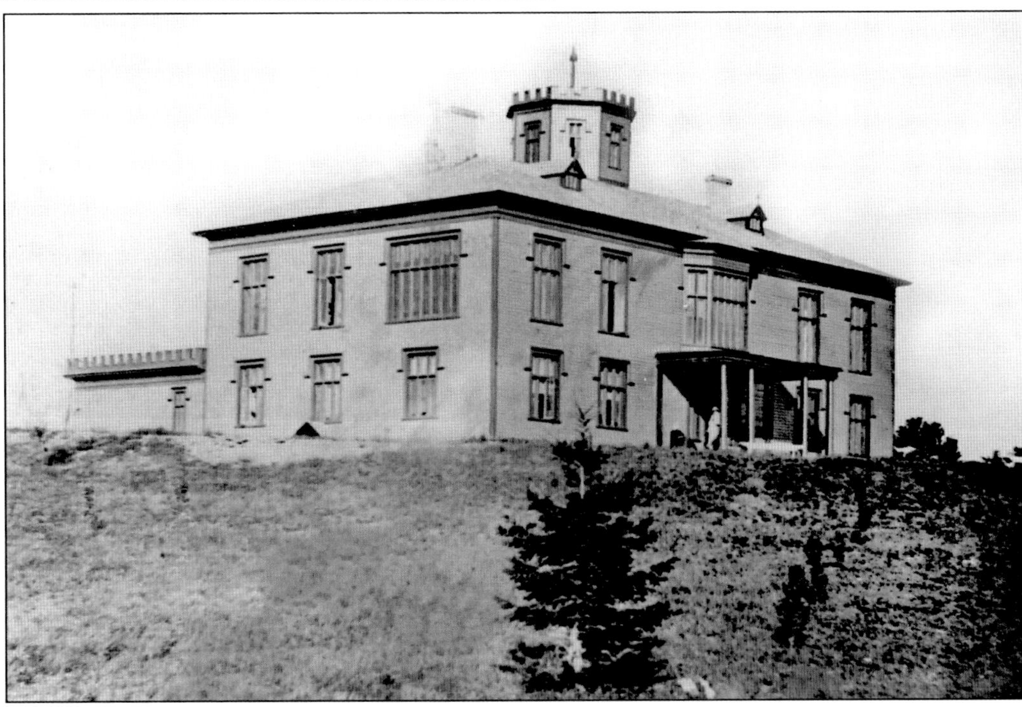

Cobham Castle, one of the most noted Warren County homes, was built between 1856 and 1863. The castle was extravagant in its design and furnishings, including a black walnut piano built by Lord Cobham and his stepsons.

Three

Southwest Warren County

Eldred, Deerfield, Southwest, Triumph, and Limestone Townships

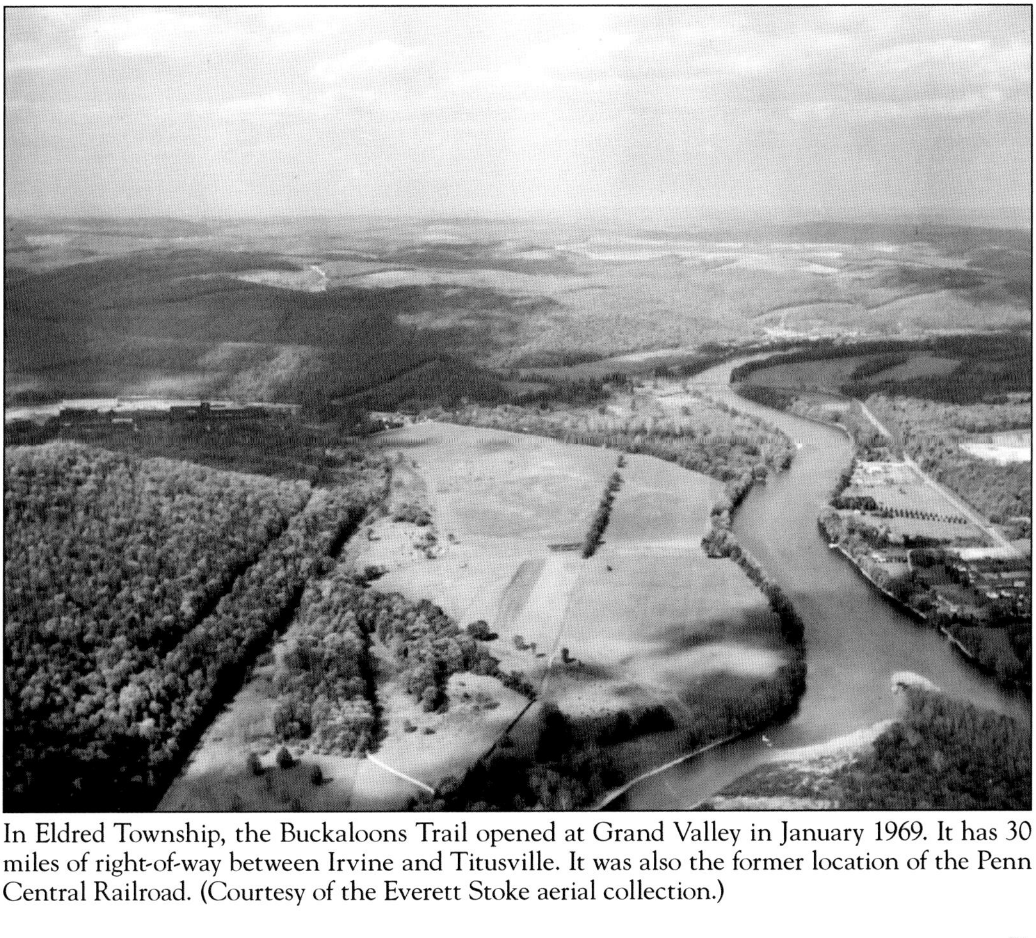

In Eldred Township, the Buckaloons Trail opened at Grand Valley in January 1969. It has 30 miles of right-of-way between Irvine and Titusville. It was also the former location of the Penn Central Railroad. (Courtesy of the Everett Stoke aerial collection.)

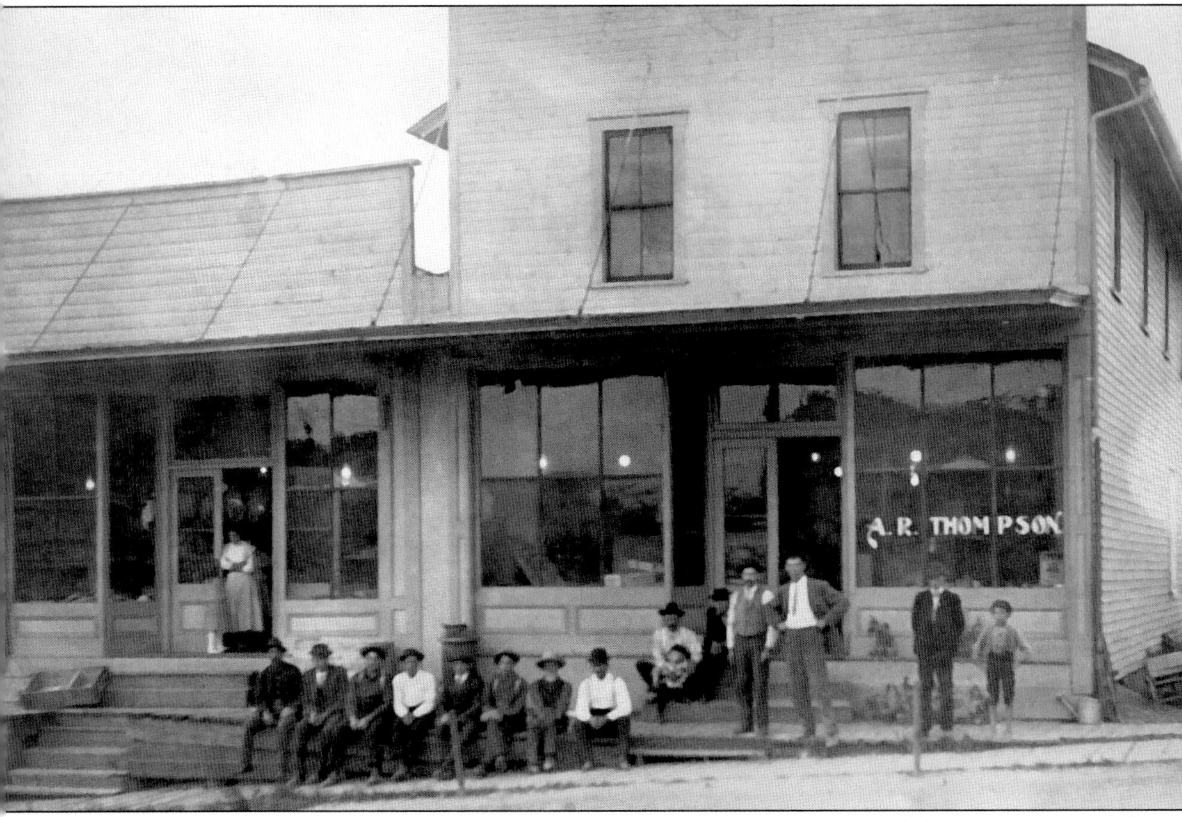

The Chambers Store was located on Route 27 across from the Grand Valley Hotel. On April 6, 1970, a fire caused by a chimney destroyed the 100-year-old hotel. Even with 70 firemen on the scene, the blaze could not be contained. Fortunately, no people were in the building during the fire.

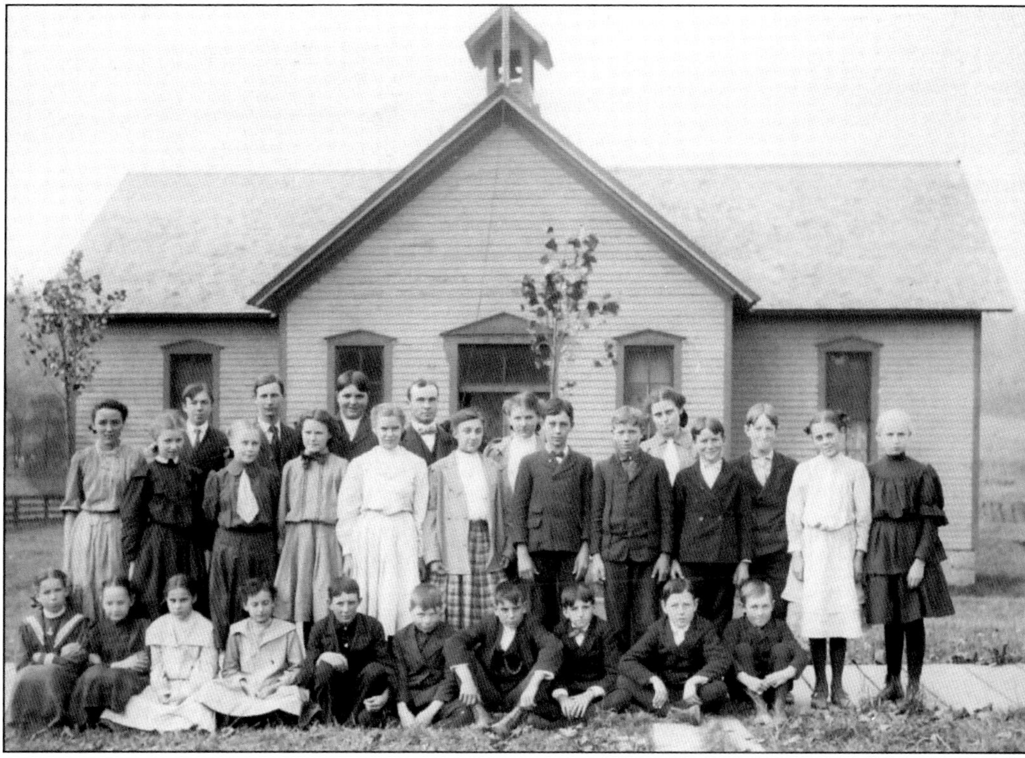

Grand Valley School, shown around 1910, offered many classes. The school wanted to be the best and took pride in hard work and planning. J.H. West, a former principal, said, "It is absolutely necessary that a systematic plan be adopted in order to accomplish the best results in school work."

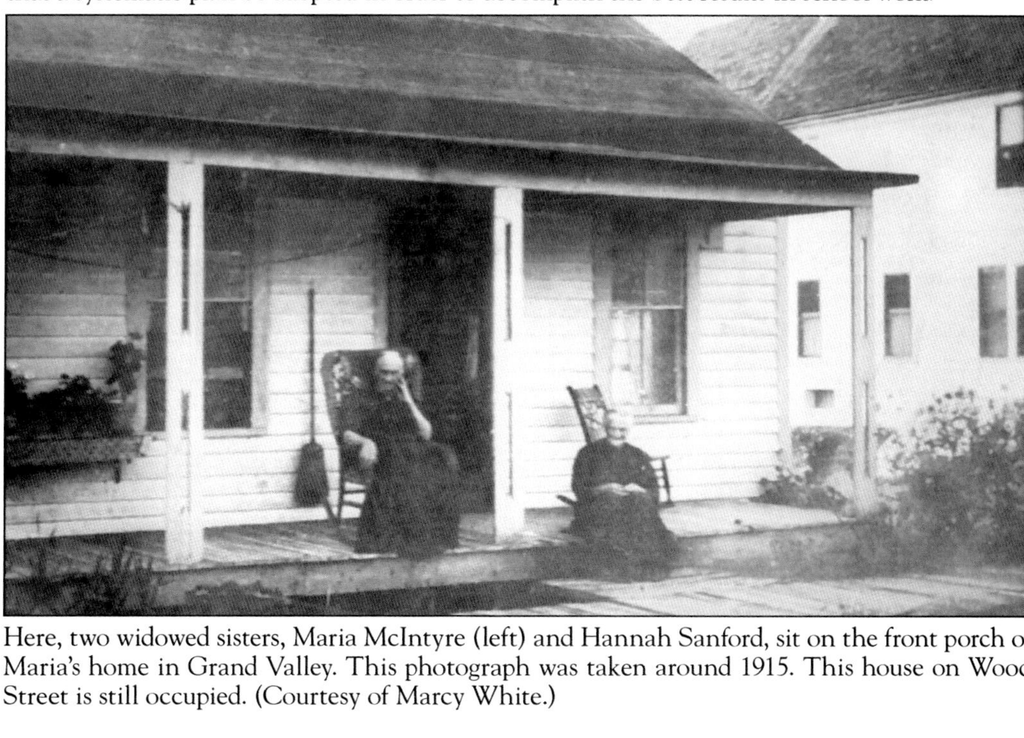

Here, two widowed sisters, Maria McIntyre (left) and Hannah Sanford, sit on the front porch of Maria's home in Grand Valley. This photograph was taken around 1915. This house on Wood Street is still occupied. (Courtesy of Marcy White.)

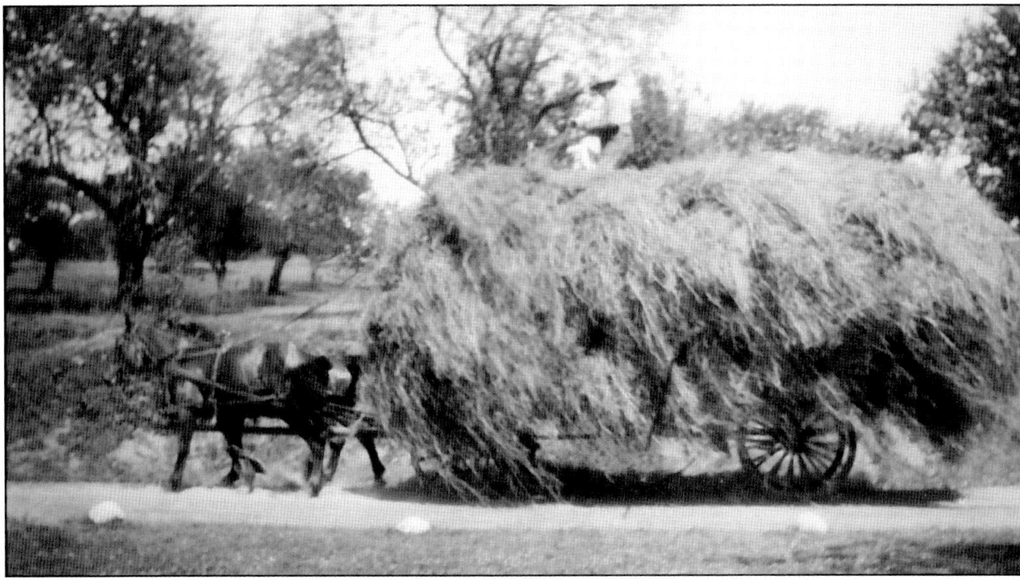

This photograph of a hay wagon pulled by team of black horses named Star and Buck was taken around 1940. The hay was forked onto the wagon by hand and later lifted off the wagon using forks and put into the hay mound. (Courtesy of Marcy White.)

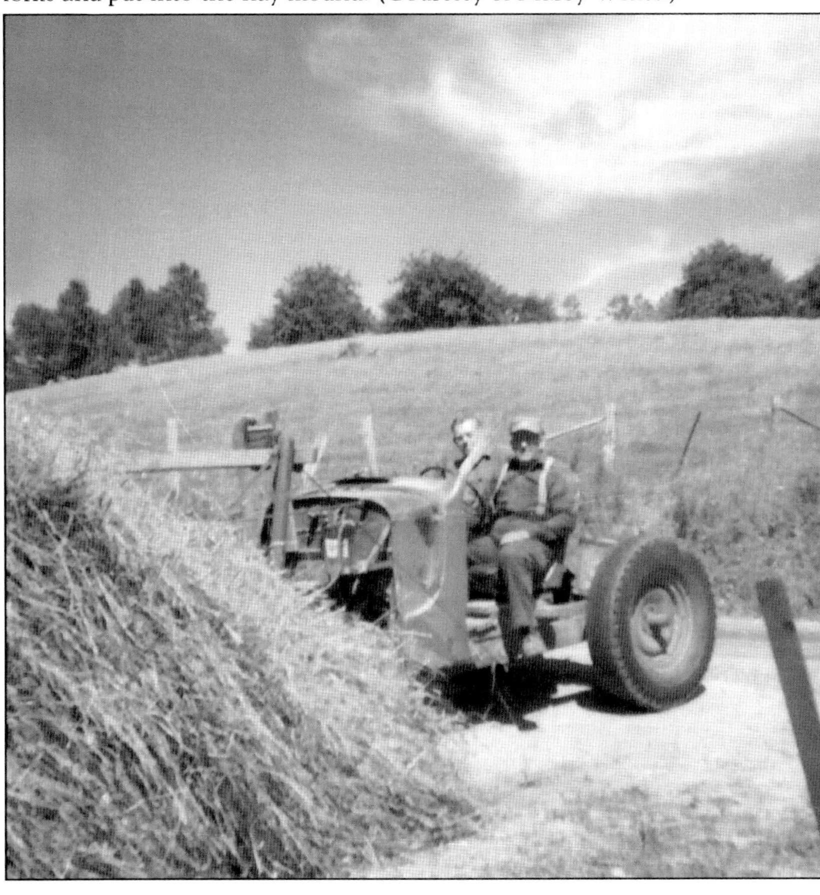

This picture is of a homemade buck rake used to bring loose hay in from the field much faster than on a wagon. The hay was dropped on the barn floor and lifted by forks into the hay mow. The vehicle was an old Hupmobile made into a tractor. A winch that lifted the forks up from the ground to travel to the barn was used in the 1950s. (Courtesy of Marcy White.)

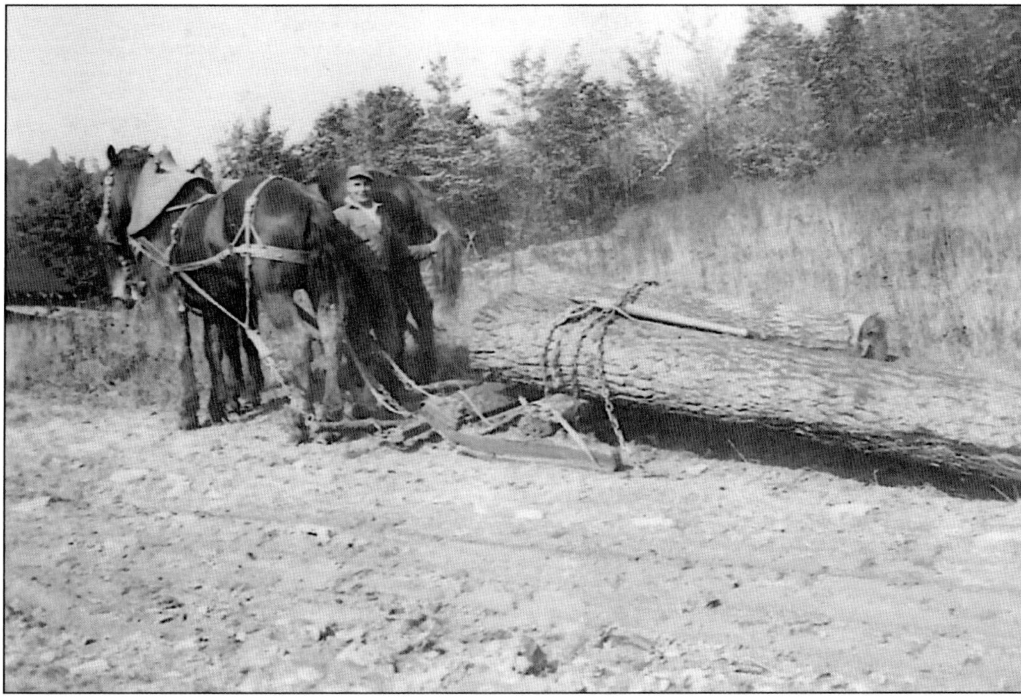

These two photographs are of Howard Cooper drawing logs out of the woods using a team of horses. These pictures were taken around 1922. (Both, courtesy of Marcy White.)

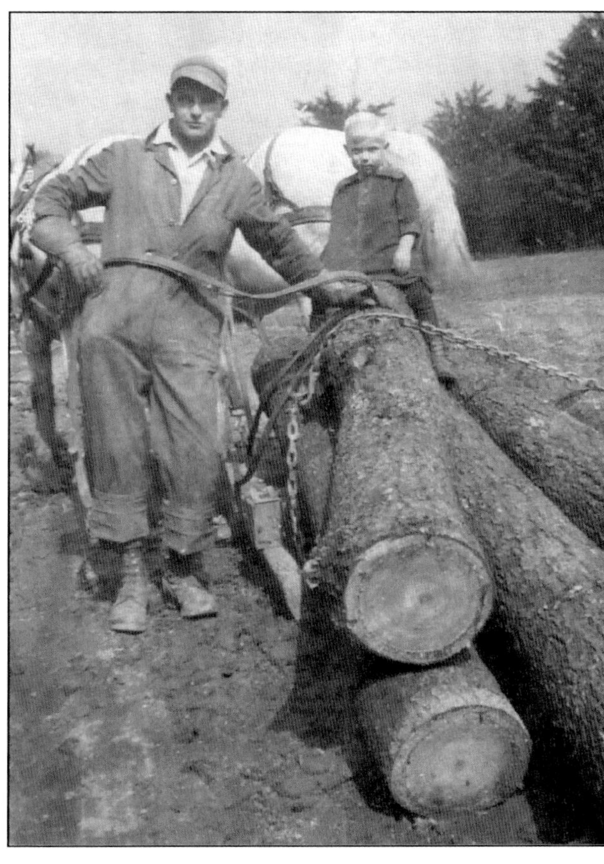

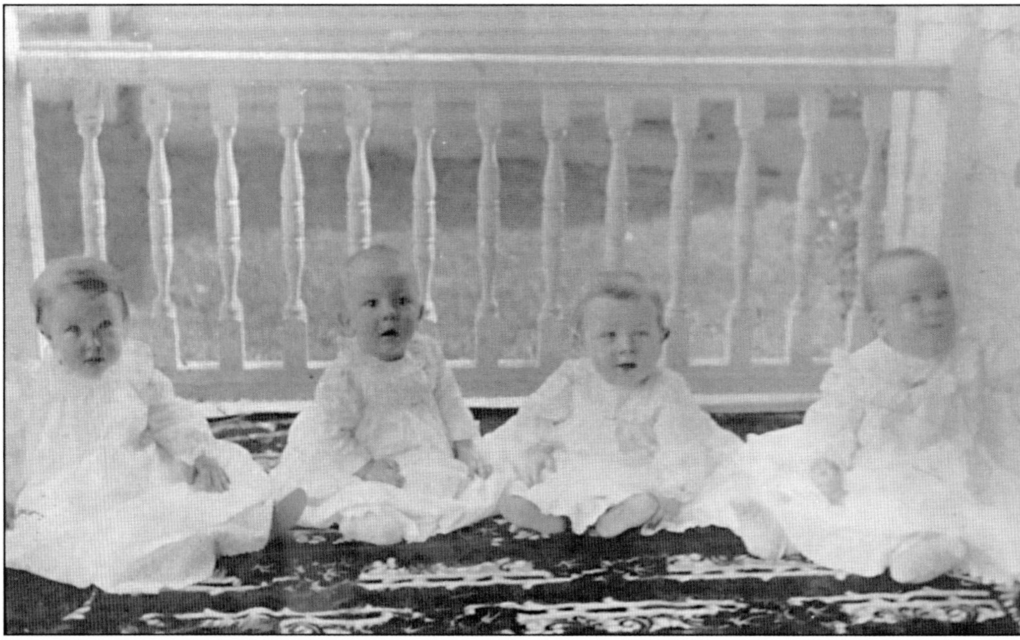

A picture captures four baby boys, all born within a few days of one another, in Sanford in 1899. From left to right are Francis Feldhausen, Herman Brown, Leo Fetterof, and Iilo Scott.

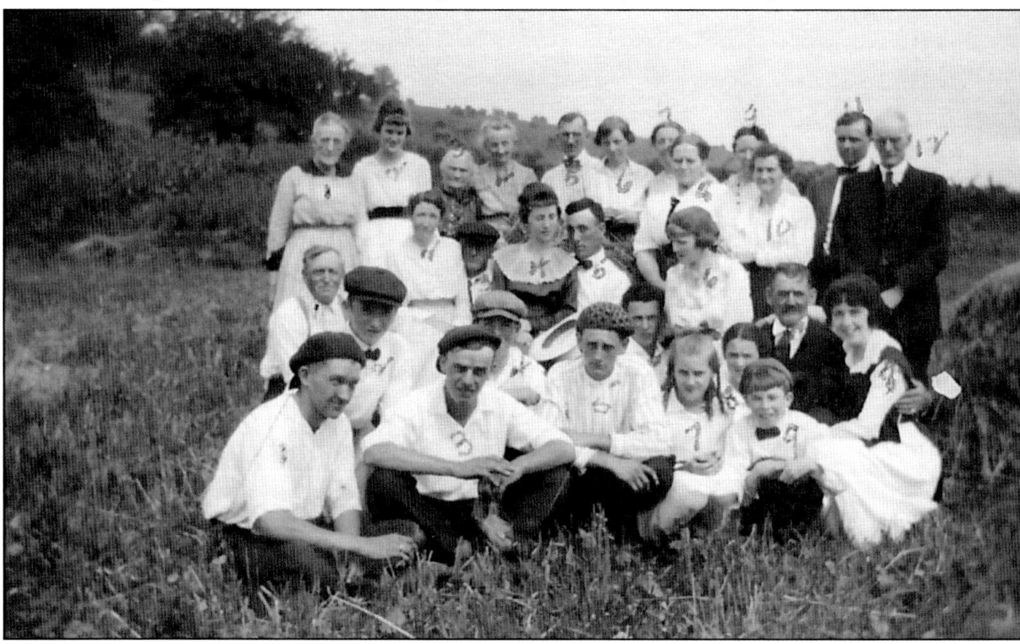

Note the recurring last names in this group photograph taken in Sanford about 1915. From left to right are (first row) Francis Feldhausen, Gilbert Sanford, unidentified Dow, Montie Scott, Paul Sanford, Iilo Scott, Bernice Sanford, Charlenne Scott, and Cleon Sanford; (second row) Charlie Scott, Carrie Sanford, Leon Sanford, Leta Meabon, Dewey Meabon, Carrie Scott, Aaron Sanford, and Madelinne Scott; (third row) Lovisa Meabon, Lulu Sanford, Hannah Sanford, Esther Jones, Will Darling, Irene Darling, Nellie Faulkner, Irene Deamer, Oma Scott, Eva Sanford, George Faulkner, and Frank Deamer. (Courtesy of Marcy White.)

In Deerfield Township, Hunter Mansion is located at 260 Main Street in Tidioute. According to *"The Favored Valley": A History of Tidioute, Pennsylvania 1806–1990*, the house was built in 1857 by oil and lumber capitalist Jahu Hunter, grandson of the pioneer settler Robert Hunter. The house remained in the Hunter family until it was sold.

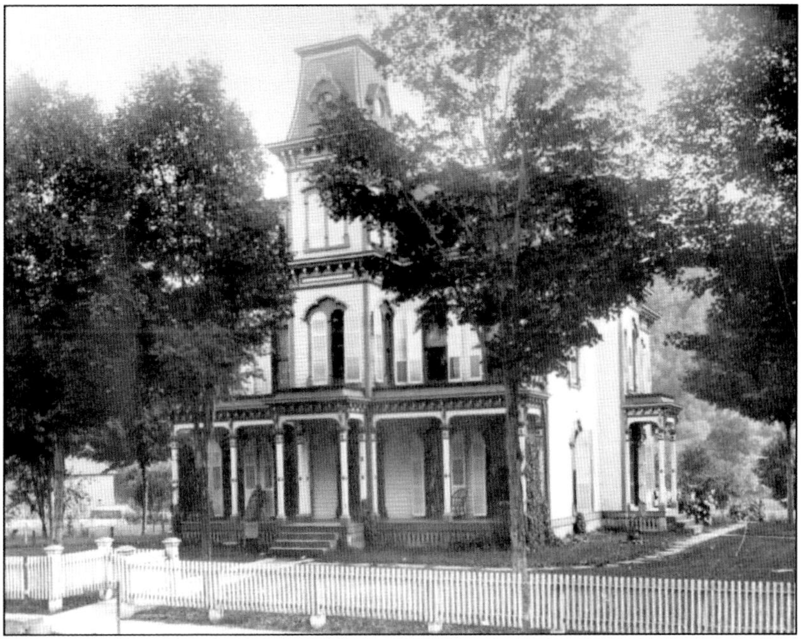

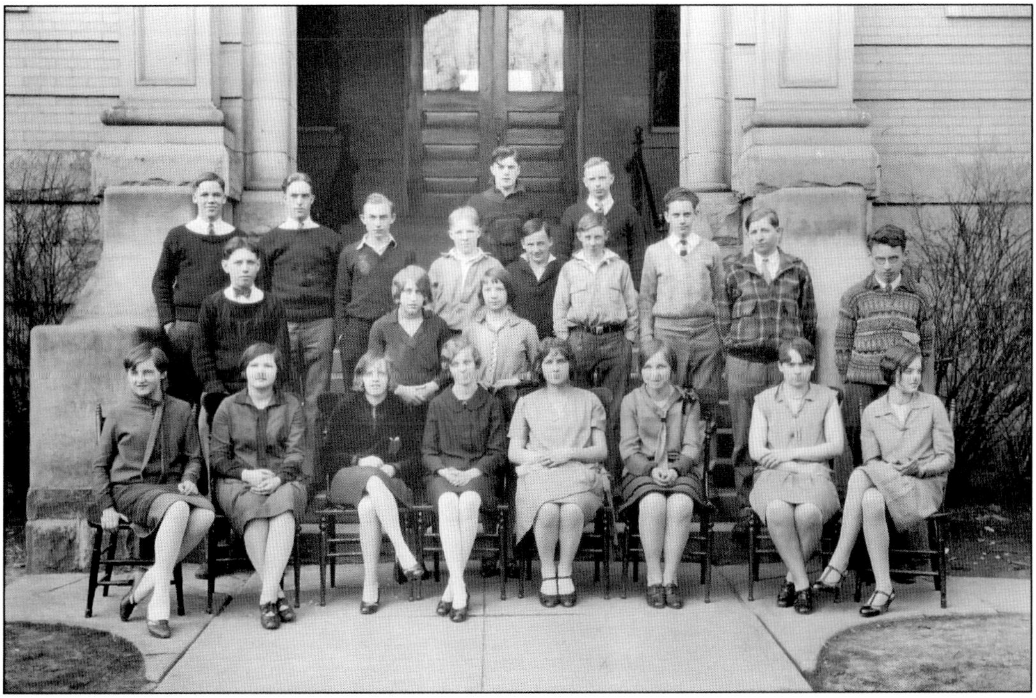

According to *"The Favored Valley": A History of Tidioute, Pennsylvania 1806–1990*, Margaret R. and Lillian L. Hunter presented Hunter Memorial School to the Town of Tidioute in memory of Jahu and Livingston L. Hunter, longtime patrons of education in the town. A yellow brick edifice was added in 1934, the same year the auditorium was added. This photograph was taken in 1928 of the Tidioute High School sophomore class.

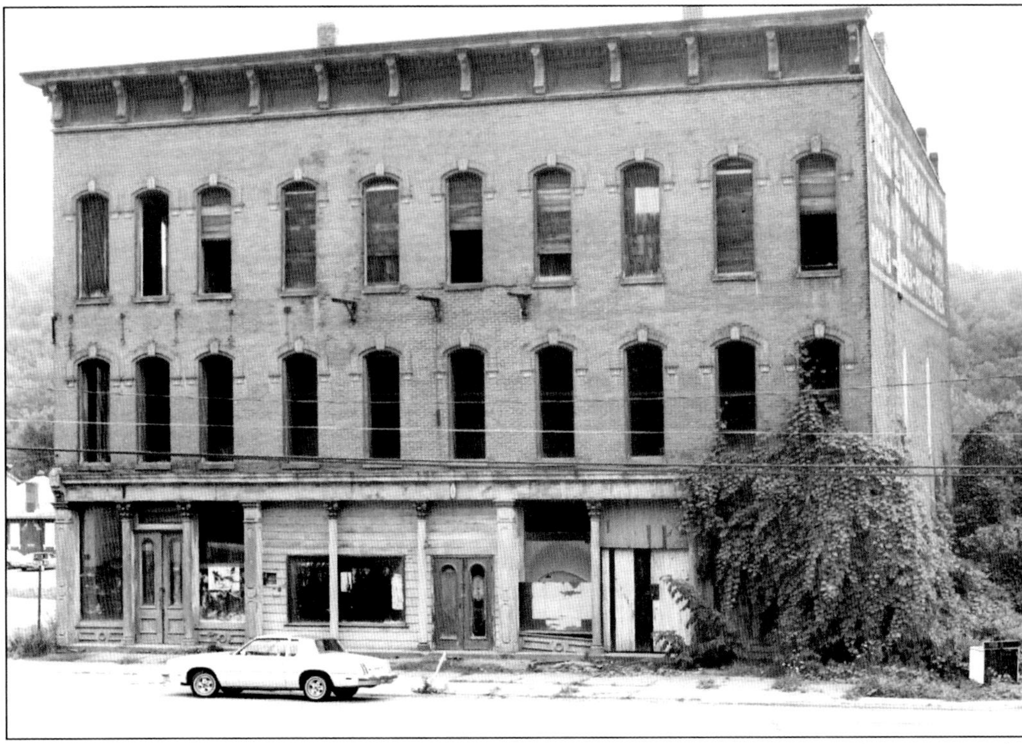

Though its first and second floors held a bank and office space, respectively, Tidioute's Grandin Block will always be remembered for the third-floor Grandin Opera House. Completed in 1872 with Grandin Brothers' oil money, the building hosted plays, bands, commencement ceremonies, and speakers, such as Elizabeth Cady Stanton, until it was condemned in the 1920s for lacking fire exits. The building was razed in 1985.

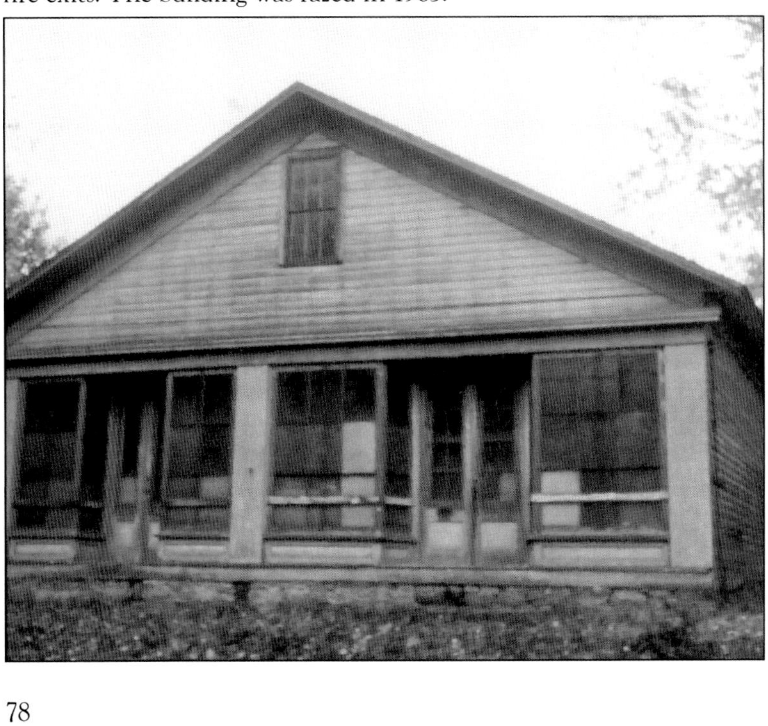

This Tidioute grocery store was opened in 1852 by a Mr. Ayer. In 1866, a 17-year-old, Julius Bourquin, began working there as a store clerk. He eventually purchased the store and ran it until it closed in 1926. Many of the Bourquin Store's artifacts were moved in 1967 (the same year this photograph was taken) to the Warren County Historical Society, where they are on display in a second-floor exhibit room.

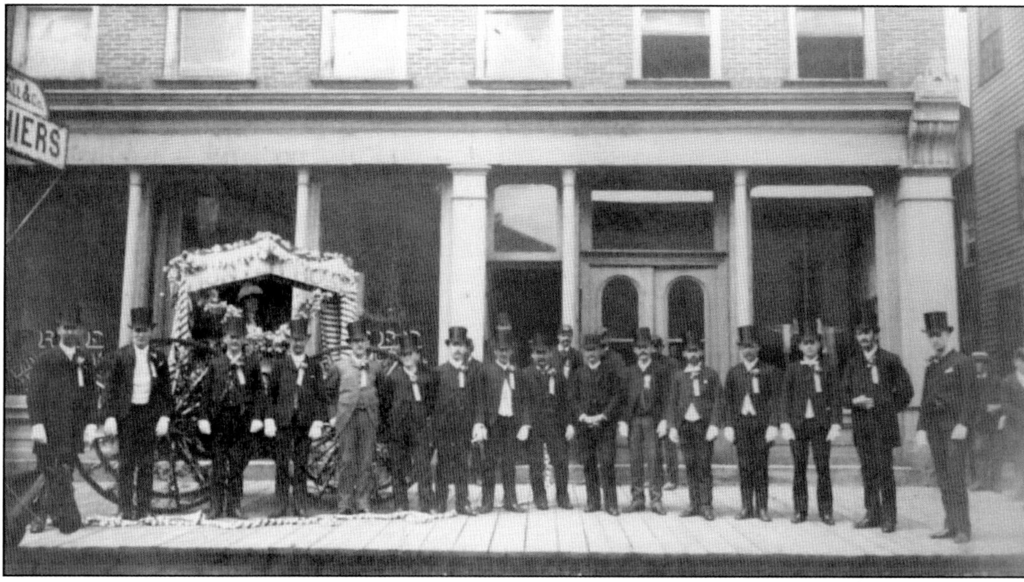

This is an 1890 image of the Tidioute Hunter Hose Company standing in front of the Grandin Opera House after the Fourth of July parade. Shown, from left to right, are Siggins, Shaw, Bowen, Kulin, Kumble, Adams, Magill, Kemble, Morrison, White, Porterfield, Clark, Eedes, Bucklin, Livingston L. Hunter, and Samuel Grandin. The soldier in the center is William Morris, and the soldier on the far right is Richard Foster. The woman in the cart is Maude Bucklin.

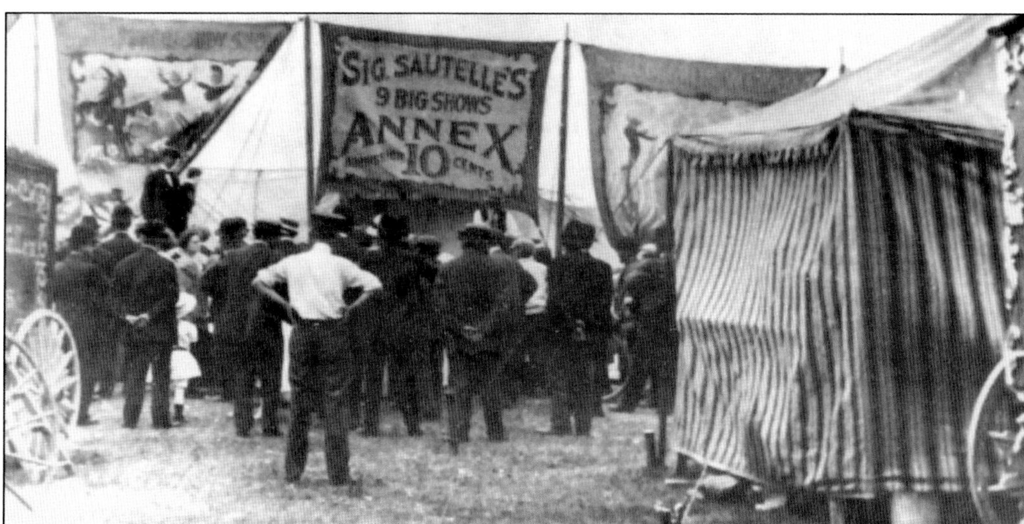

This photograph captures the crowd around the Sig Sautelle–Welsh Brothers Consolidated Circus, which visited Tidioute in June 1905. The circus featured elephants, lions, clowns, magicians, a Wild West show, and numerous tents on the midway. Despite the entertainment, no fewer than three riots erupted between circus folk and townspeople over alleged cheating in the shell game.

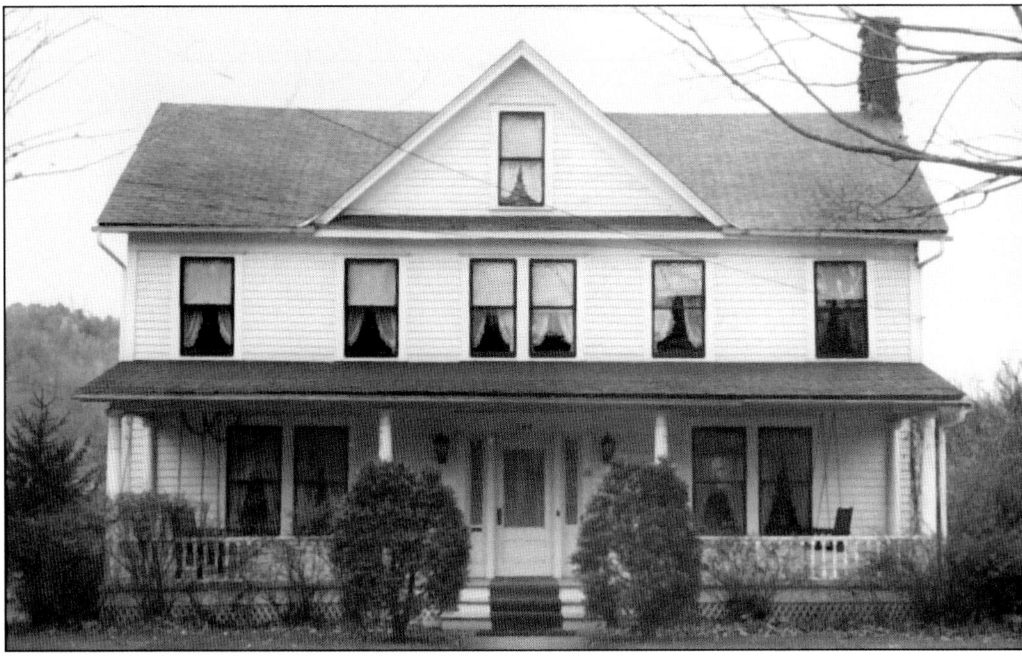

In 1806, Thomas Arters came with his father, Richard, from Lewistown, Pennsylvania, and settled at the mouth of the Tidioute Creek on 400 acres along the Allegheny River. The house Thomas built in the center of what would become the borough of Tidioute in 1824 became known as the Arters House and is said to be the oldest frame house in this part of the county.

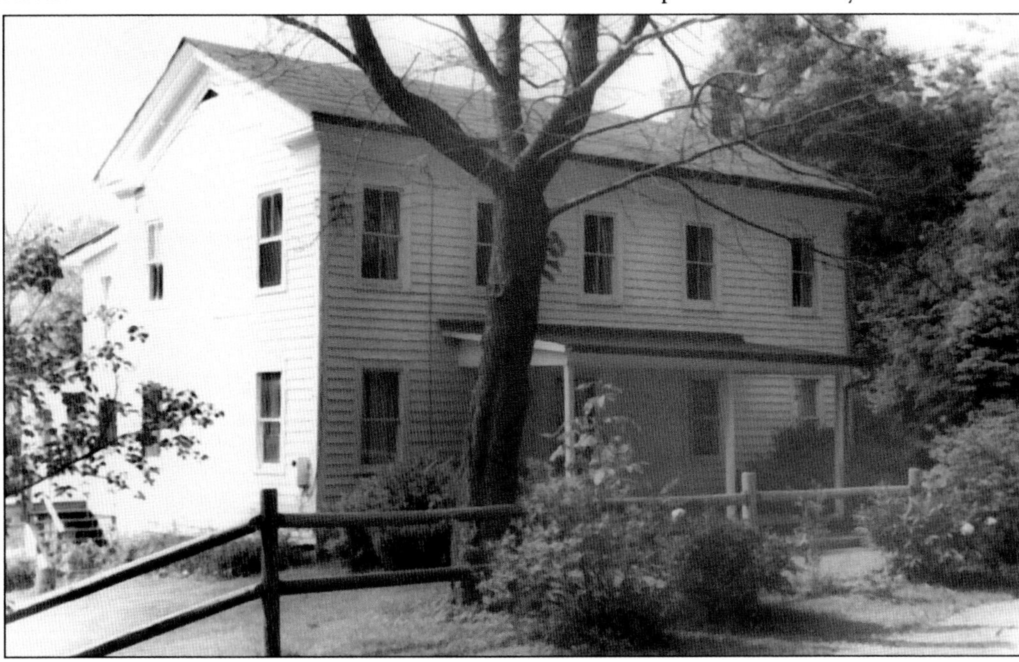

In 1825, Anthony Courson came to Deerfield Township from Centre County, where he was born in 1788. Settling on 400 acres of land near Tidioute, Courson for many years was engaged as an innkeeper, serving raftsmen returning from downriver. This house was built by Anthony's grandson, Ward, in Deerfield Township. It was demolished around 1990.

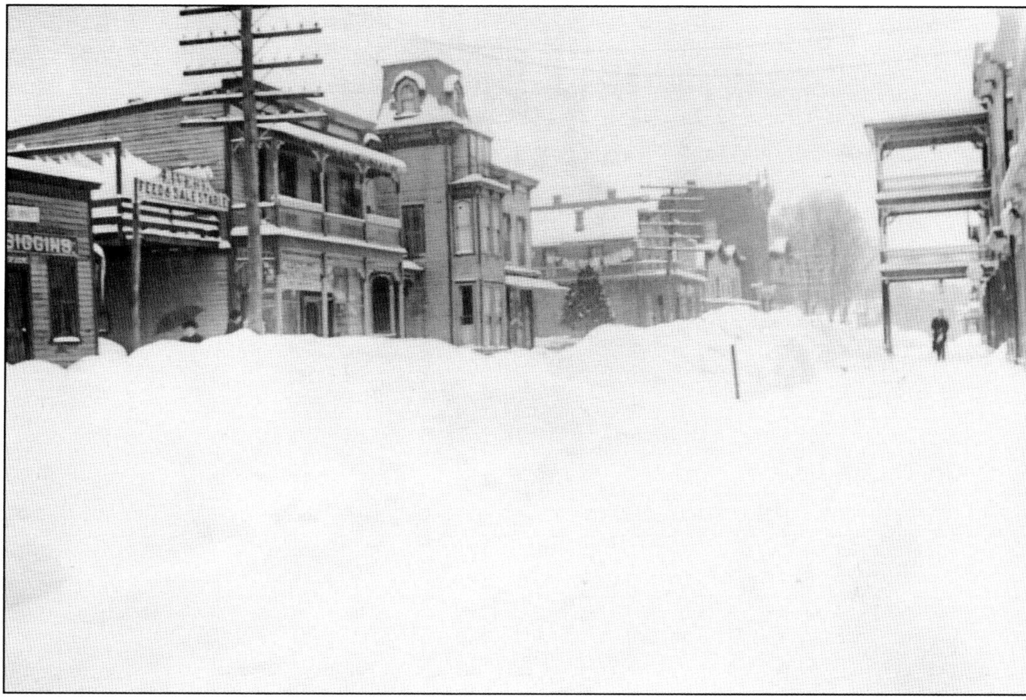

In a scene typical of the hard winters of years past, this 1909 photograph documents Main Street in Tidioute utterly blanketed by a mantle of snow. Although the town of Tidioute began as a prosperous little lumber town, it exploded after July 1860 when the successful drilling of oil wells transformed the sleepy hamlet into a bustling town with an extensive Main Street business district.

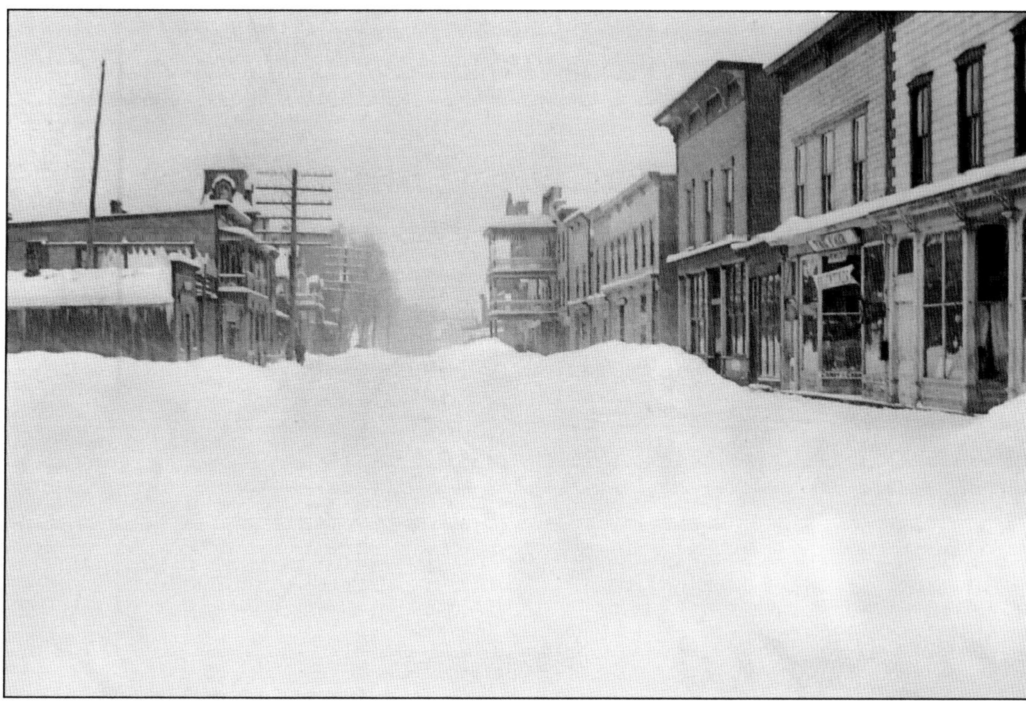

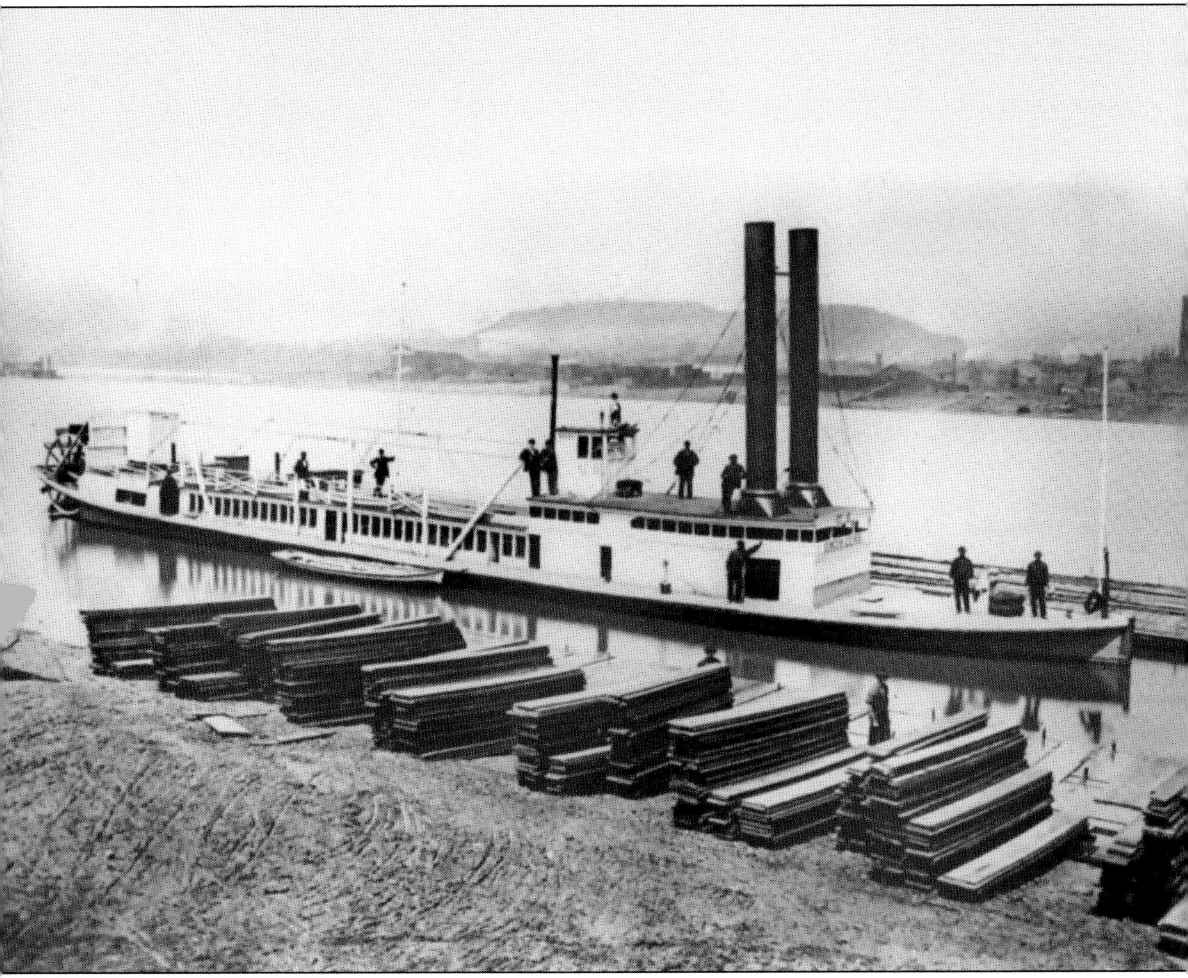

During the oil excitement of 1865, Capt. Amasa Dingley, for whom a branch of Gordon Run was named, built an extraordinary steamboat on the river bank at Tidioute. The boat, which Dingley named for the town, drew a scant eight inches of water and was described as the "fastest and lightest steamboat of this region" by Capt. Frederick Way Jr. of the *S&D Reflector*.

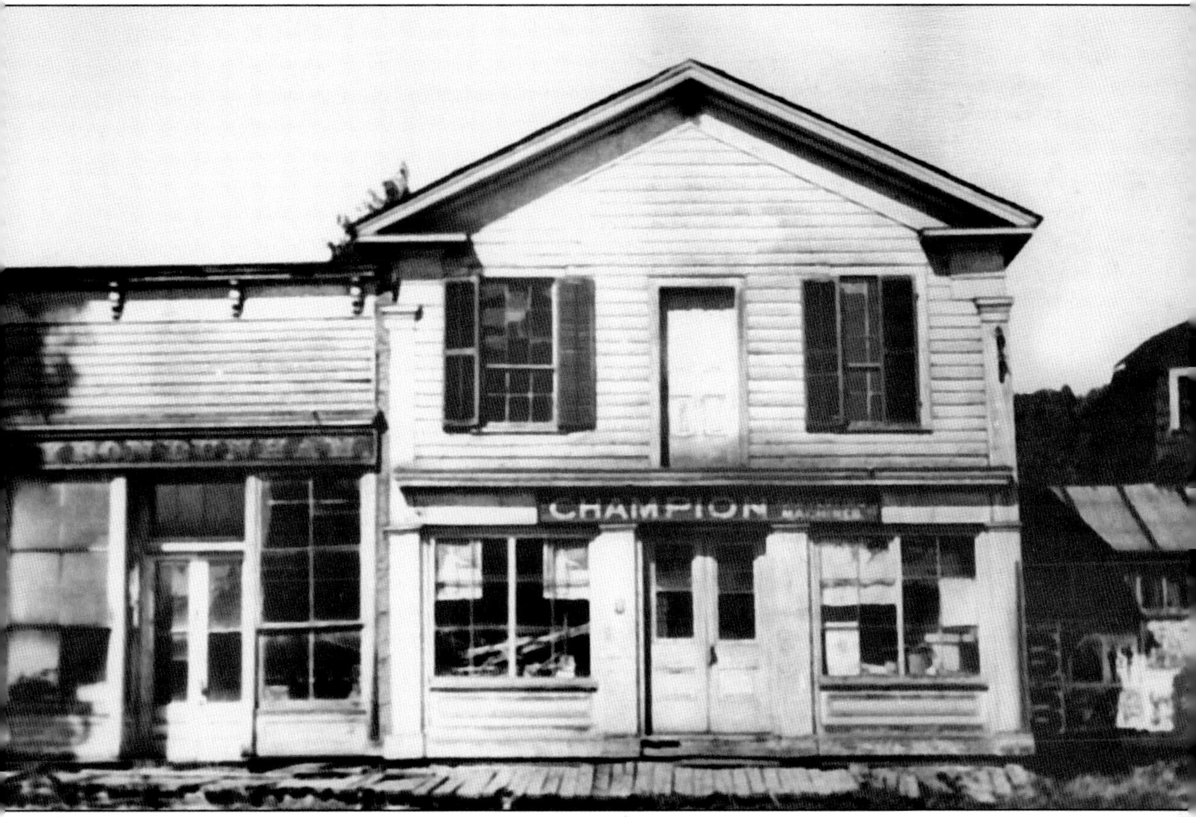

In Southwest Township, the village of Enterprise is located in the southernmost part of the township. In the 1840s, the village was booming with sawmills, general stores, and enterprising citizens, hence its name. According to the National Archives, the first post office at Enterprise commenced on February 23, 1874, with Myron Dunham as postmaster. Looking much worse for the wear, this is the Myron Dunham Building in Enterprise.

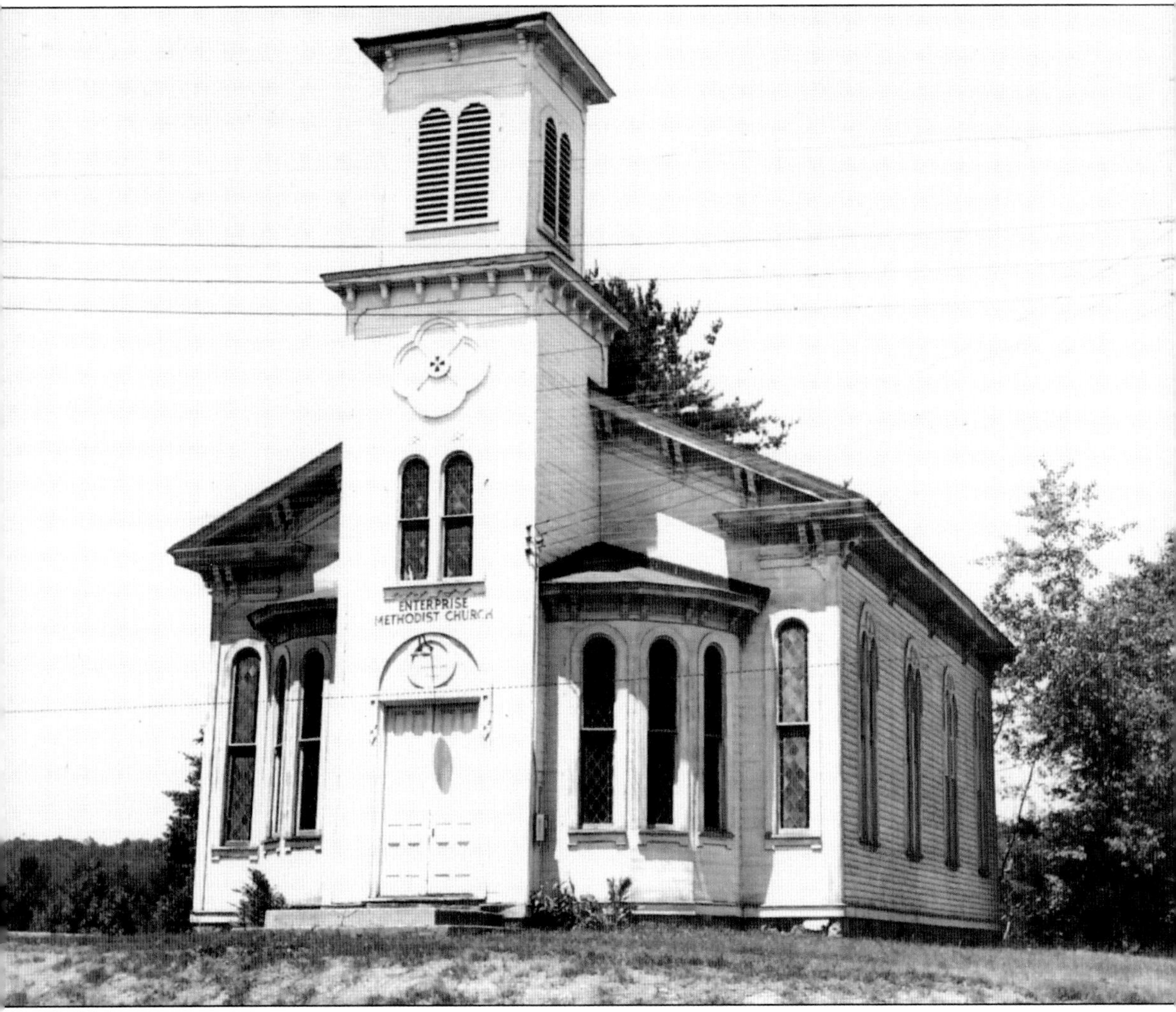

The Enterprise Church was dedicated on August 5, 1872. It became the Enterprise Methodist Church in 1900. The *Titusville Herald* credited "the enterprising citizens of the community" for casting the church's bell, which "was heavy on one side and had a weird ring." It was hung on July 4, 1876, and so became known as the "Freedom Bell."

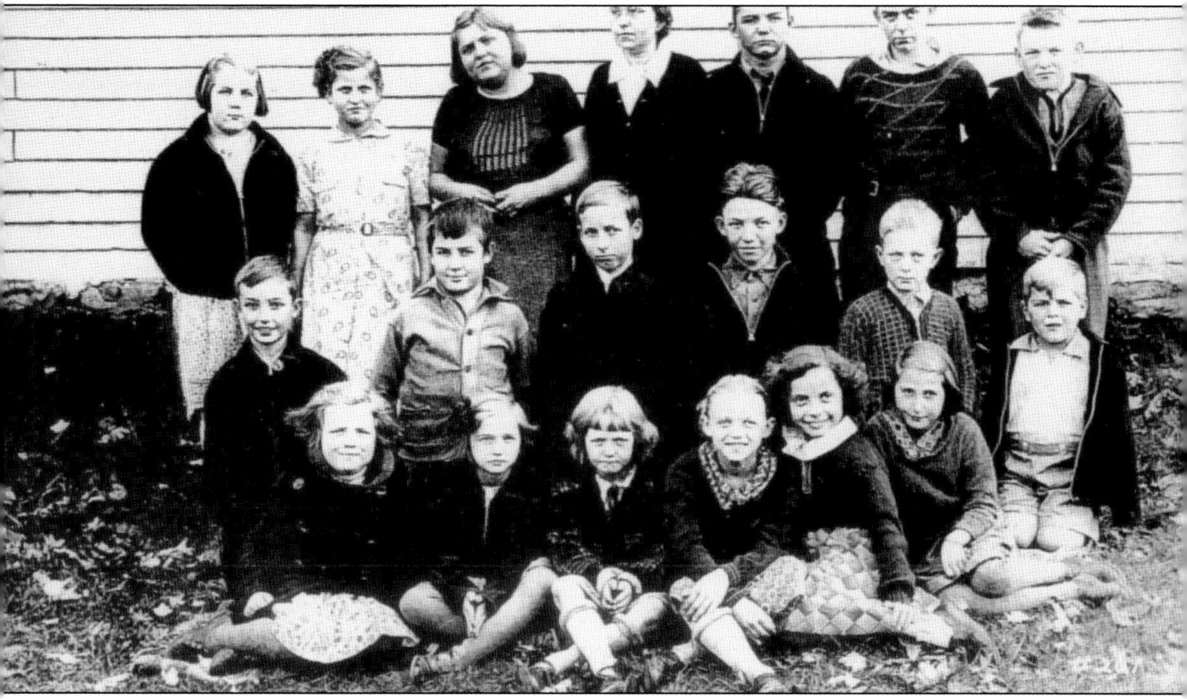

Students who attended Hunter School in Southwest Township in 1937–1938 are, from left to right, (front row) Betty Drake, Mary Lou Mowris, Lucille Cheney, Faye Cheney, and Dorothy Dreyer; (second row) Harold Mowris, Merle Snavley, Wayne Mowris, Herb Cheney, George Sprinks, and Neil Snavley; (third row) Joyce Snavley, Virginia Allen, Mary Allen, Mrs. Orphia Stewart (teacher), Harold Cheney, Carl Wolfe, and Walter Spinks. (Courtesy of Joyce Snavley.)

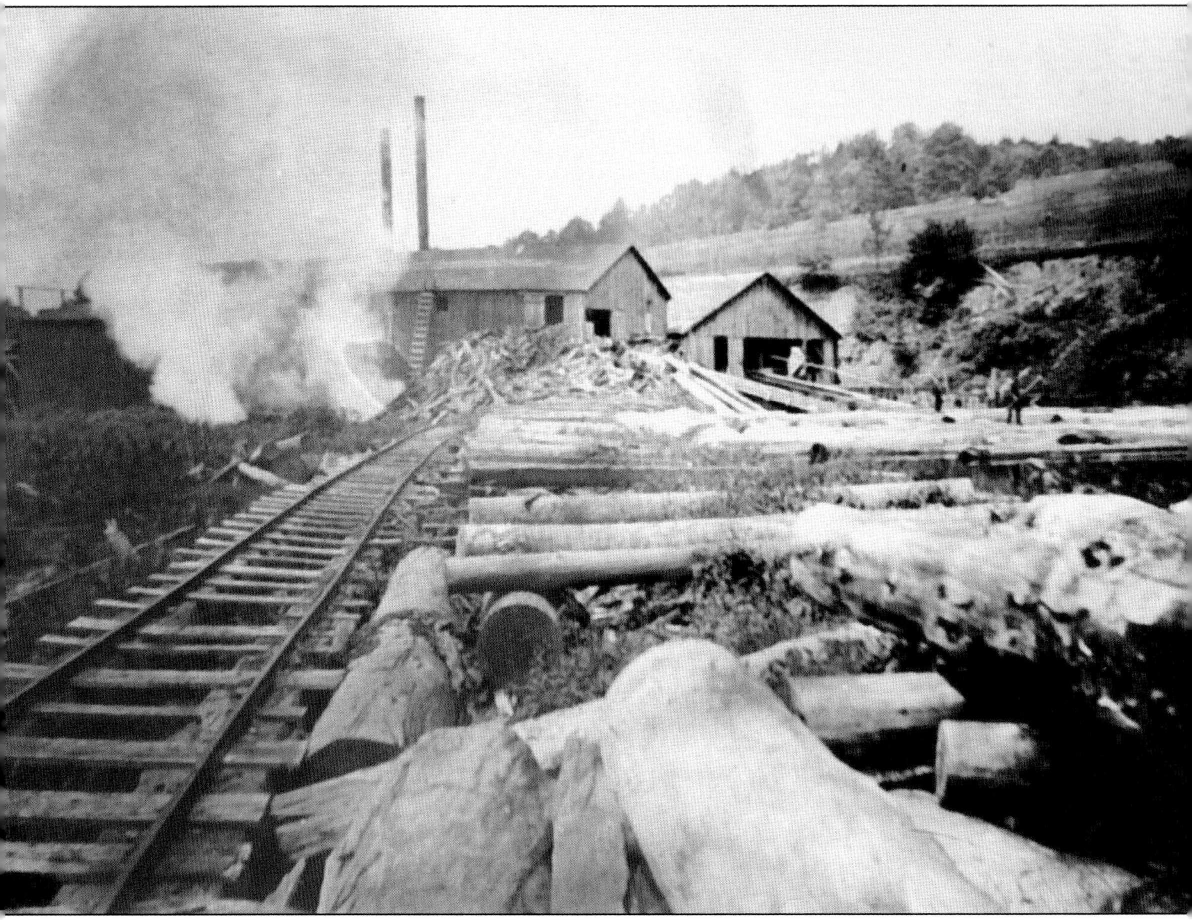

This mill was located in Enterprise and was known as the I.L. Shank and Company. According to the Thomas T. Taber III collection, Shank had a mill along Pine Creek at Enterprise that started in the 1880s. Sometime in the 1890s, a 36-inch-gauge railroad was built from East Titusville to the mill and then about eight miles up Pine Creek to a place called Seldom Seen. There were several branches off it. The mill ran until shortly before 1900, when it closed down.

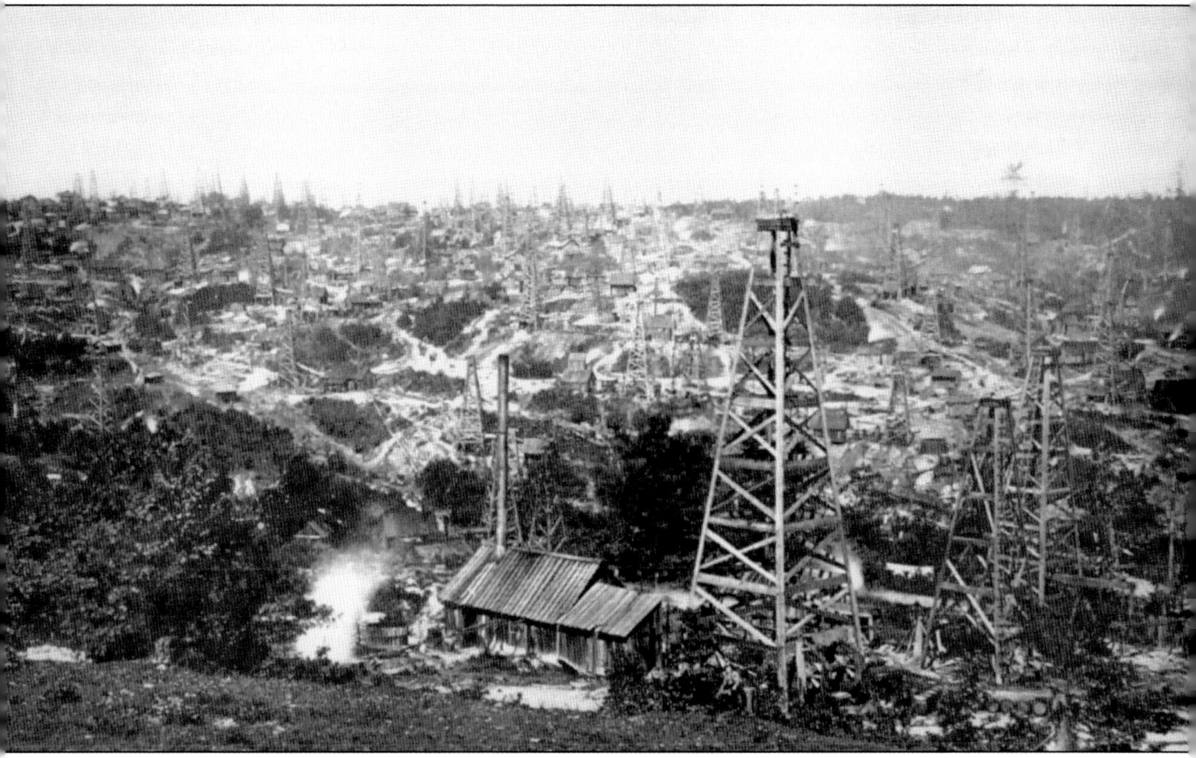

In Triumph Township, the turbulent years of the Civil War did not thwart development in the oil-rich regions of Warren County. By 1865, the oil excitement from Tidioute had crept up Dennis Run to Triumph Hill, where a town, Triumph City, was erected. It had a population of more than 1,000 until it was destroyed by fire in 1868.

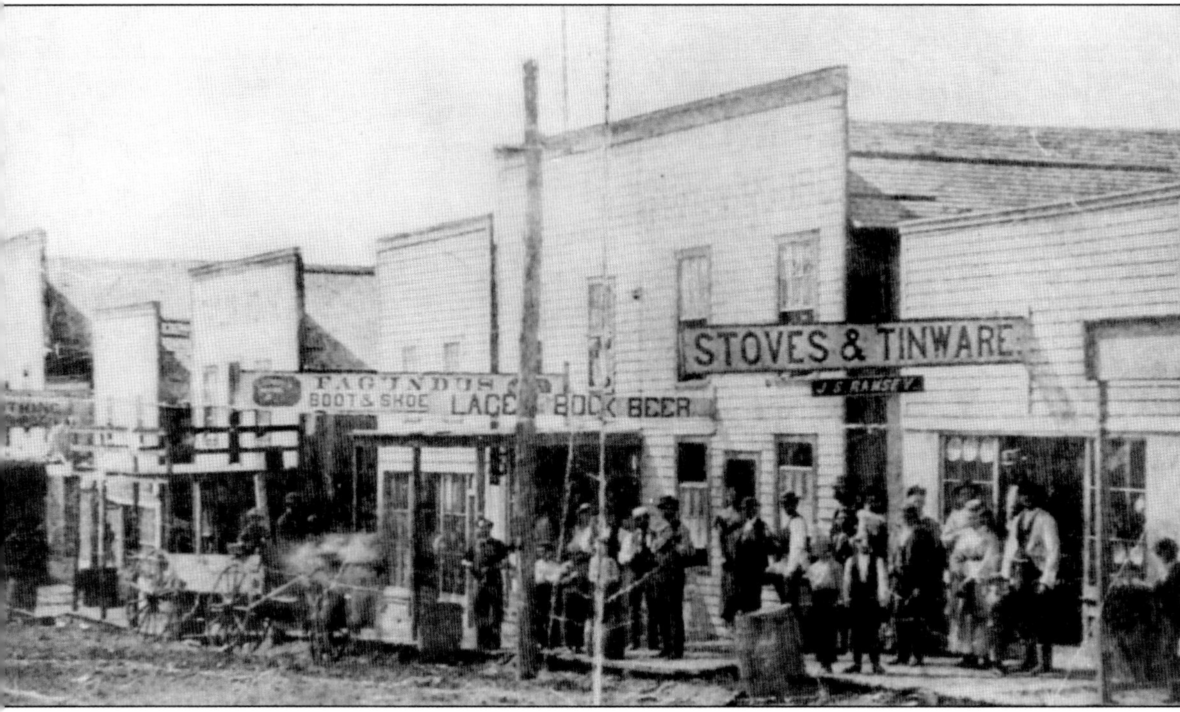

Originally named Battle City, Fagundus took its name from the Fagundus Farm, where in 1870, oil was discovered by wildcatters. Soon, the Fagundus Farm well was producing upwards of 2,000 barrels daily, and a town grew that included a newspaper, a bank, and five hotels. This rare photograph captures those boom years before the bust began in 1876. (Courtesy of the Gustav and Everett Borg photograph collection.)

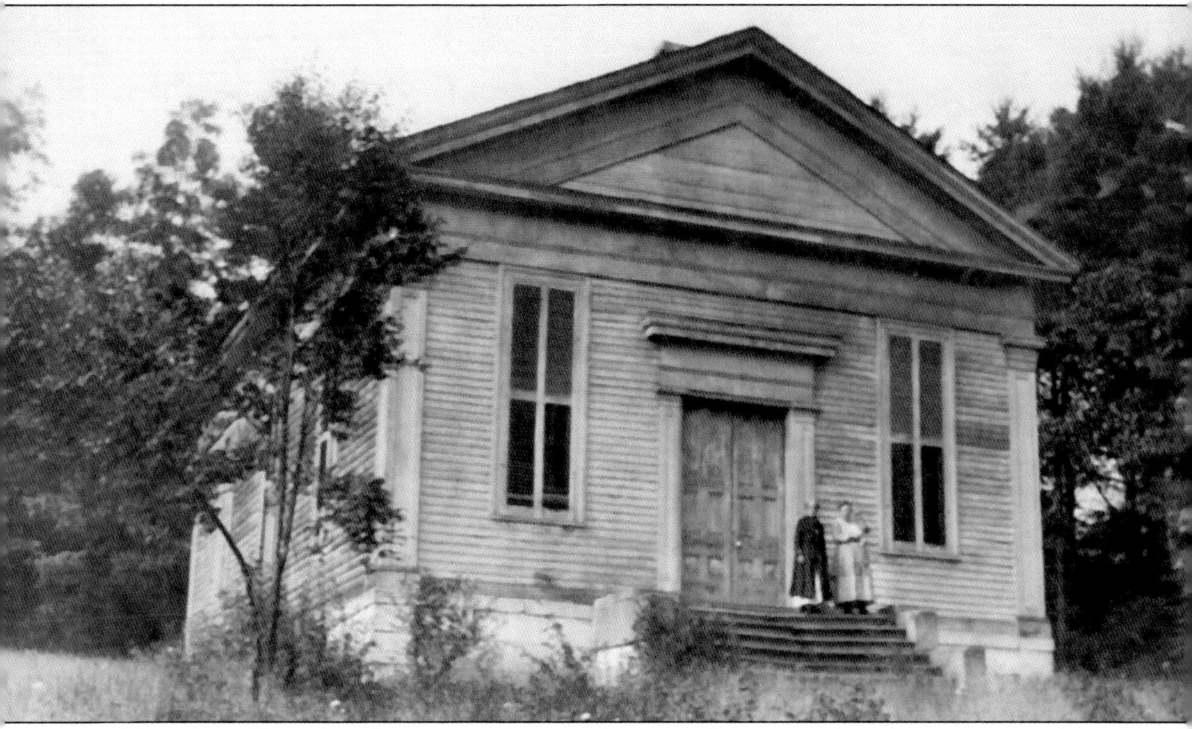

The old Funk Hollow Church in Triumph Township is no longer standing, but visitors to the Valentine graves nearby might still be able to find its foundation. Capt. A.B. Funk, a riverman, lumberman, and oil entrepreneur who visited Colonel Drake's well, lived in this vicinity.

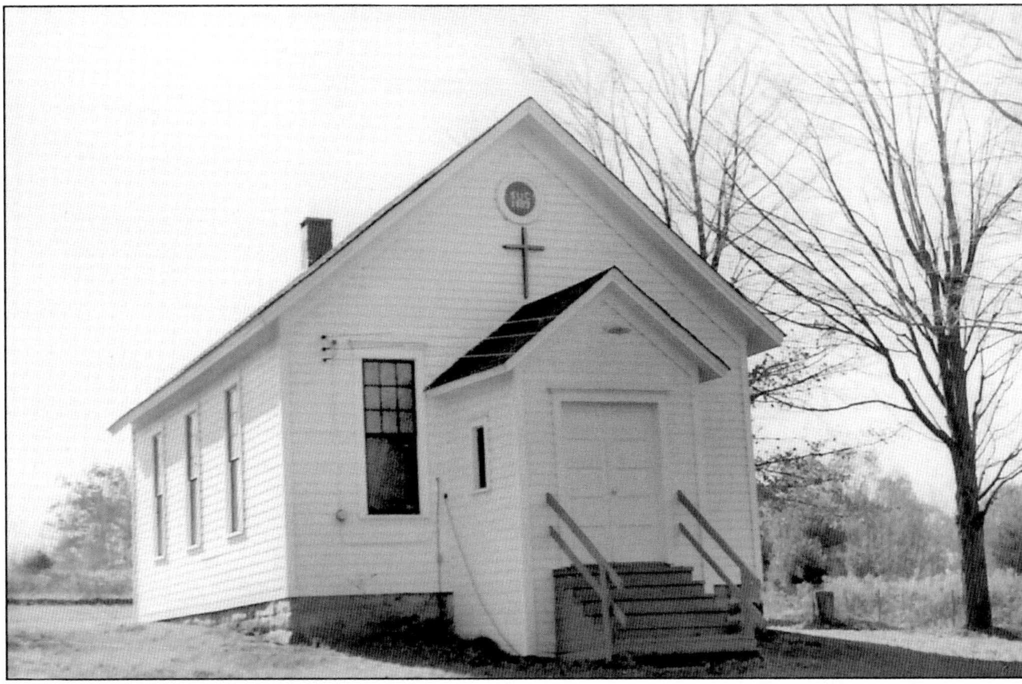

The Triumph Oil Company reportedly built the Swede Road Church for the settlers, among them droves of Swedish immigrants, who flocked to Triumph in the 1860s hoping to strike it rich in black gold. When the oil fields ran dry in the 1870s, the oil company liquidated its assets and in 1887 gave the church to the Swedes, who then moved the church from Triumph to their settlement a mile away.

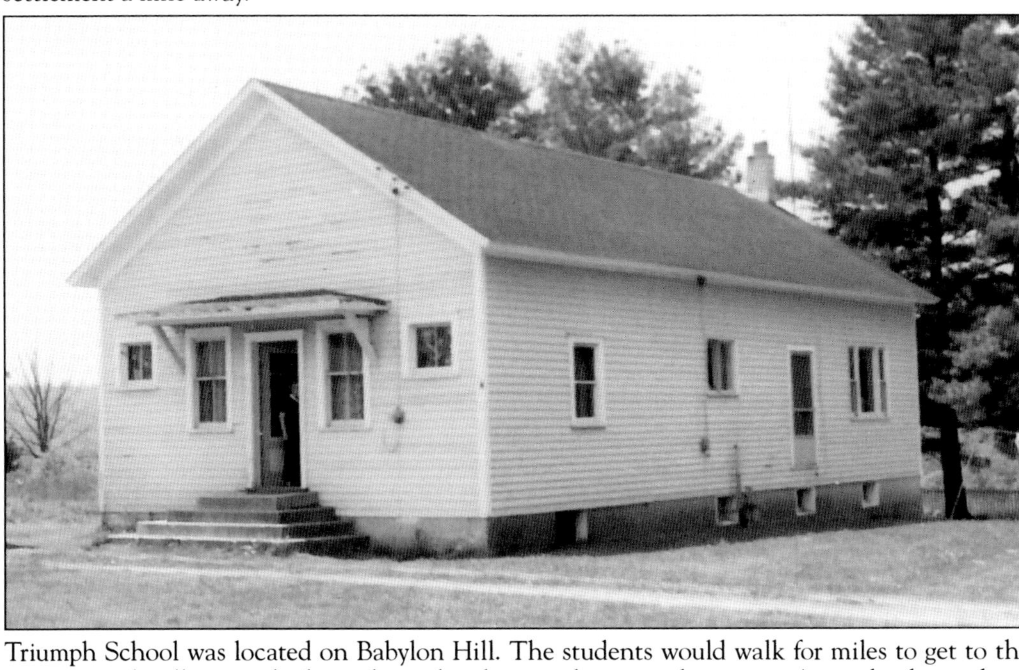

Triumph School was located on Babylon Hill. The students would walk for miles to get to the one-room schoolhouse, which was heated with a woodstove in the winter. As a rule, the students ranged from first through eighth graders.

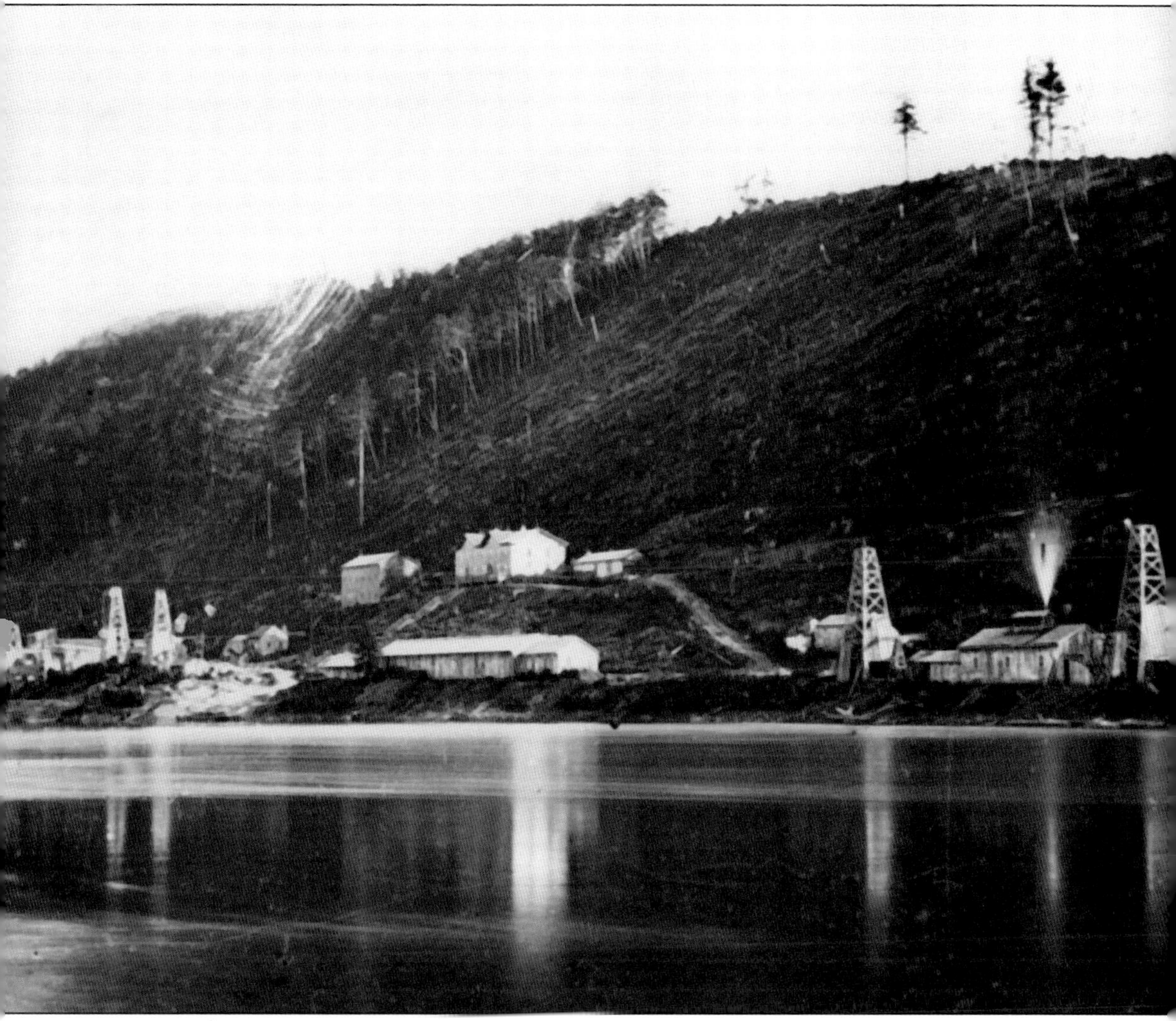

In this image from Limestone Township, the large house in the center of the photograph is the birthplace of Anna M. Grandin, formerly of Tidioute. US Route 62 now runs along the hillside speckled with the freshly cut stumps. This photograph was taken around 1860 by pioneer oil photographer John Mather.

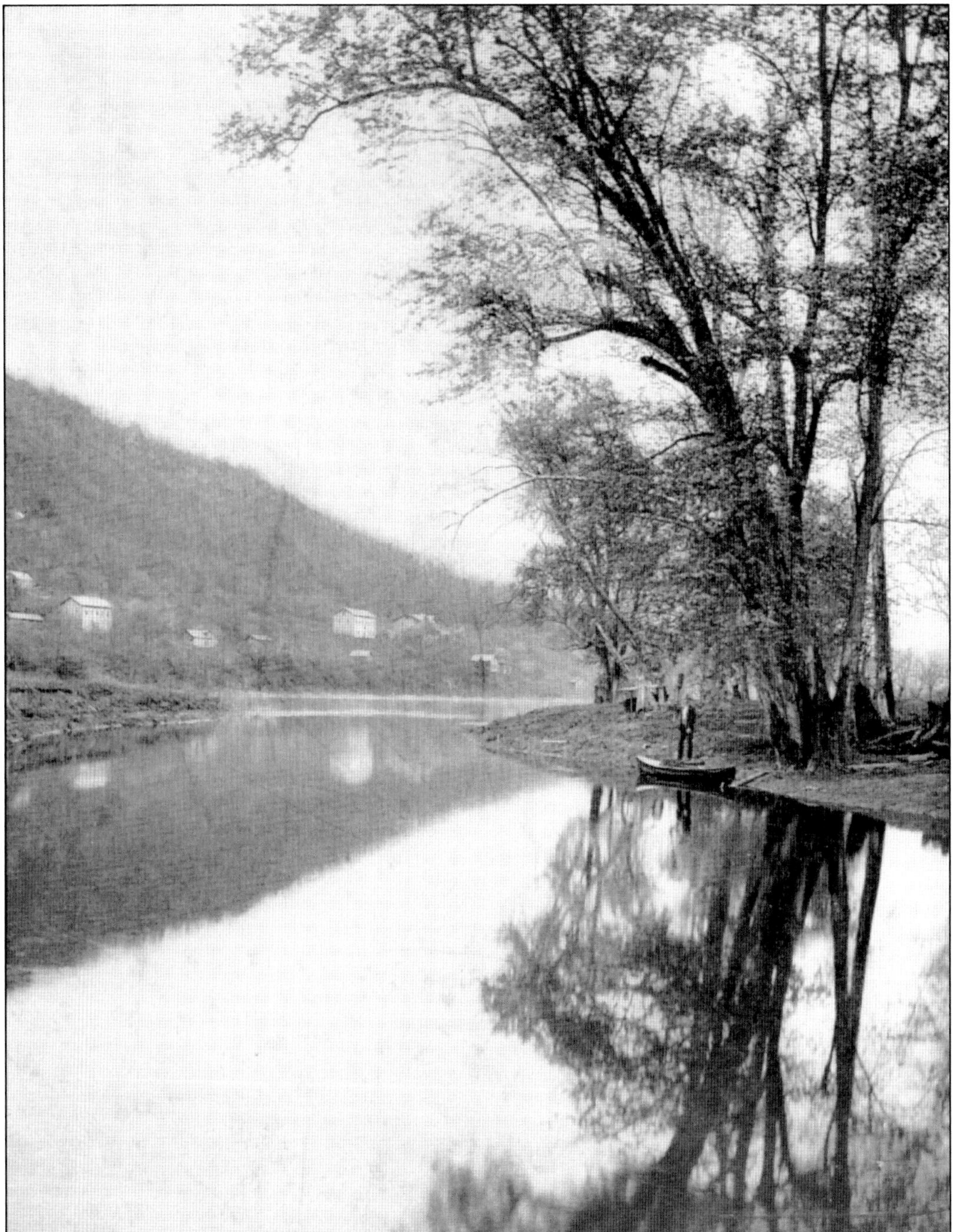

In the distance, one can see the house and barn of the Economites, a hardworking, religious group. In the 1850s, the Economites purchased 2,000 acres of land, and shortly after William Davidson went bankrupt, they purchased his 4,000 acres of timberland at a sheriff's sale. The Economites were also known as the Harmonists and reaped the benefit of Limestone Township's natural resources. After Colonel Drake struck oil in 1859, they made millions from oil production.

Four

Southeast Warren County

Pleasant, Mead, Watson, Cherry Grove, and Sheffield Townships

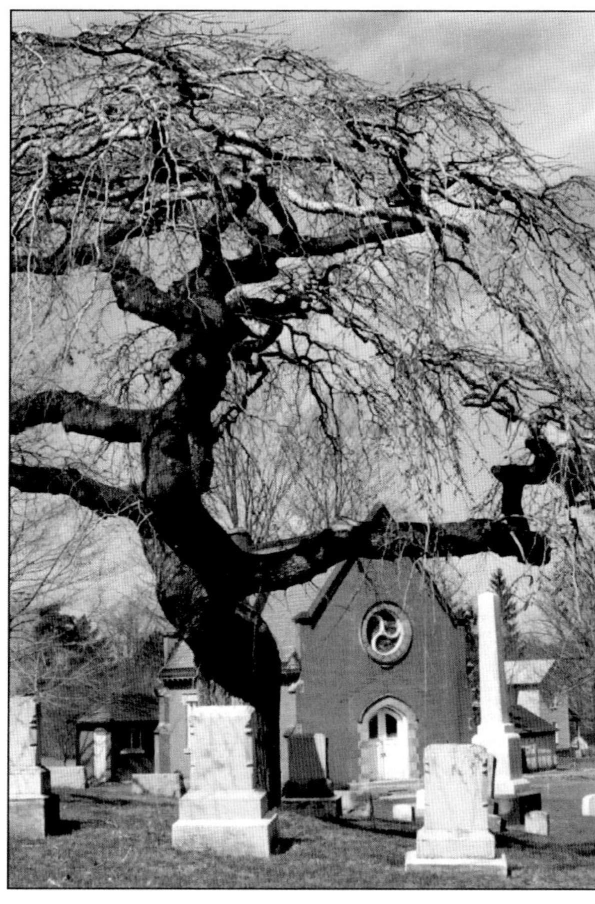

In Pleasant Township, Oakland Cemetery was founded in 1863 when the original cemetery on Water, East, Fourth, and Fifth Streets reached capacity. Many of the bodies were disinterred and moved from their final resting places at that location to Oakland Cemetery across the Allegheny River. However, as not all graves were marked, not all graves were moved. (Courtesy of *Oakland* by Charles R. Tranter.)

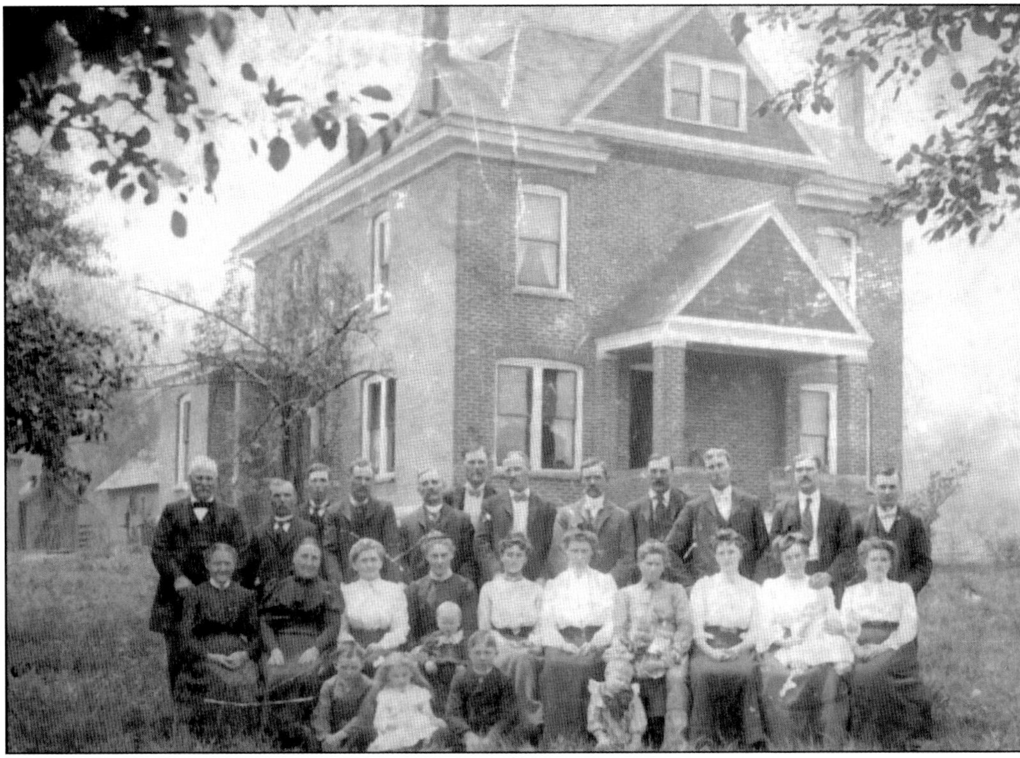

Ernest and William Highhouse worked in a German brick factory before coming to America in 1848. Upon hearing of the clay in Pleasant Township, they started their own business, Highhouse Brick Factory. It passed through their family until closing in 1939 due to the high cost of using gas. (Both, courtesy of Nicki Tremblay.)

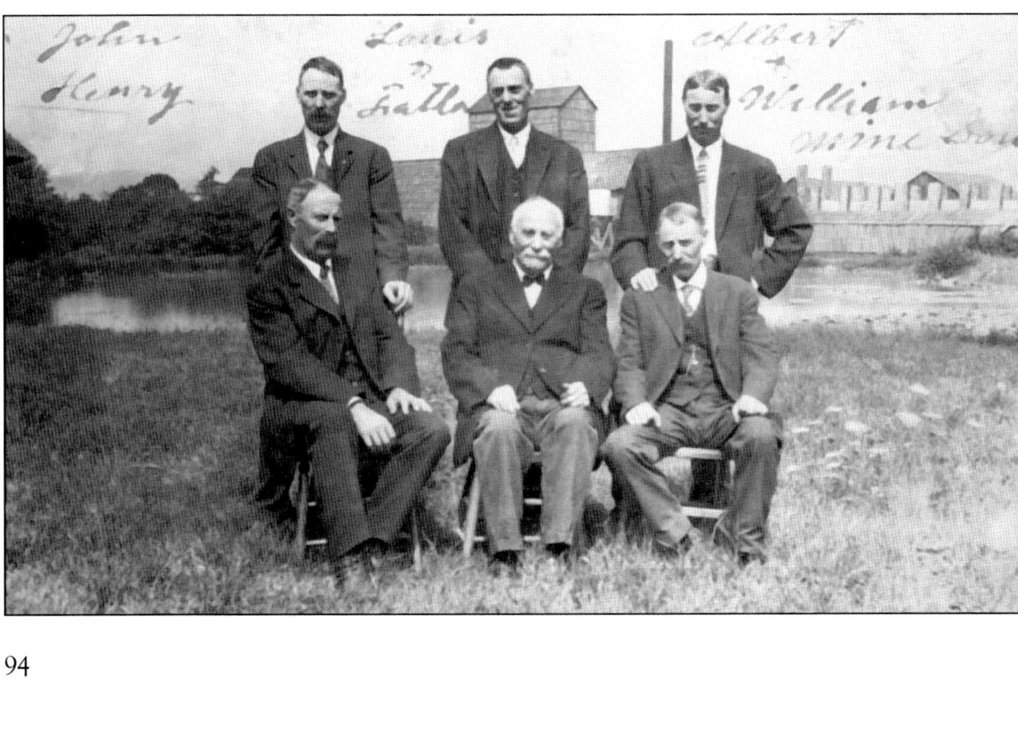

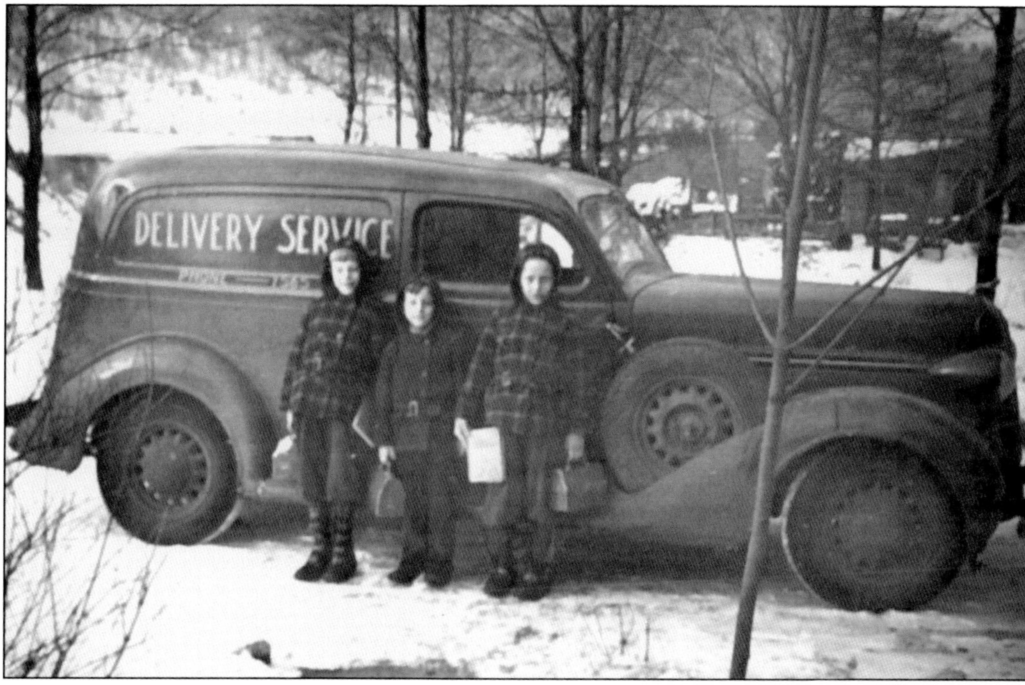

The Yaegle delivery business began around the mid-1930s. It delivered almost anything people needed. A lady living on Water Street in Warren would make heavenly pies that were often a delivery item. The business ended around 1940 because George Yaegle, who owned and ran the truck, began working for the Pennsylvania Railroad. (Courtesy of Edward Yaegle.)

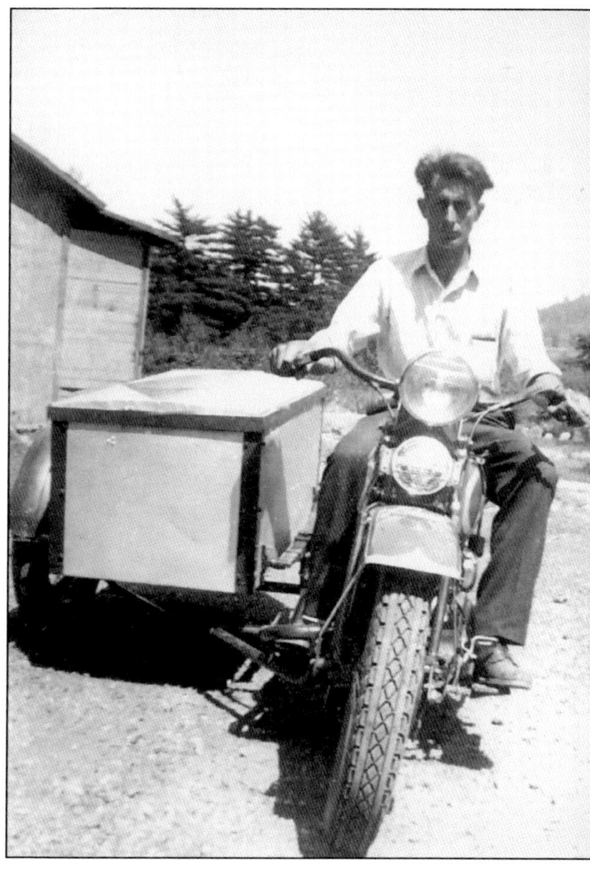

Prior to the delivery truck, Lloyd Yaegle ran a motorcycle shop in Pleasant Township that not only sold motorcycles but also tuned them up. Most motorcyclists of this period rode their motorcycles because they were a cheap form of transportation. They could be bought for just a couple hundred dollars. (Courtesy of Edward Yaegle.)

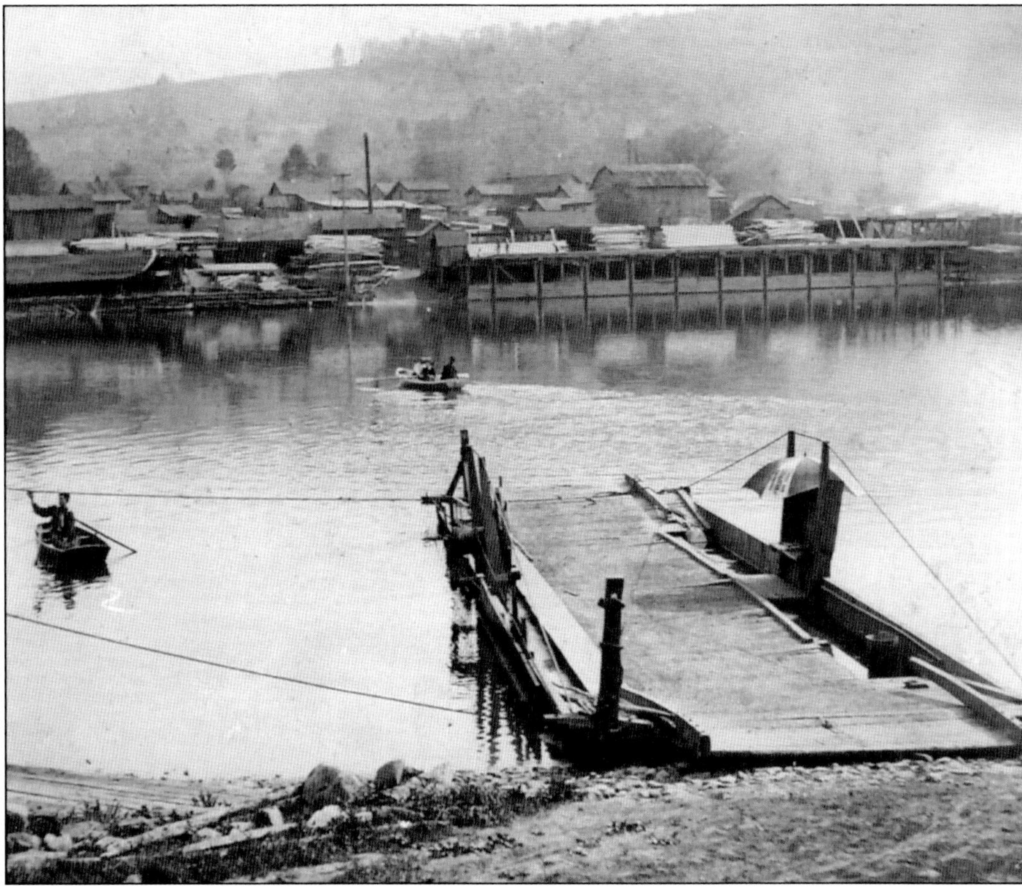

The Grunderville Mill began when a man by the name of Lawrence and a banker from Tionesta bought a 400-acre tract of timber. With it, they constructed 10 square timber rafts. The rafts were sold to Alec McClure of Pittsburgh. Eventually, the mill was dismantled and moved to an area where timber interest for the company was greater.

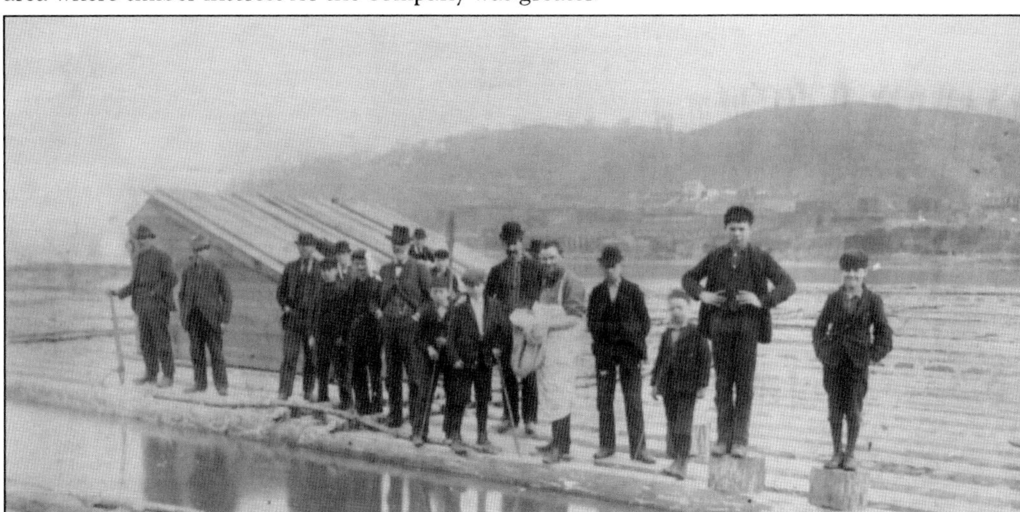

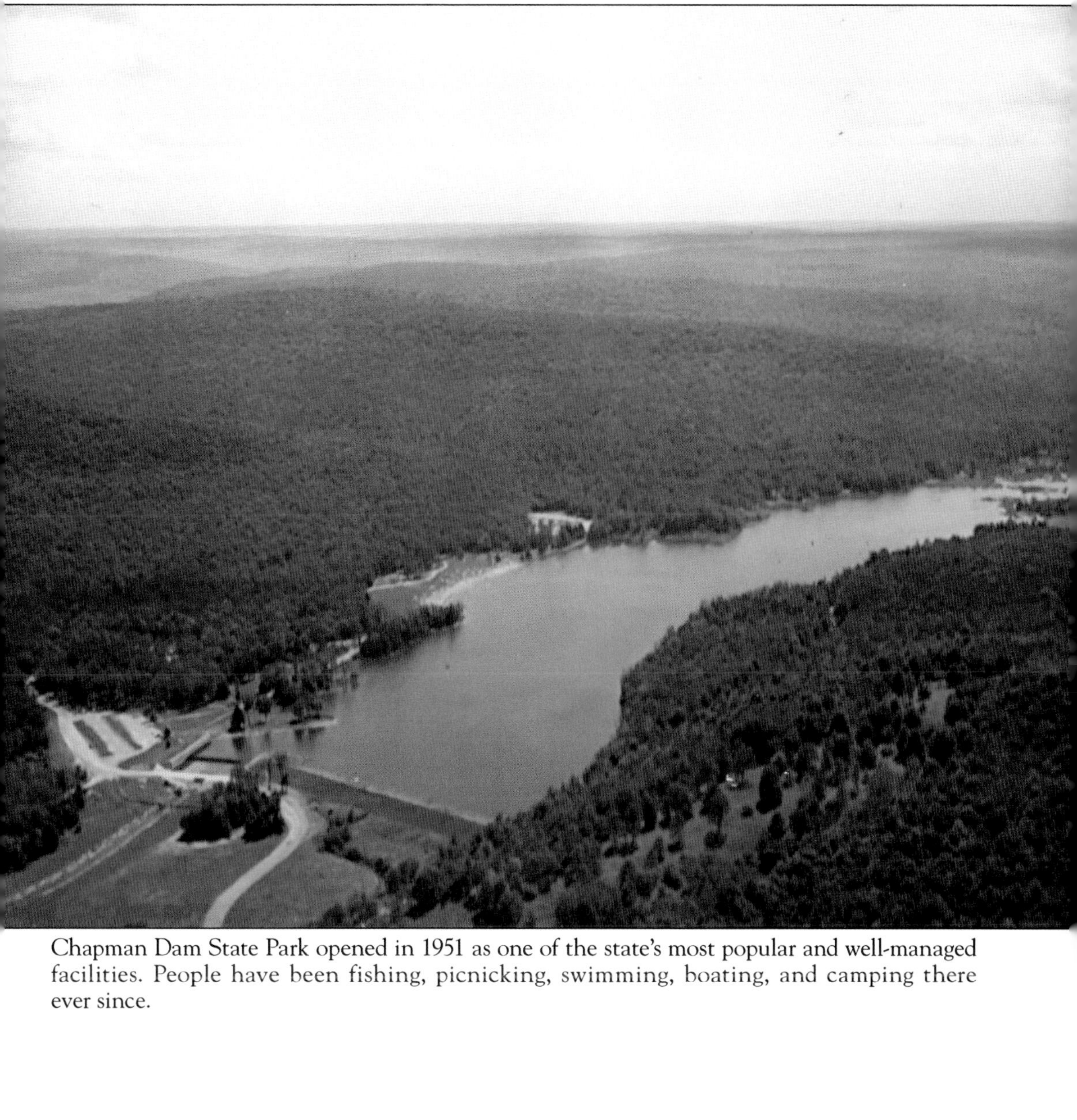

Chapman Dam State Park opened in 1951 as one of the state's most popular and well-managed facilities. People have been fishing, picnicking, swimming, boating, and camping there ever since.

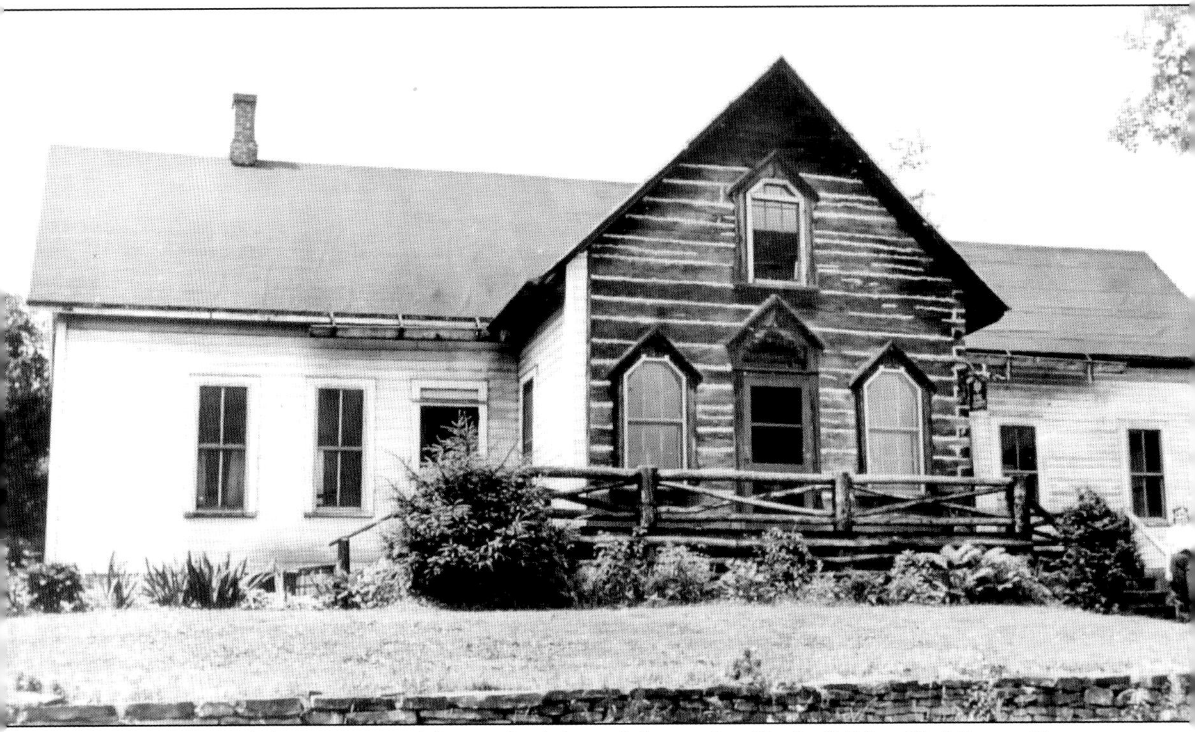

This image of the Homestead (caretaker's home) located at Birdsall Edey Girl Scout Camp on Grunderville Road was taken by photographer David Correll in June 1999. In 1934, the Homestead was included in the US Forest Service's (USFS) acquisition of a project area where a men's transient labor camp was built. The Gothic-style windows and the square, cut-log structure may date to the early or middle 1800s. A part of the only example of Depression-era military-style architecture in the Allegheny National Forest and the only work relief camp associated with the State Emergency Relief Board and the Works Progress Administration, it remains intact today. (Photograph courtesy of David Correll for the 60th anniverary of Camp Birdsall Edey – June 1999.)

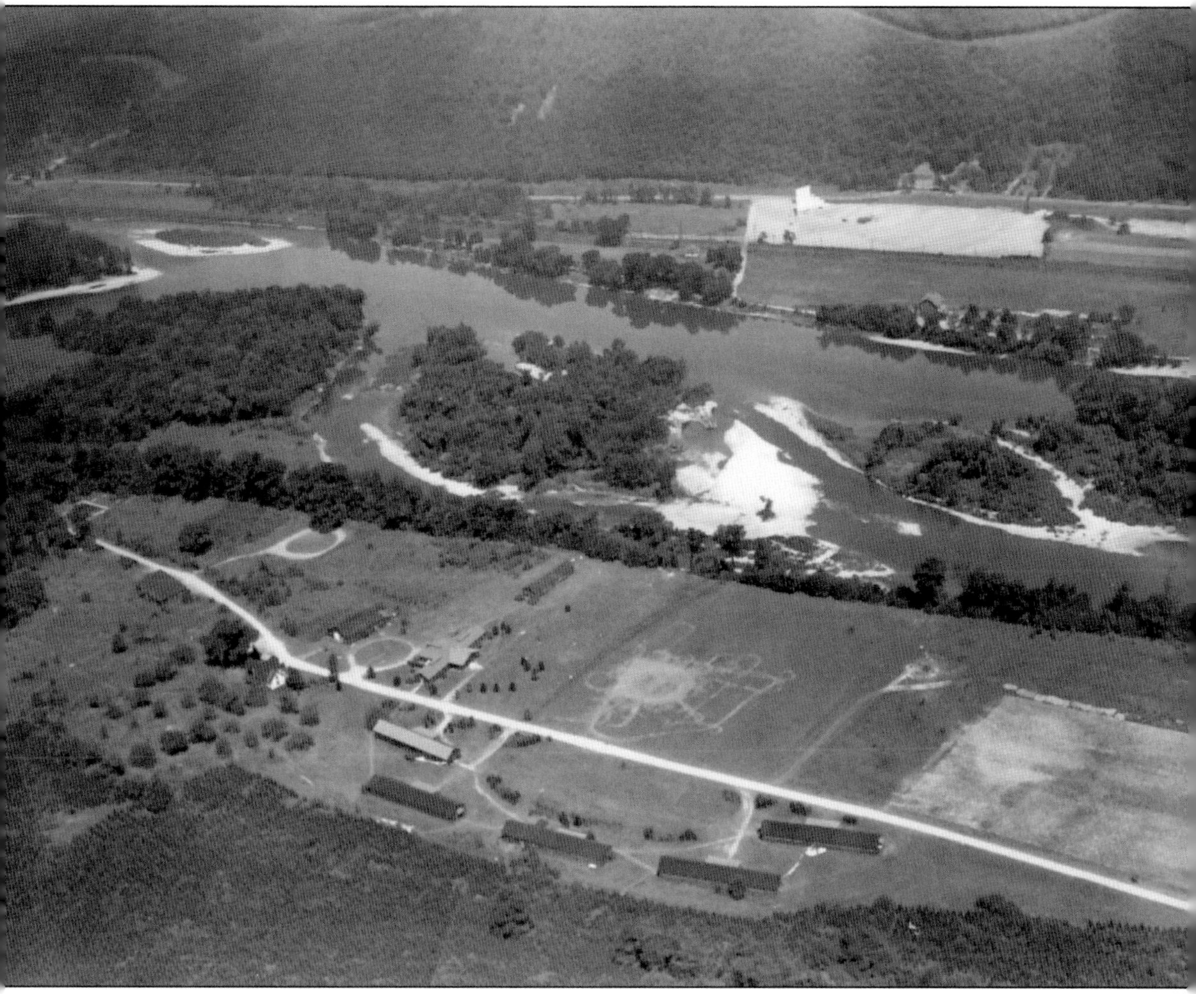

Birdsall Edey has not been used since 2010, when the Girl Scout camp closed after leasing from the USFS since 1939. (Courtesy of the Everett Stoke aerial collection.)

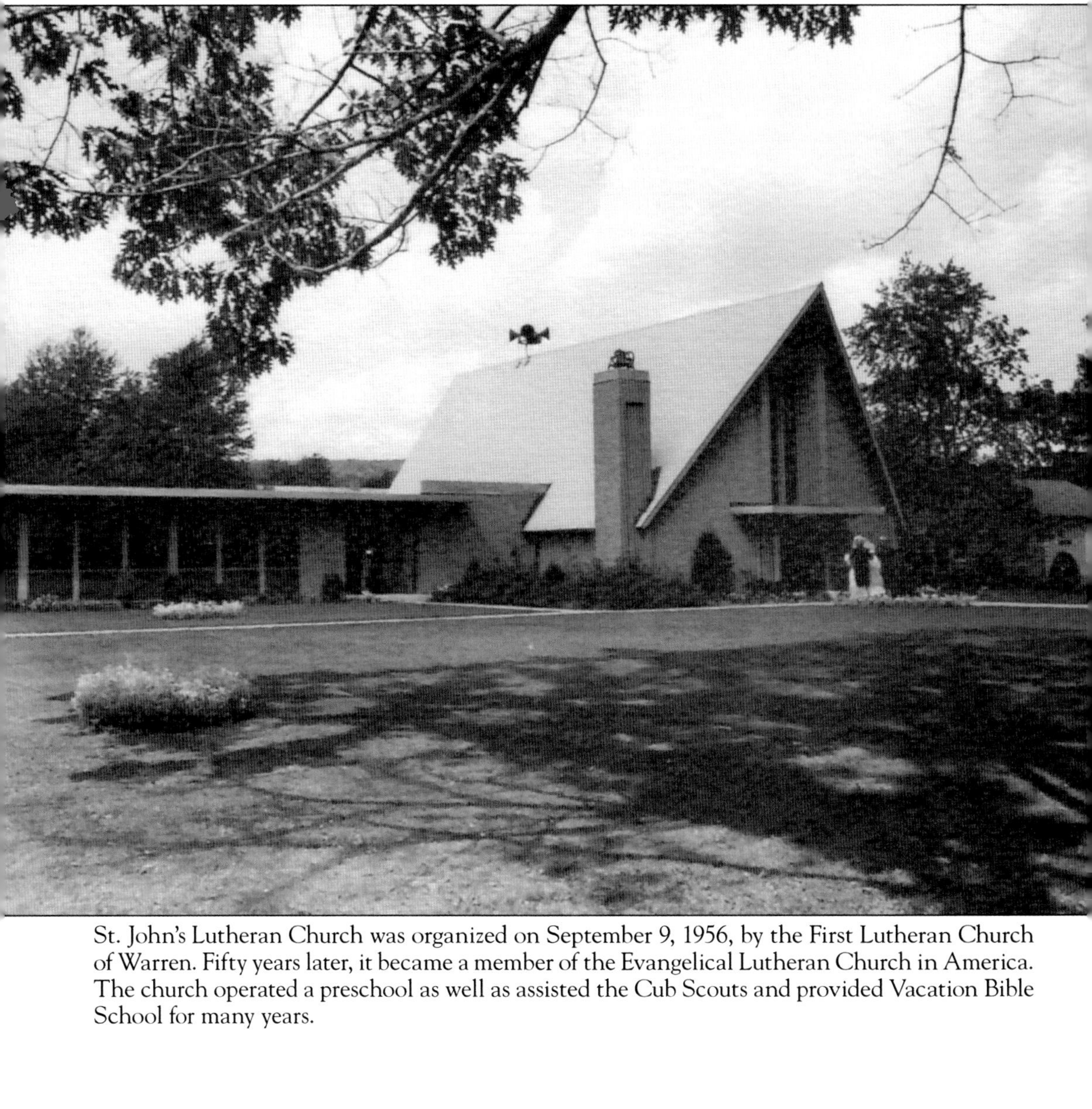

St. John's Lutheran Church was organized on September 9, 1956, by the First Lutheran Church of Warren. Fifty years later, it became a member of the Evangelical Lutheran Church in America. The church operated a preschool as well as assisted the Cub Scouts and provided Vacation Bible School for many years.

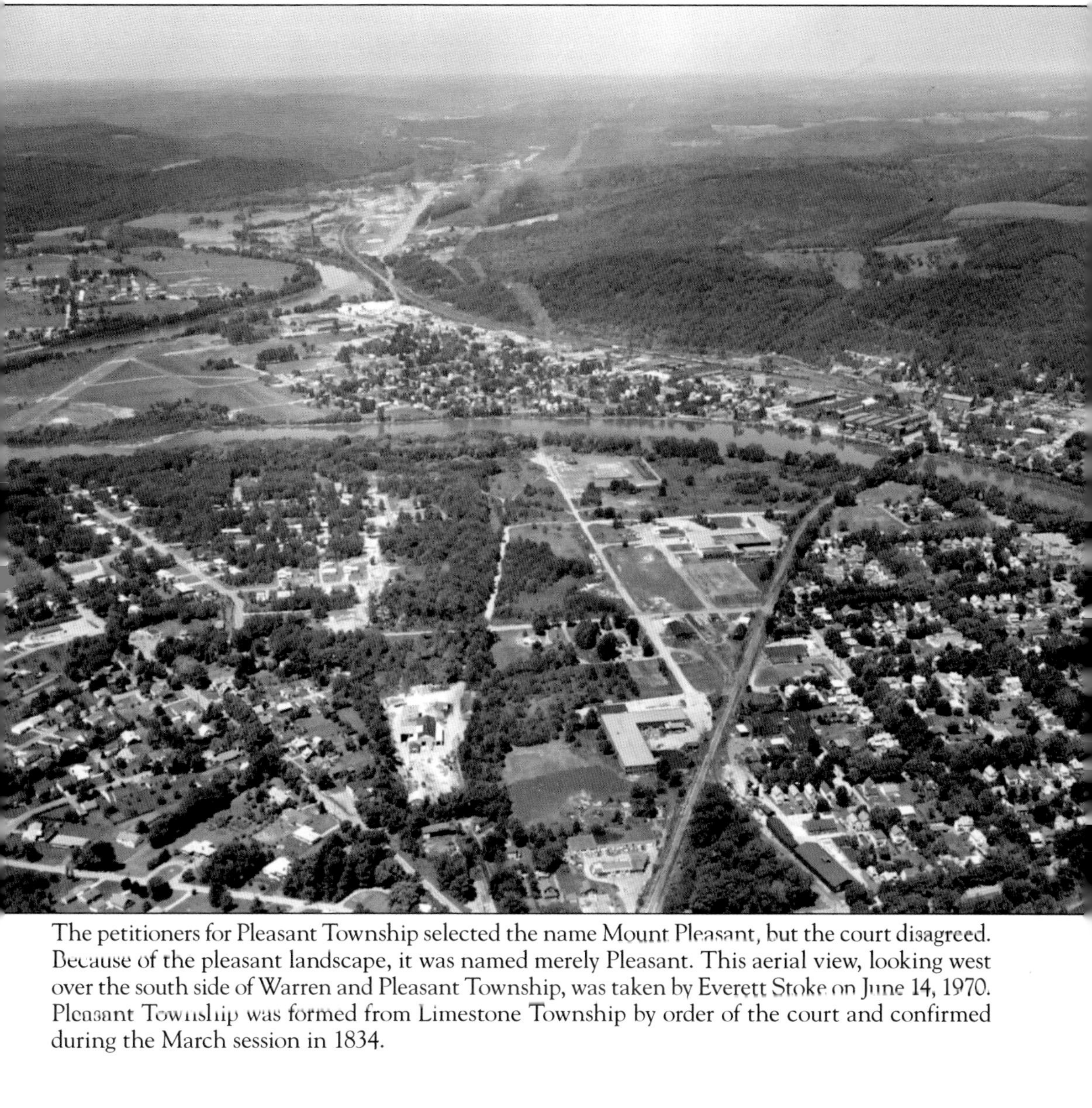

The petitioners for Pleasant Township selected the name Mount Pleasant, but the court disagreed. Because of the pleasant landscape, it was named merely Pleasant. This aerial view, looking west over the south side of Warren and Pleasant Township, was taken by Everett Stoke on June 14, 1970. Pleasant Township was formed from Limestone Township by order of the court and confirmed during the March session in 1834.

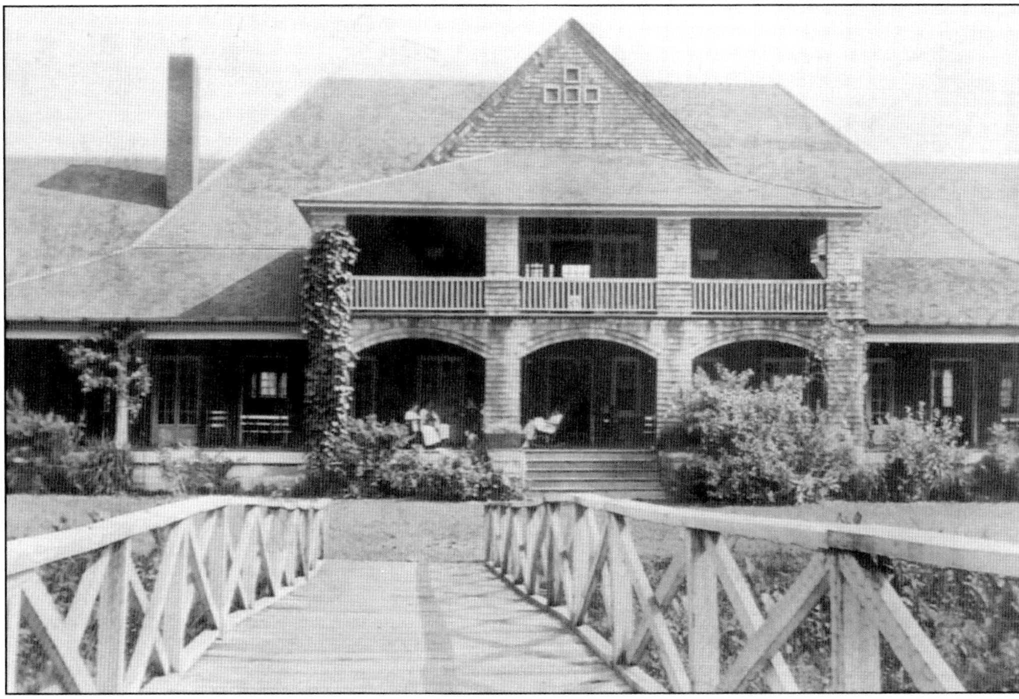

In Mead Township, the Warren Outing Club was made in the hopes that the members would "promote social activities and an interest in outdoor pleasures." It was located at the riverfront property known as "Hertzel's Ferry" in Mead Township and hosted dinners, dances, parties, and picnics.

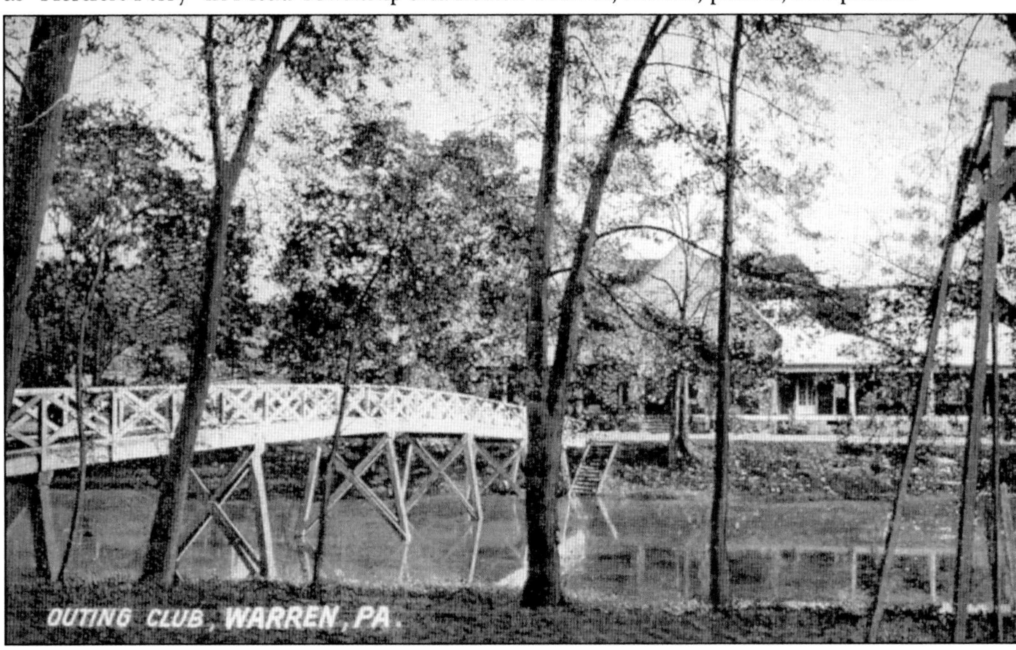

The Warren Outing Club provided a getaway from the city. People spent their downtime fishing, hiking, swimming, rowing, and playing team sports there. Eventually, the Warren Outing Club was sold to become the Marconi Club. Part of the building was burned in a fire, and it then became a restaurant.

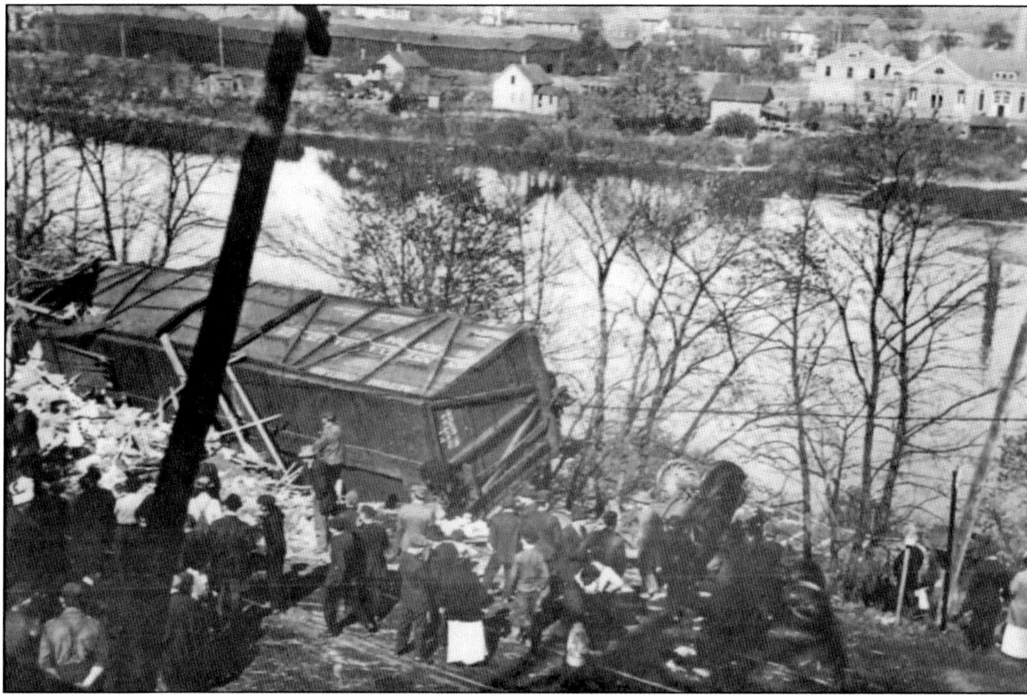

This is a 1910 freight wreck on the Philadelphia and Erie Railroad. This railroad was completed in 1864 and alleviated transportation problems found in this part of the county. Previously, it could take up to four days to travel from Warren to Sheffield.

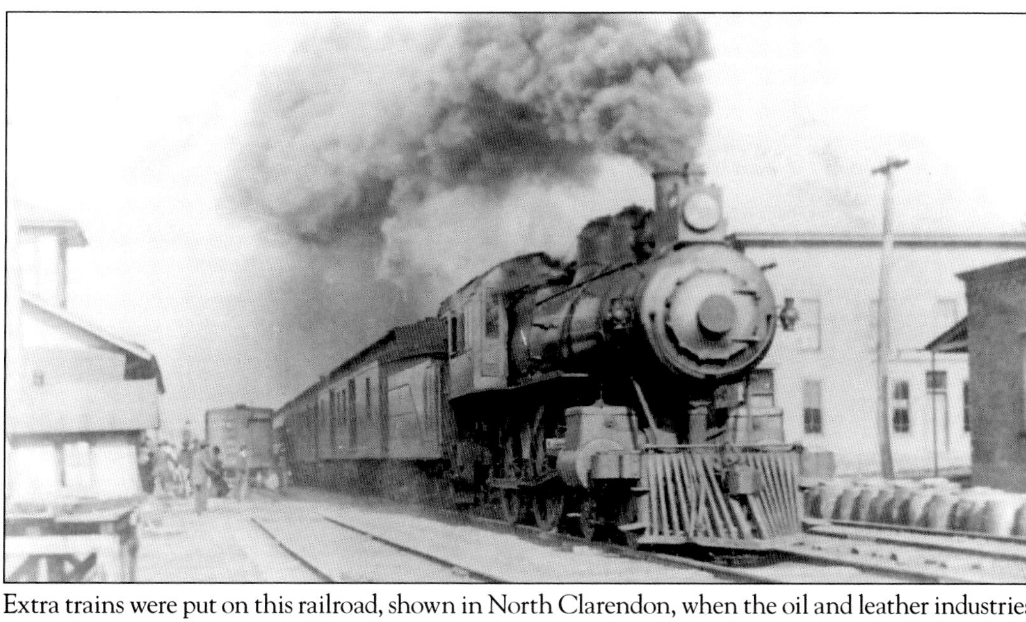

Extra trains were put on this railroad, shown in North Clarendon, when the oil and leather industries started to grow in the area. The railroad would carry workers from Warren to the oil fields. From Clarendon, the Philadelphia & Erie Railroad continued on to Stoneham and Rogertown.

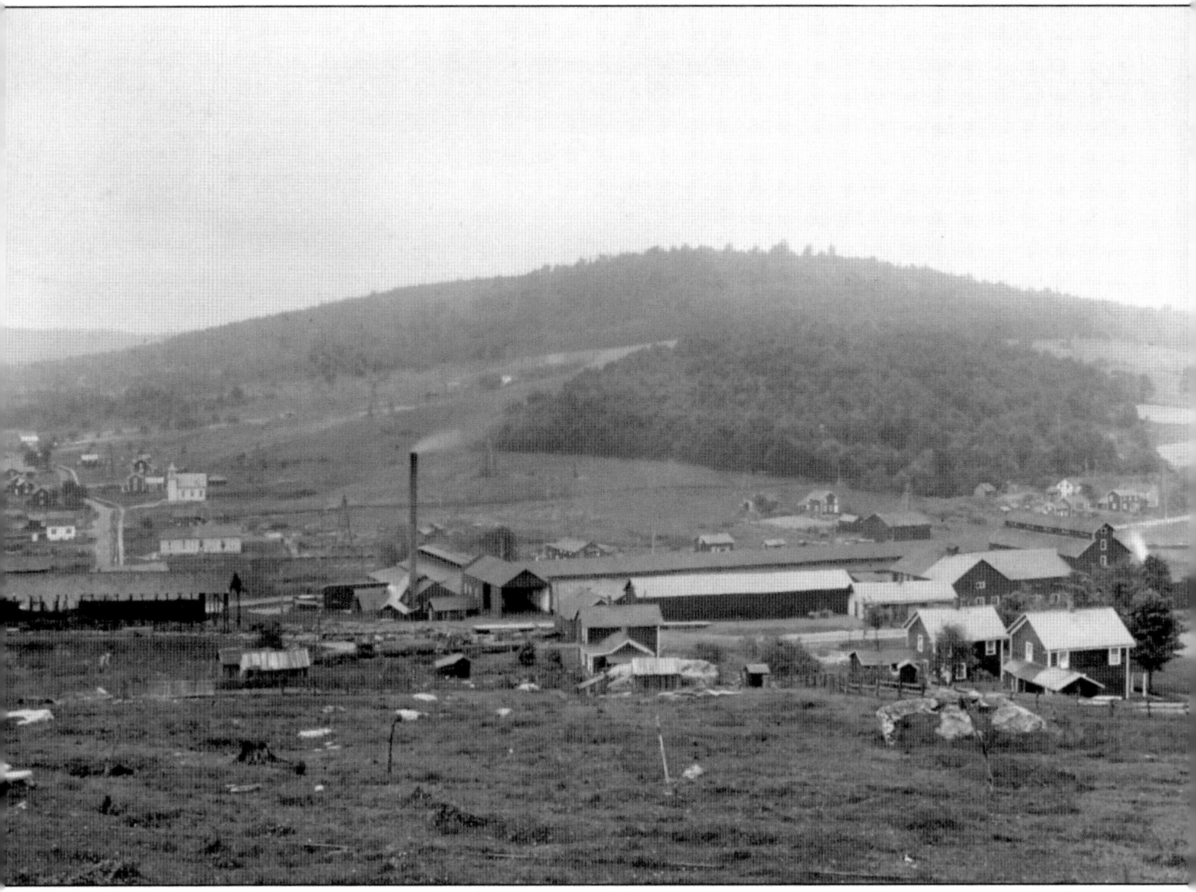

At one point in time, the Stoneham Tannery sold its leather to the British army to use for boots. The leather was ordered, shipped, and heavily salted and made the company very profitable. When the United States Leather Company was formed, the Stoneham Tannery was sold to it.

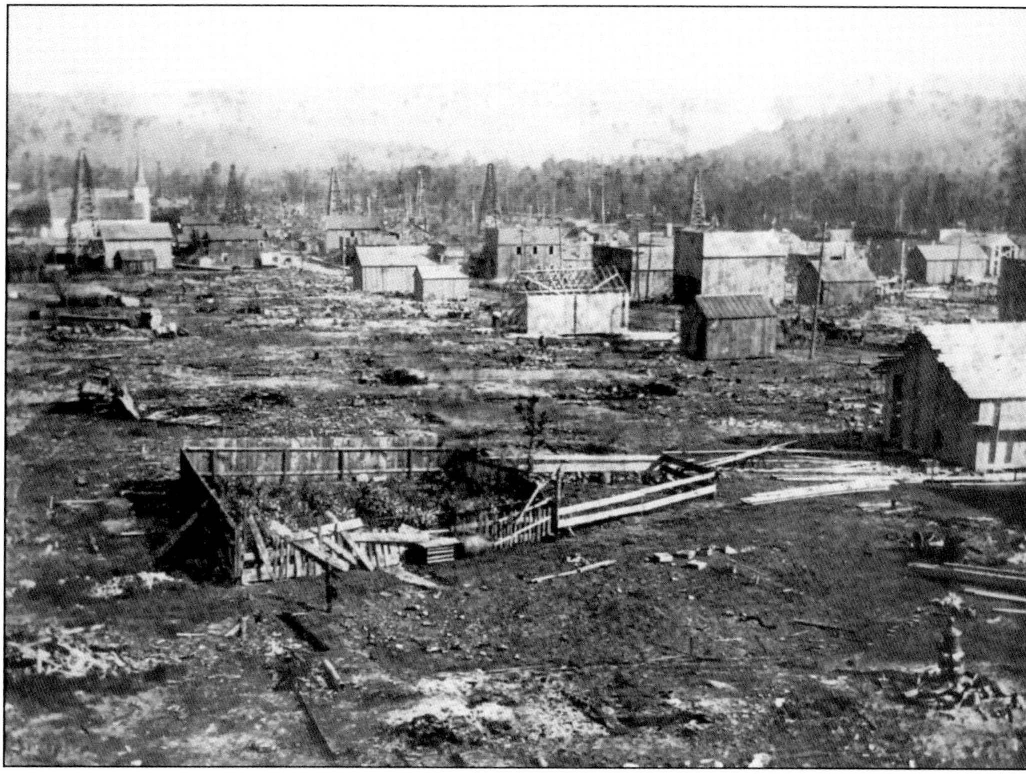

In 1887, a fire in Clarendon started at the old Brown Mill. Just as firefighters got it under control, another one started at Beaver House. Firefighters called for reinforcements, but by the time they put the fire out, the destruction was tremendous.

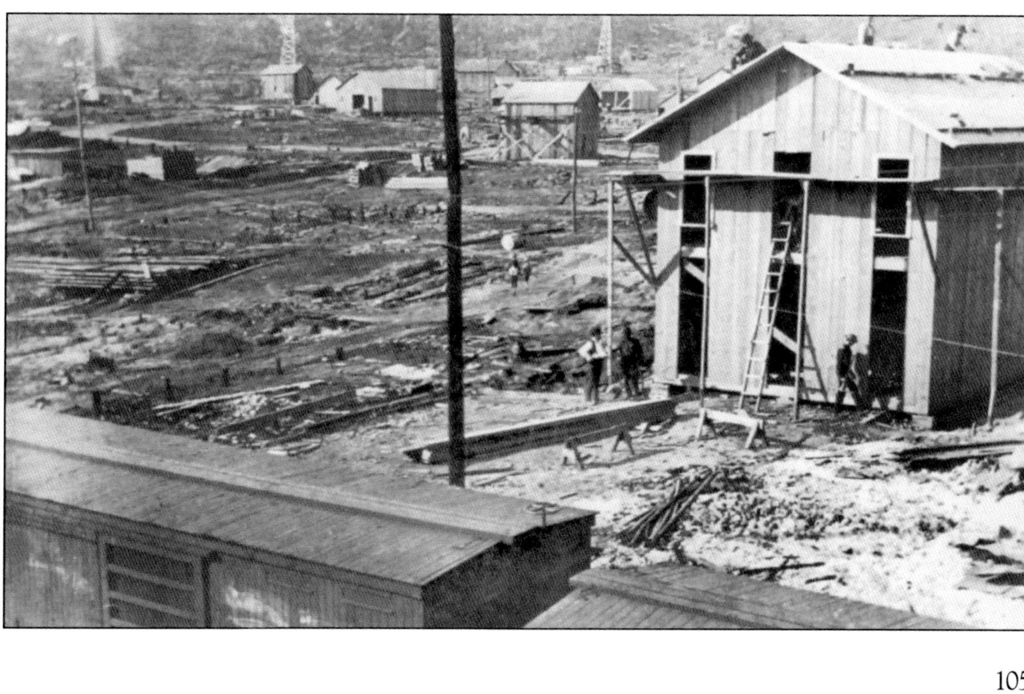

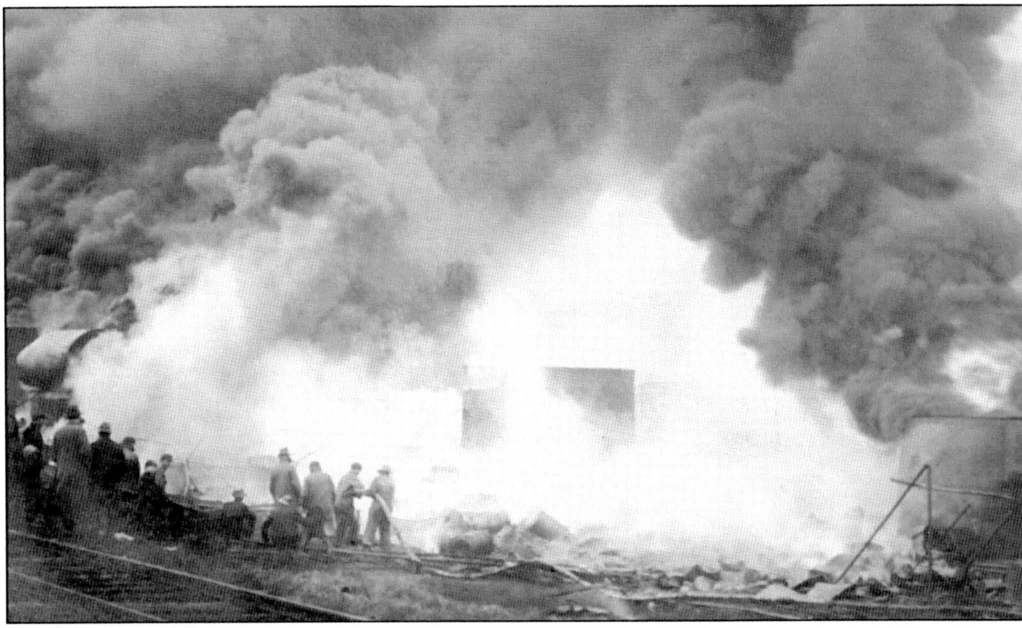

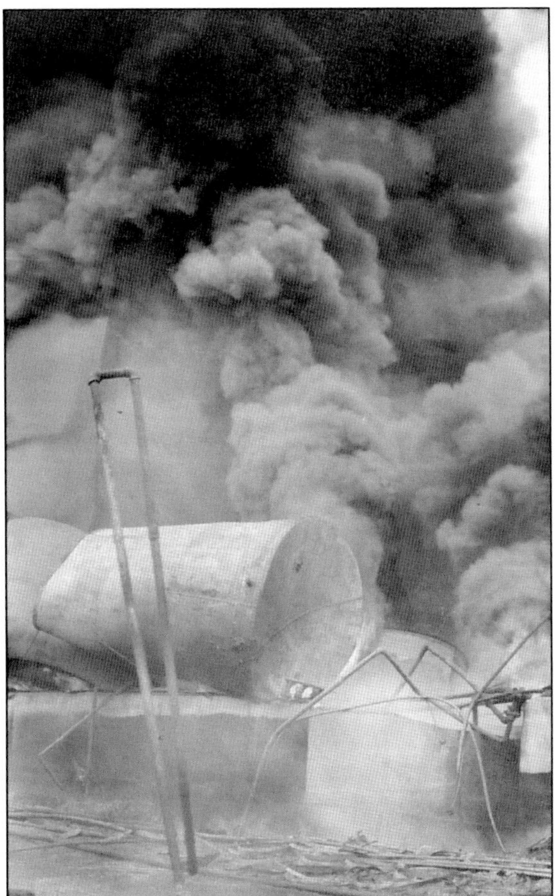

In the 1880s, the activity of oil wells in Glade and North Warren diminished, but those in Clarendon continued to flourish. Clarendon's oil refinery used large wells in the area, making the company very successful and helping the town to grow rapidly. It eventually merged with Stoneham, producing 350 barrels a day.

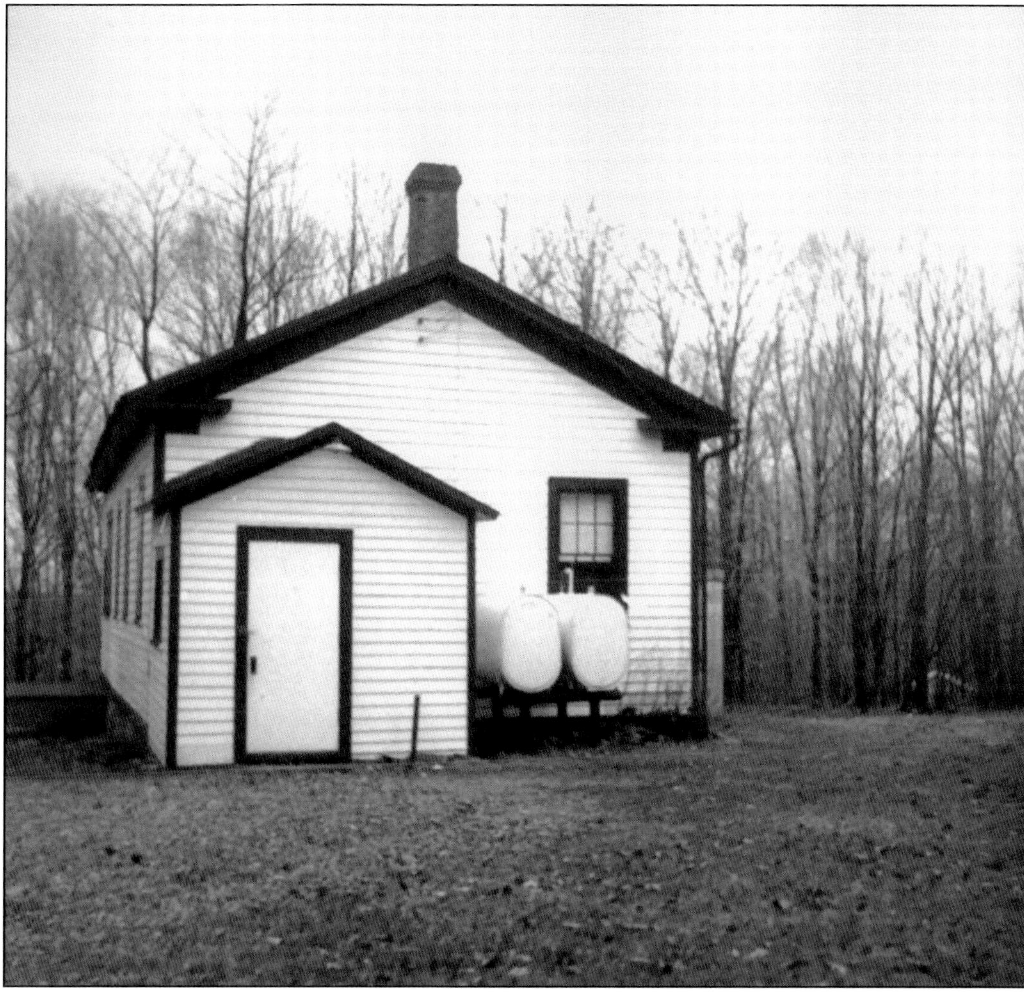

In Watson Township, the Plank Road One-Room Schoolhouse serves today as the Watson Township Community Center. The Warren County School District donated the building to the Watson Township supervisors in 1969. The school was built around 1885 and named for the plank road built by Henry Baxter that ran 30 feet from the entrance of the school.

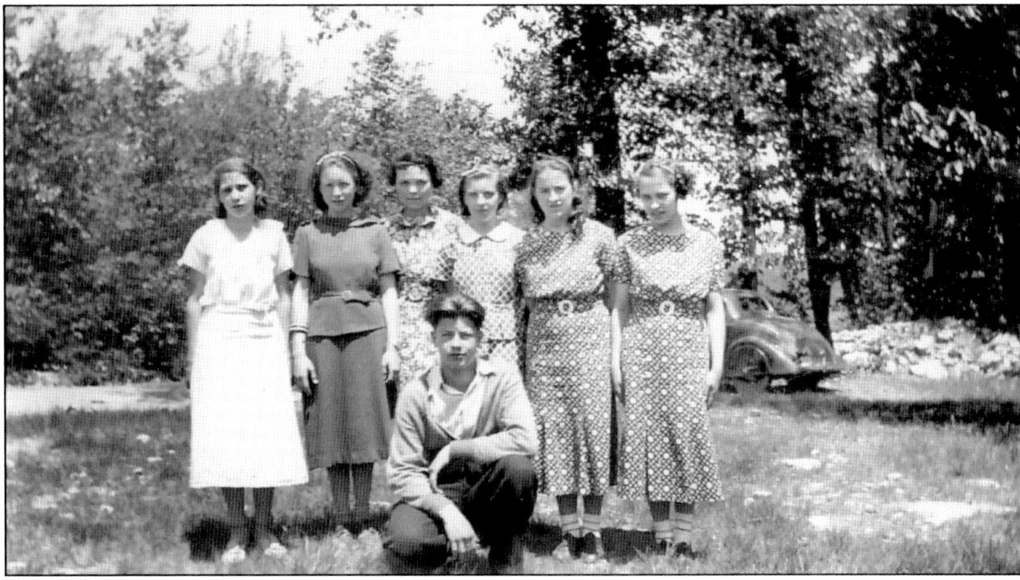

In 1936, eighth grade students of Plank Road School pose for a portrait. Pictured are (first row) Alfred Westfall; (second row) from left to right, Sophie Glotz, Betty King, a Mrs. Knapp (teacher), June Reynolds, Doris Mickelson, and Dorothy Mickelson. (Above, courtesy of Watson Township; below, courtesy of Hannah Fry.)

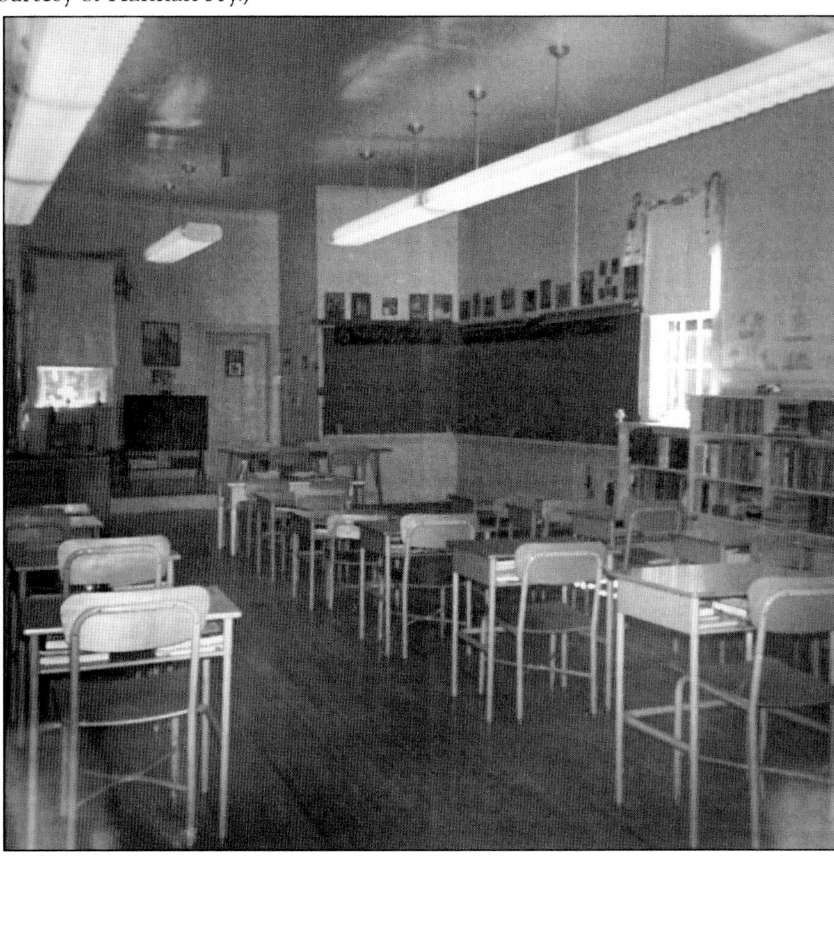

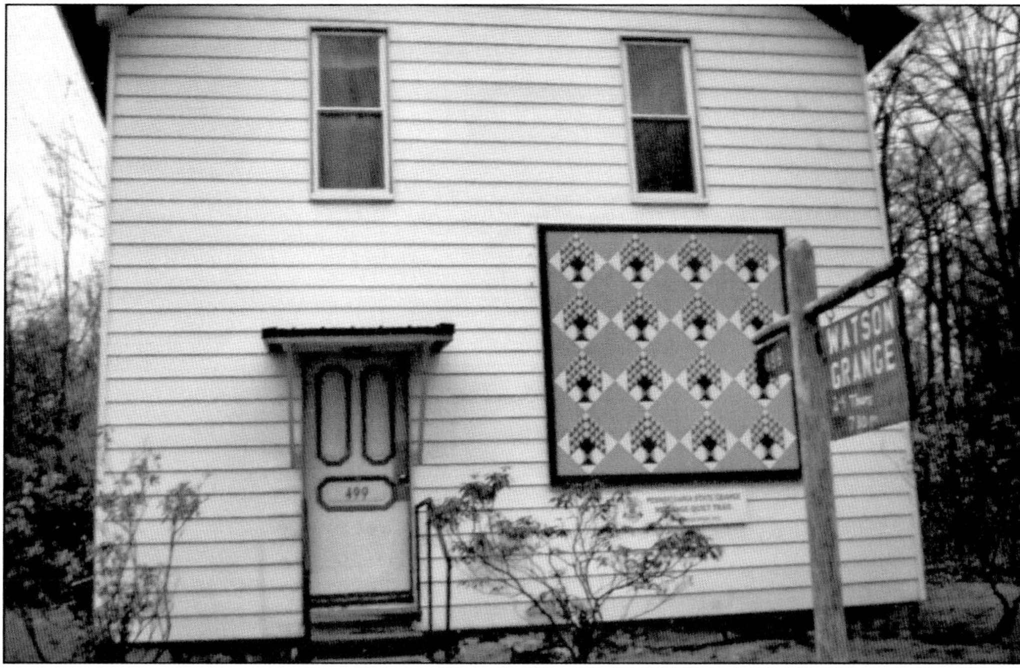

Watson Grange 1068 was organized on July 6, 1892. The first meetings were held in the Good Templars Hall located on the Gillis Farm near the Plank Road School. In January 1899, the Grangers voted to build their own hall, with the first meeting held there on April 16, 1900. Electricity was installed in 1949, and a water well was drilled in 1950. Pictured here is the Society of Farm Women organized at the Grange Hall on May 3, 1919. (Both, courtesy of Mrs. W.B. McCormick.)

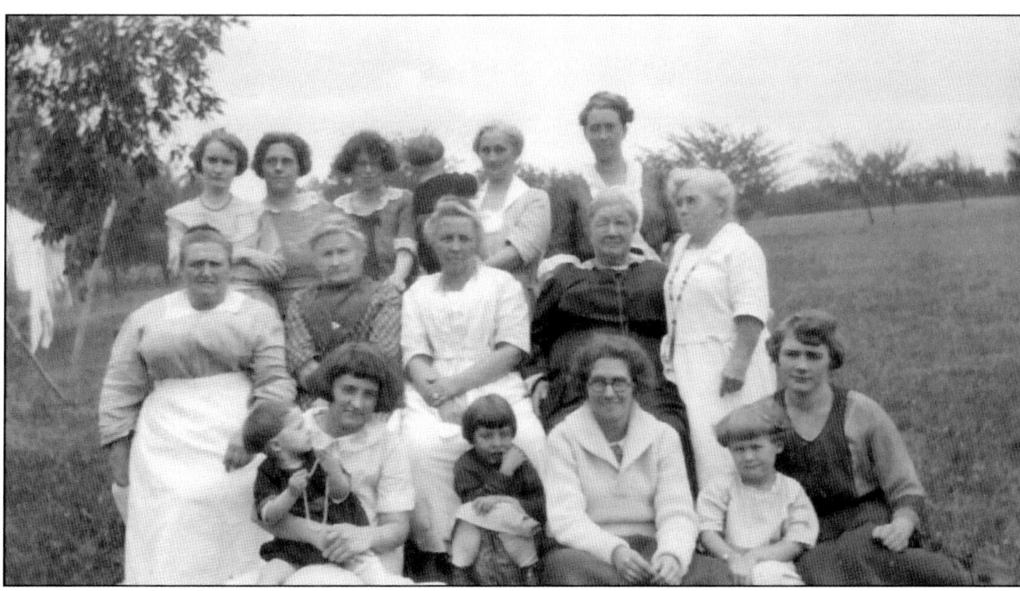

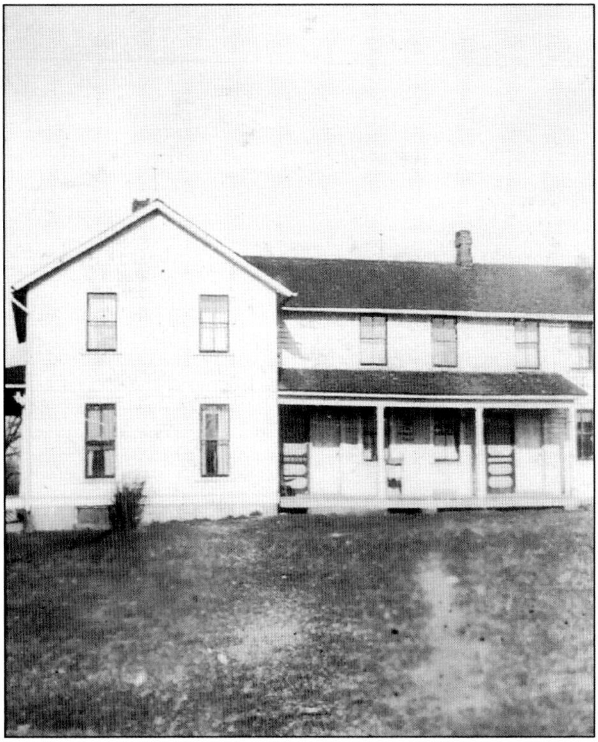

The Wilkins Farm dedication was a gift of land from the State Federation of Pennsylvania Women to the Allegheny National Forest (ANF) for public use and enjoyment. The formal presentation was made by the Northwestern District on June 14, 1934. This photograph is noted as showing "the house in the middle of the garden spot of the world." (Courtesy of Hannah Fry.)

In 1977, the ANF dedicated the land as a national landmark, today known as the Hearts Content Scenic Area. The photograph below was taken at the dedication ceremony on July 5, 1977. Pictured, from left to right, are Benjamin J. Zerby (National Park Service), Fr. Joseph Kapusnak (St. Michael's, Sheffield, Pennsylvania), John P. Butt (ANF supervisor), and Hon. Joseph S. Ammerman (23rd District congressman).

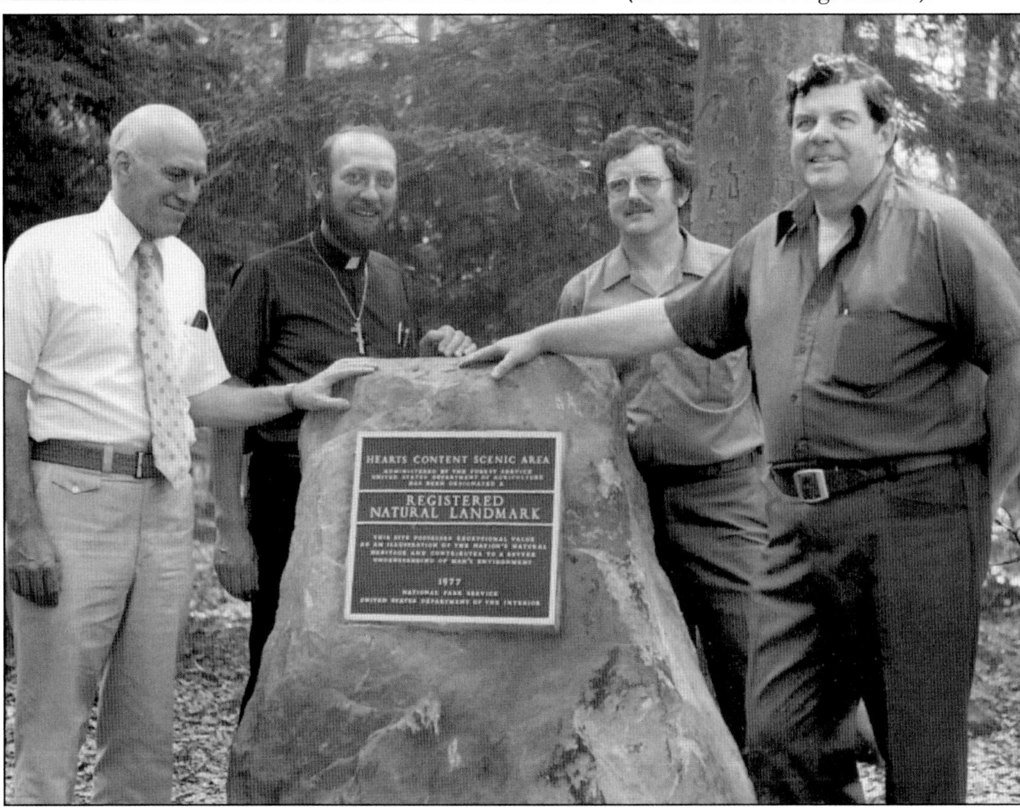

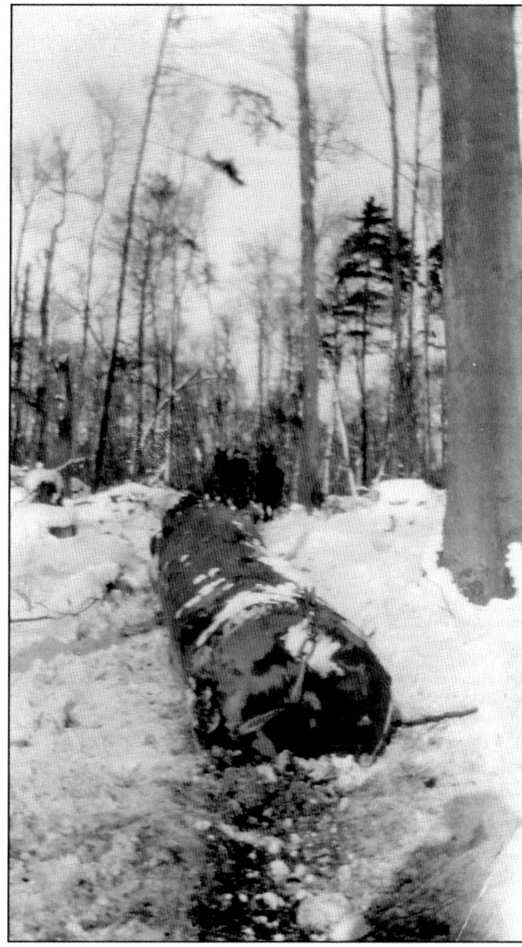

Hearts Content was never a town. The first record of the name appeared in the book *Pine Knots and Bark Peelers* by W. Reginald Wheeler. The Wheeler and Dusenbury Lumber Company began operations in 1834. The men pictured below are Deb Osborne and Nels Jamieson from lumber camp no. 15. Lumber operations ceased in 1922, and the Wheeler family donated that area to the federal government. (Both, courtesy of Hannah Fry.)

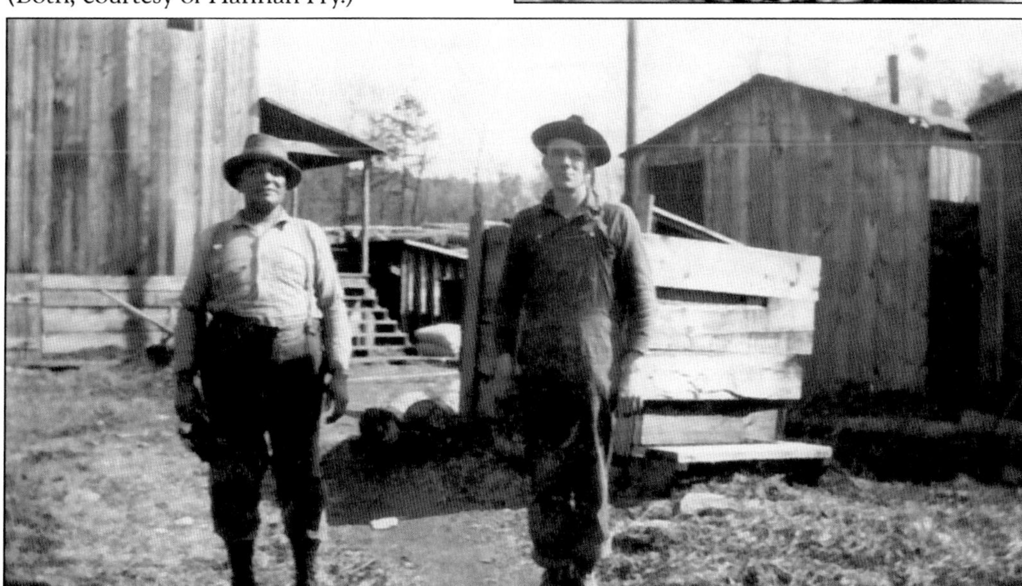

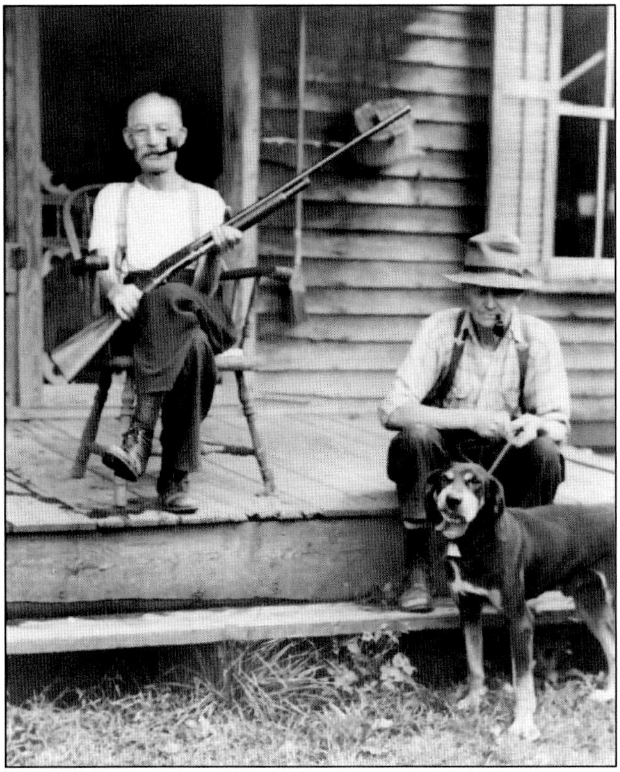

Watson Township still maintains some of the country's finest timber tracts. In the 1870s, the township's eight steam sawmills averaged over 2,500 feet of timber per day. Lumber camps like camp no. 15 existed in Hearts Content for many years. Lemon Thompson, pictured on the right, was one of the bosses for Wheeler and Dusenbury Lumber Company, and Davey Kerr (camp cook) is pictured on the left. (Courtesy of Hannah Fry.)

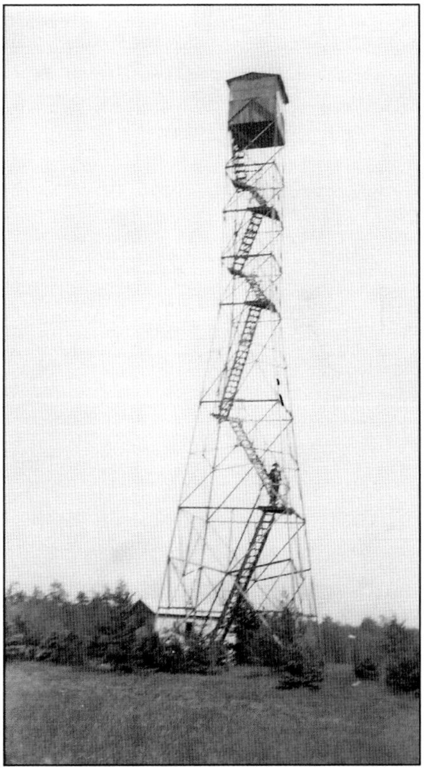

This fire tower located at Hearts Content Recreation Area was constructed in 1922. It is 30 feet tall and provides an unobstructed view of over 15 miles in all directions. Hearts Content is home to 120 acres of 400-year-old timber left undisturbed by the US Forest Service for inspiration and scientific study. All fires are forbidden!

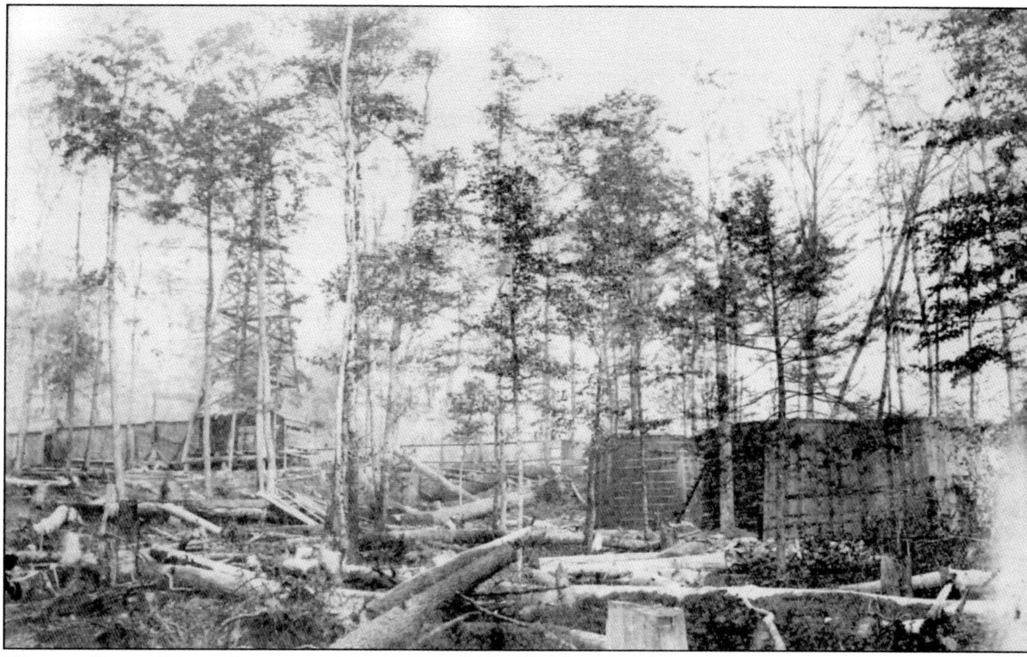

Cherry Grove Township was carved out of Sheffield Township on December 7, 1847. Sheffield, Mead, and Cherry Grove Townships were originally included in the old Kinzua Township. Cherry Grove is best known for the no. 646 well. Two men by the name of Morck and Falconer purchased land that was promised to produce oil. The men leased the land to the Jamestown Oil Company in hopes of prosperity. By 1882, secret plans were formulated to shoot well no. 646 with torpedoes, but on the day of the torpedoing, with spies all about and hundreds gathered to watch, nothing happened. The shells were empty and the cans had no glycerin to ignite the charge. Many left disappointed and thought well no. 646 was a failure, but by May, it was gushing 2,000 barrels a day. The public had been fooled!

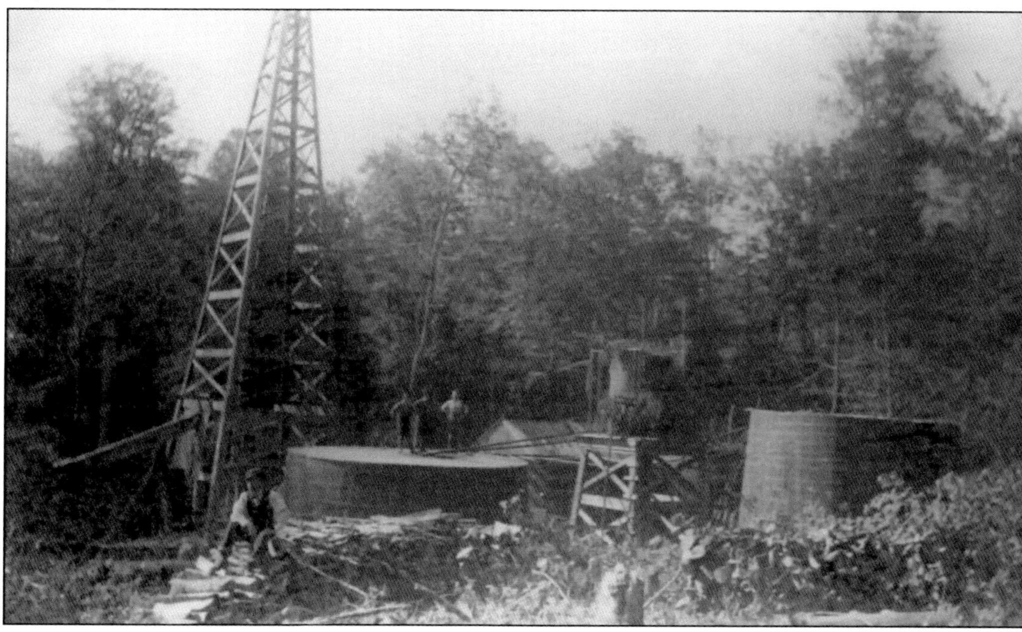

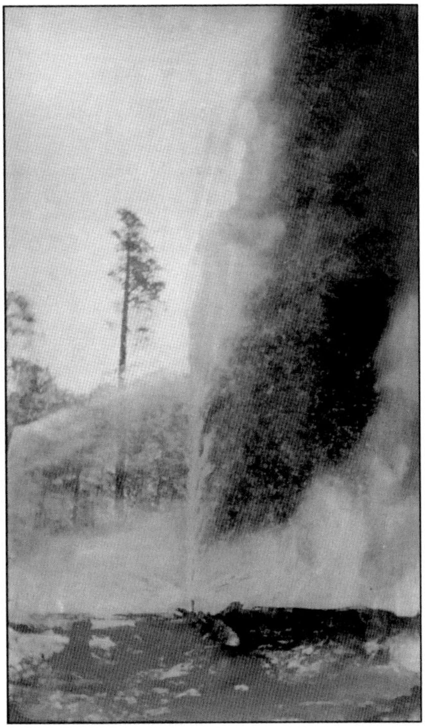

The no. 646 well, along with Murphy's gusher, brought the oil pack rushing into the new field like hungry wolves. Crowded quarters were the rule, not the exception. At first, tents and barns were used to house the many workers, then rough board shanties were put up for the oil-seekers. A true boomtown ensued. (Photograph by Bairstow.)

Two plank roads and numerous pipelines were put in from Sheffield out to the oil fields. In 1882, a railroad line was hurriedly installed to haul the heavy oil-producing equipment. The railroad survived the oil bust as it carried passengers and supplies and was then later used to haul lumber and bark for the local tanning mills.

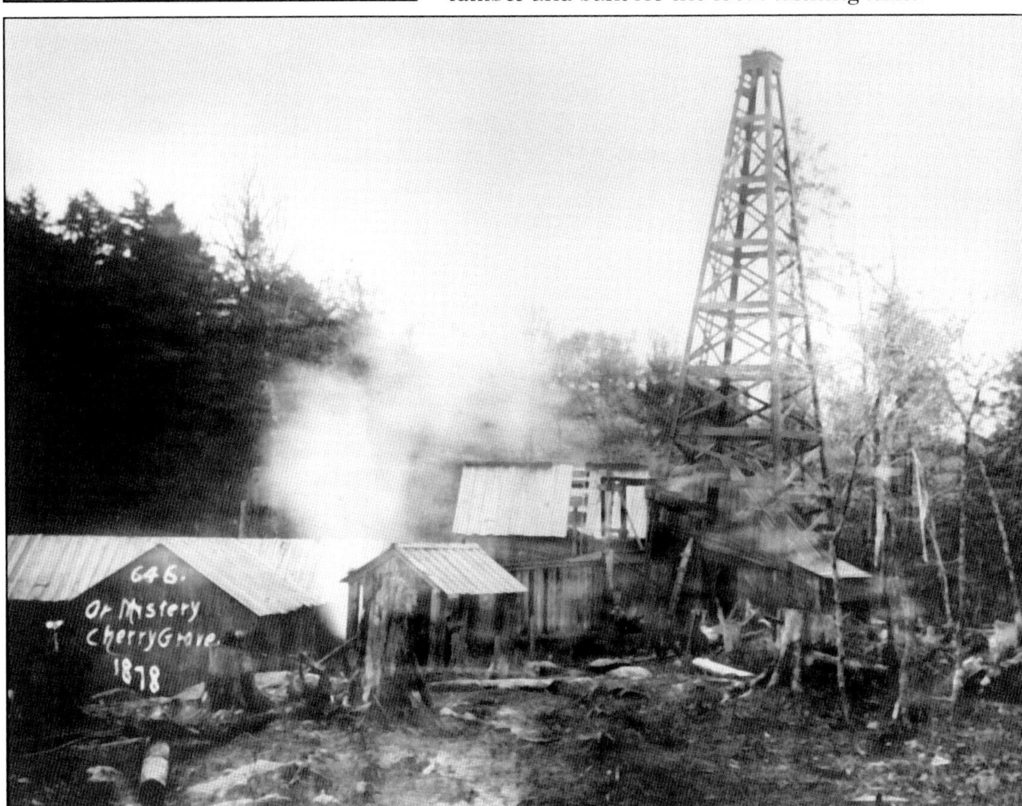

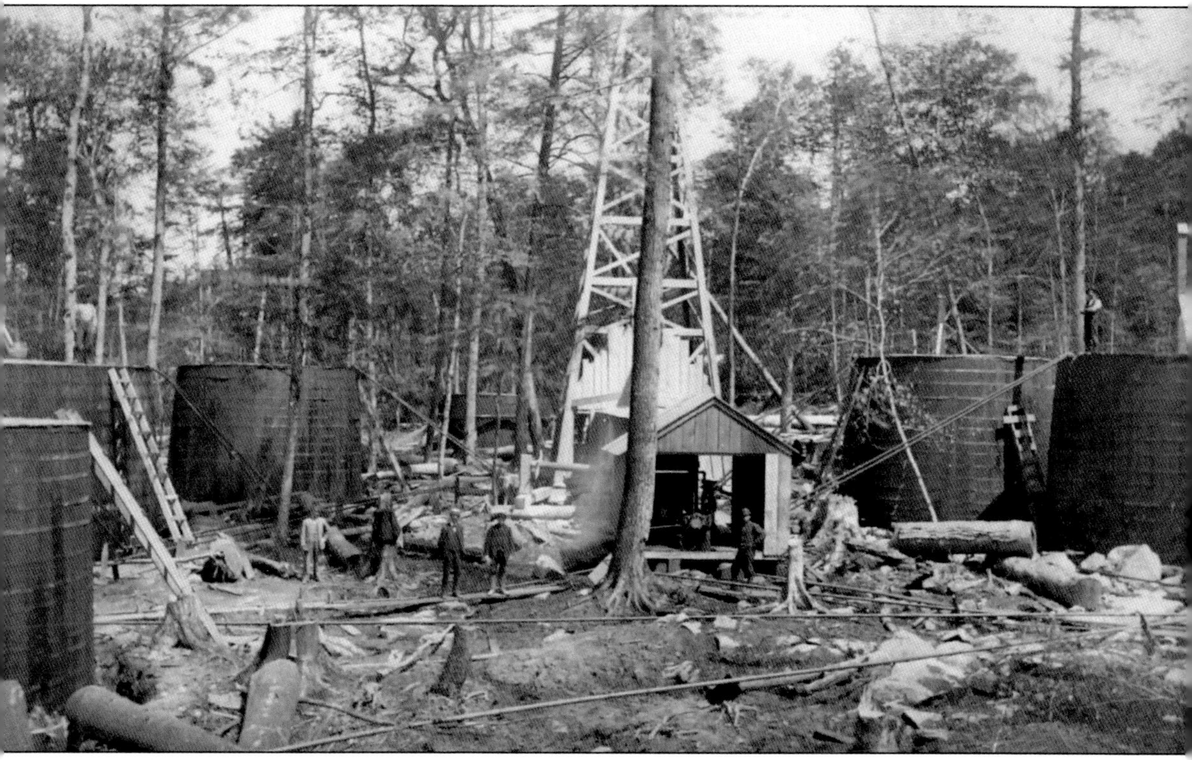

Before the sudden collapse of the oil business, Cherry Grove had won a national reputation as being part of the greatest oil boom in Pennsylvania. By January 1883, one-fourth of the wells were dry. Now, Cherry Grove is part of a natural, beautiful rural area of Pennsylvania.

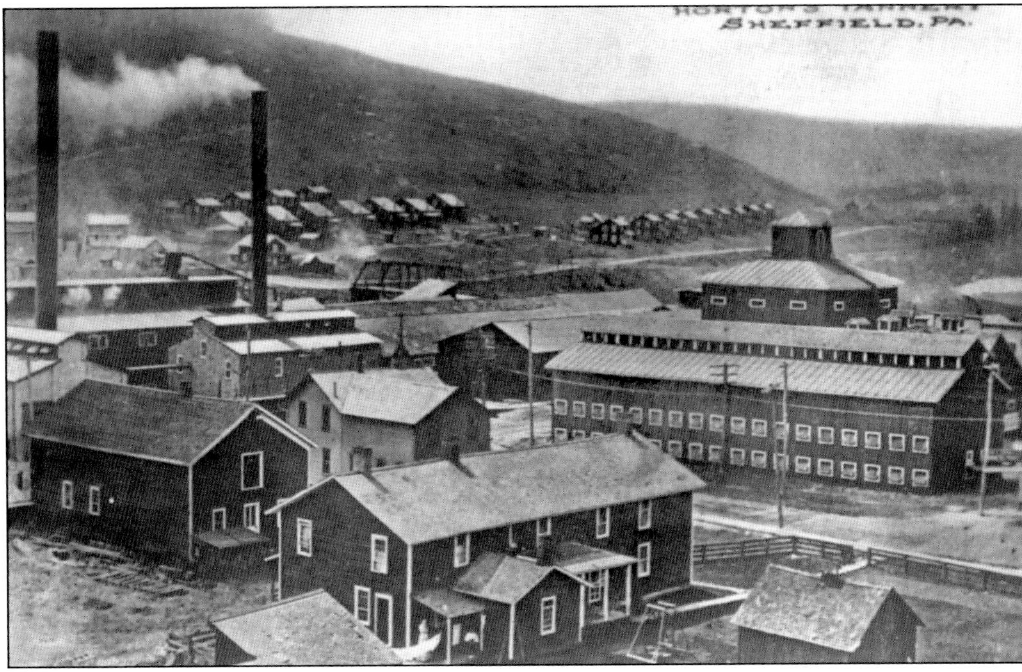

In Sheffield Township, Horton, Crary, and Company either built, bought, or had a controlling interest in Sheffield's three large tanneries. It took almost a year for an animal hide to be tanned, during which time the hide soaked in manure, salt, and water; was applied with hemlock bark acid; and was finally dried and molded. Horton, Crary, and Company built the tannery above in 1867 and purchased the Brooks tannery, seen below, in 1880.

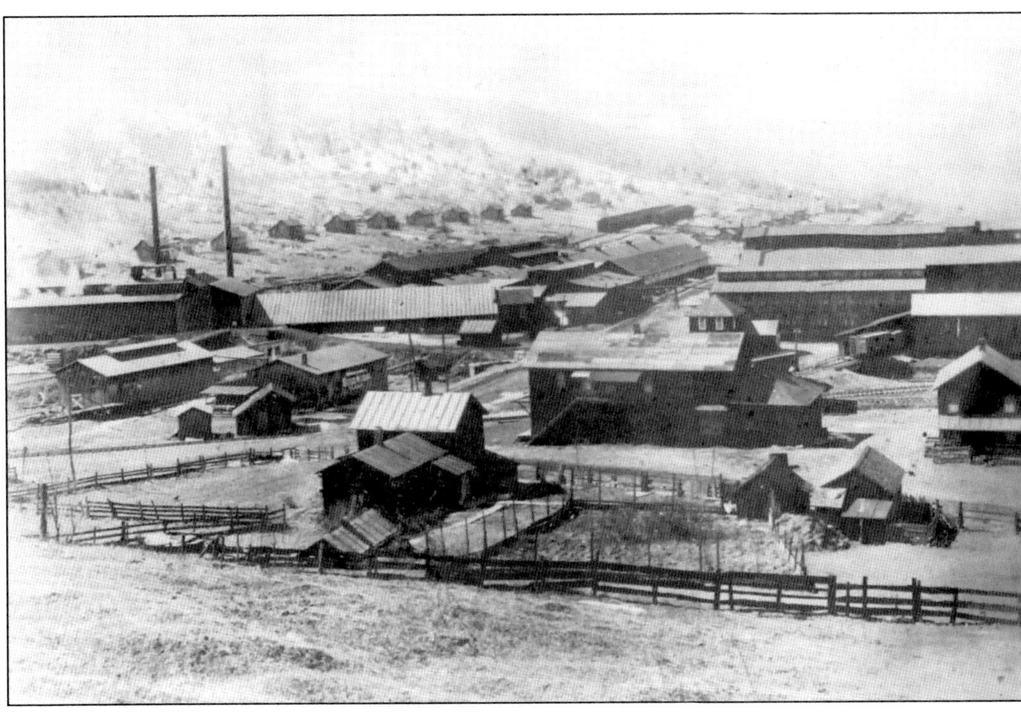

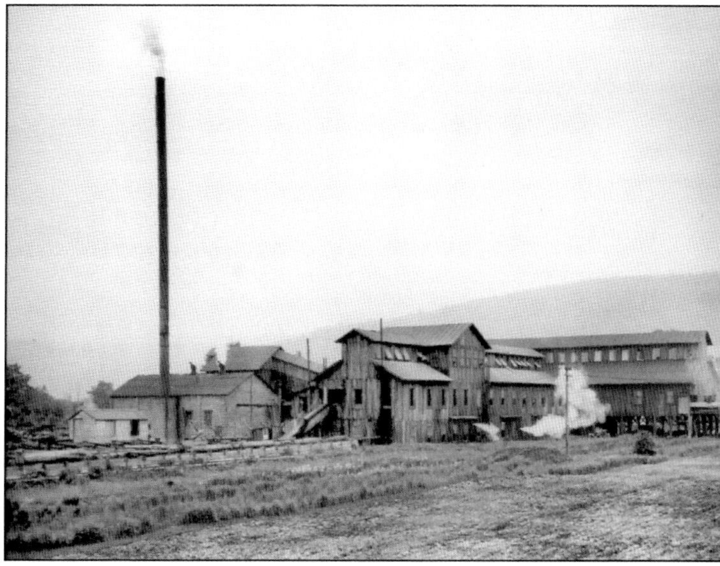

The tanning process required tree bark, but what to do with the remaining lumber? Owned by the Central Lumber Company of New York, the Central Pennsylvania Lumber Company was an answer to that question. According to the *Sheffield Centennial*, the CPL had operations throughout the state, including this hardwood mill in Sheffield, which provided millions of feet of lumber after its establishment in 1907.

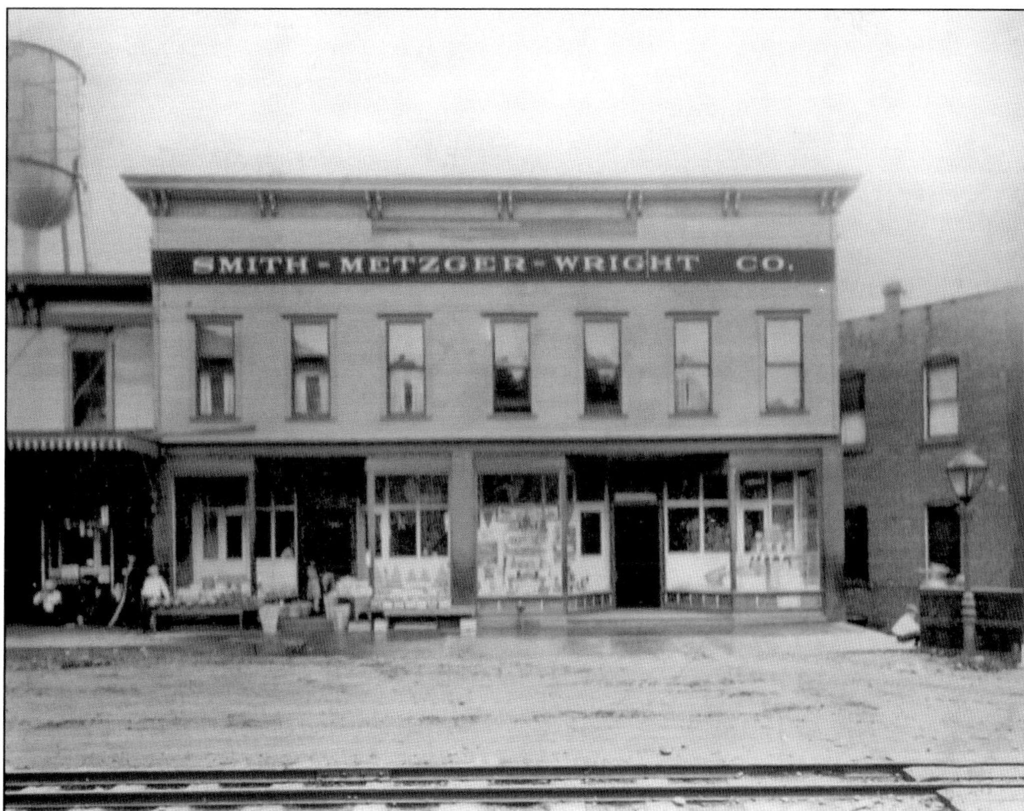

The *Historical Collections of Sheffield Township* notes that around 1864, Horton, Crary, and Company founded a retail store in Sheffield. The venture passed through many hands before it eventually encompassed a block of real estate and comprised eight different departments. In 1895, as C.H. Smith Company, Limited, it was called the largest department store between Erie and Williamsport. It eventually became the Metzger-Wright Company before its demise.

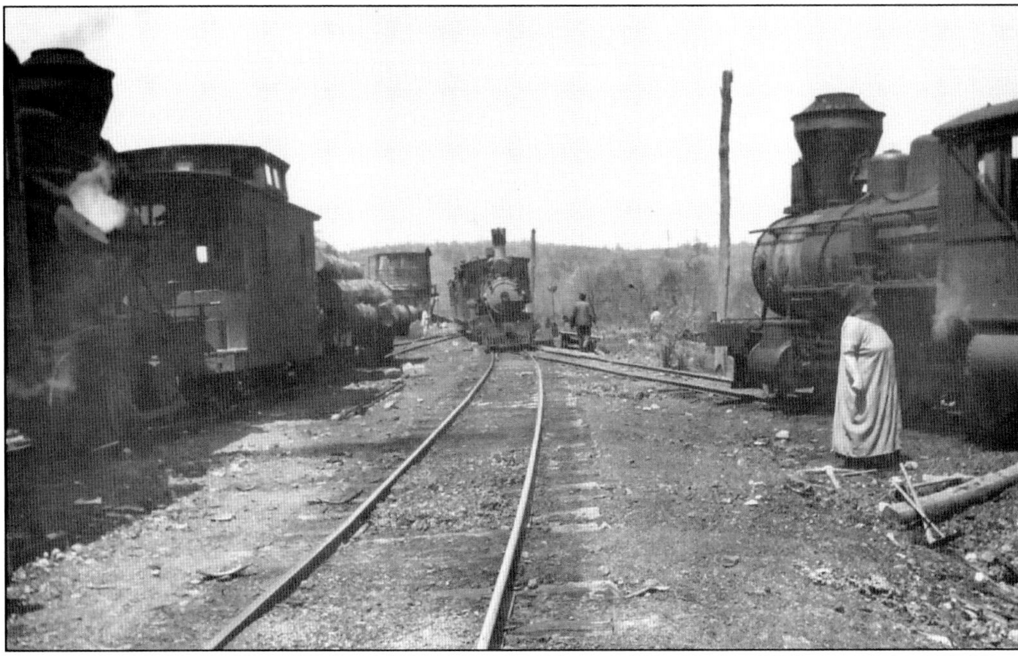

According to Thomas T. Taber III, the Tionesta Valley Railroad operated from 1882 to 1942 and was the biggest and most colorful of the narrow gauges in Pennsylvania. It initially served the tanneries, then the lumber mills, and finally the chemical companies. It was built by the Horton and Crary families, who later formed the Central Leather Company and Central Pennsylvania Lumber Company. Pictured above is a Brooks locomotive, nicknamed "Wild Pigeon"; it was built about 1880 and remained on the roster until 1935. Pictured below is another TVRR locomotive, built by Wyoming Valley in 1882 and sold to Warren & Farnsworth Railroad in 1902. (Both, courtesy of the Thomas T. Taber III collection.)

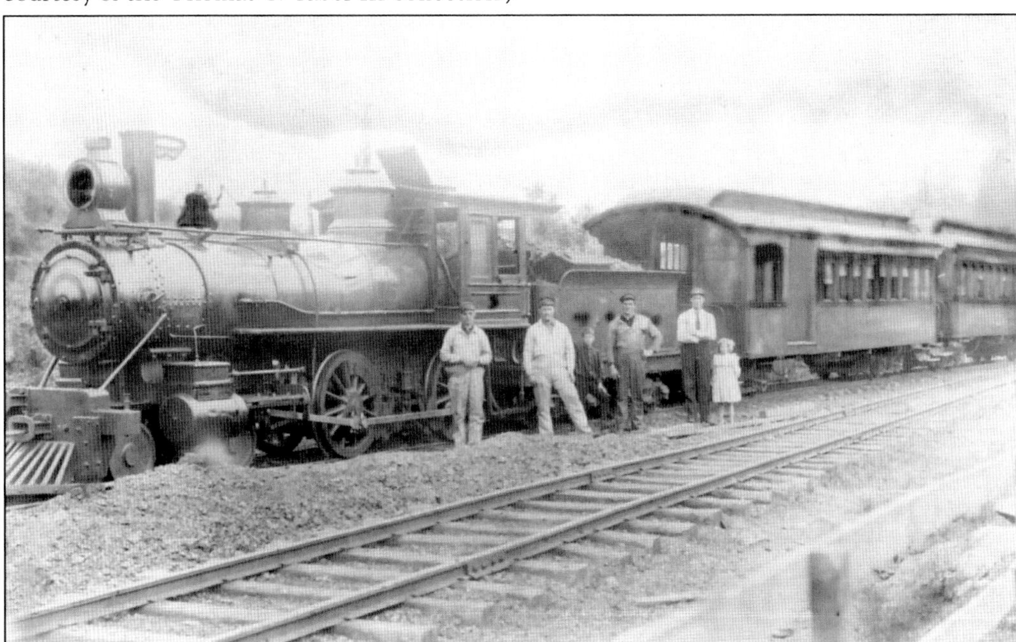

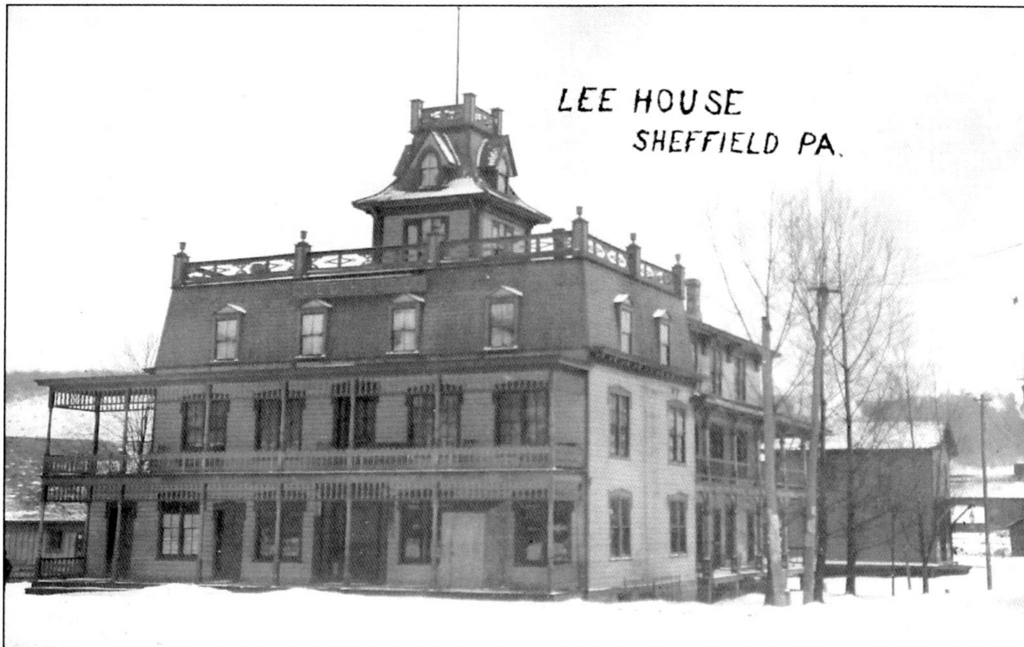

According to the *Sheffield Centennial*, this landmark was established by Amos Lee in 1873. During this period of rapid growth, the Lee House served as a hub for businessmen making their way through town in search of fortunes in the lumber and tanning industries. In 1880, it hosted Greenback Party presidential candidate Gen. James B. Weaver. This c. 1915 postcard image shows the building before time began to take its toll.

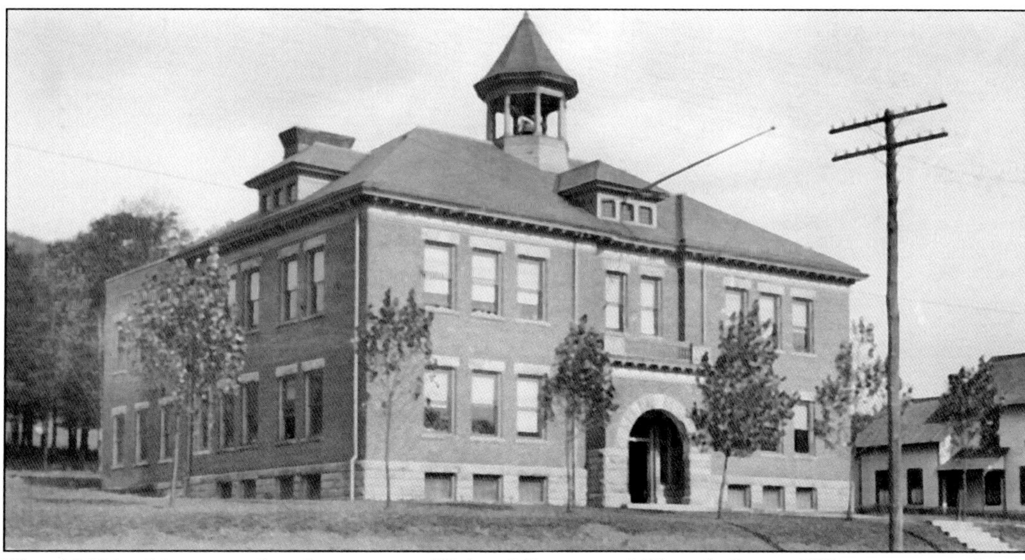

This 1912 building stood at the corner of School Street and Church Street. When it was replaced by a newer structure along Route 6 in 1975 and finally razed in 1978, it took a place in a long succession of Sheffield schools that includes the original 1836 Dunham School on West Main Street, the "Washington School," the "Lincoln School," and a school specifically for mill workers' children on Deerlick Hollow.

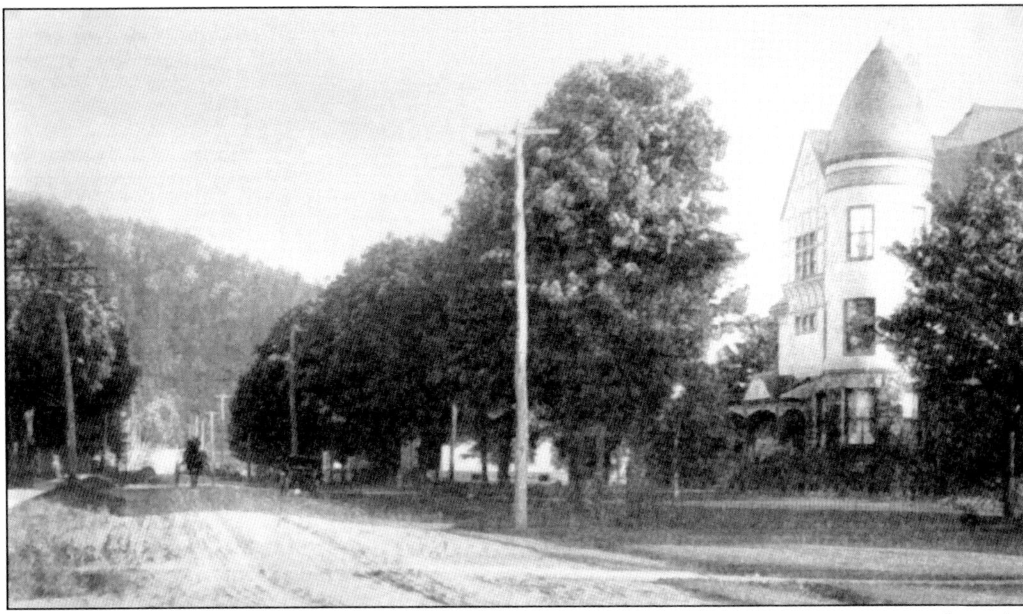

This 1902 postcard shows the road to Barnes, with the home built by George Horton on the right. Horton had seen similar dwellings on a trip to Chicago and employed the same Chicago architect of those homes, Alfred Smith, to construct such a residence in Sheffield in 1888.

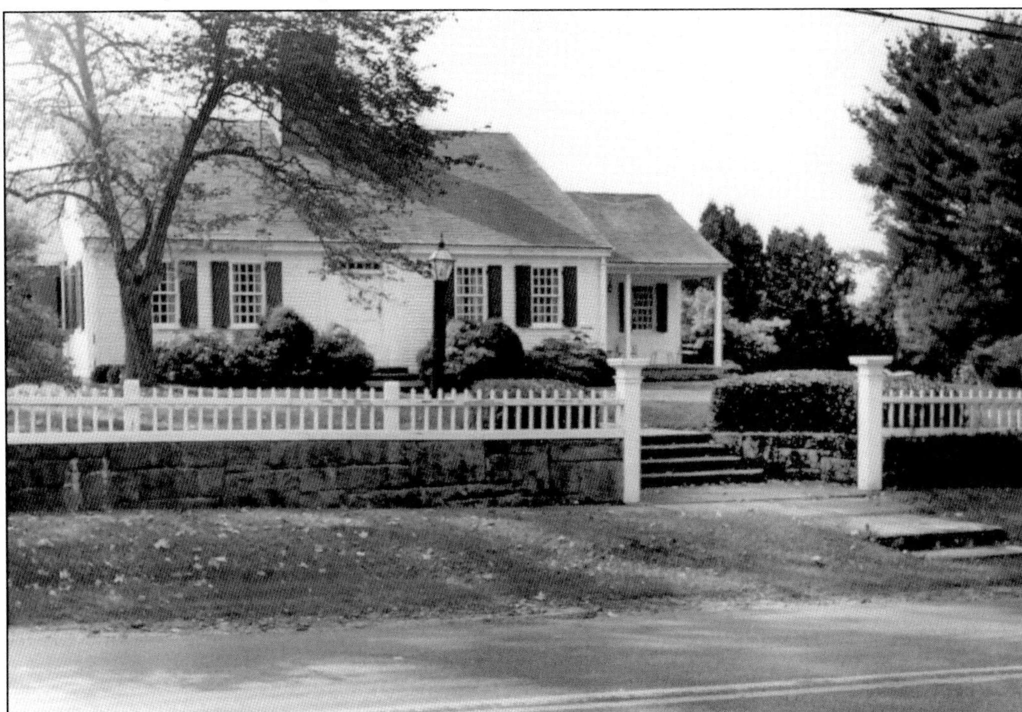

Built in 1847 by Erastus Barnes—son of Timothy Barnes, for whom the village of Barnes is named—this home is one of the oldest still standing in Sheffield Township. Erastus served as a Warren County commissioner. In an 1856 letter, Erastus left proof that he hid a fugitive slave in this home in that year.

Five

Gone but Not Forgotten
Kinzua and Corydon Townships

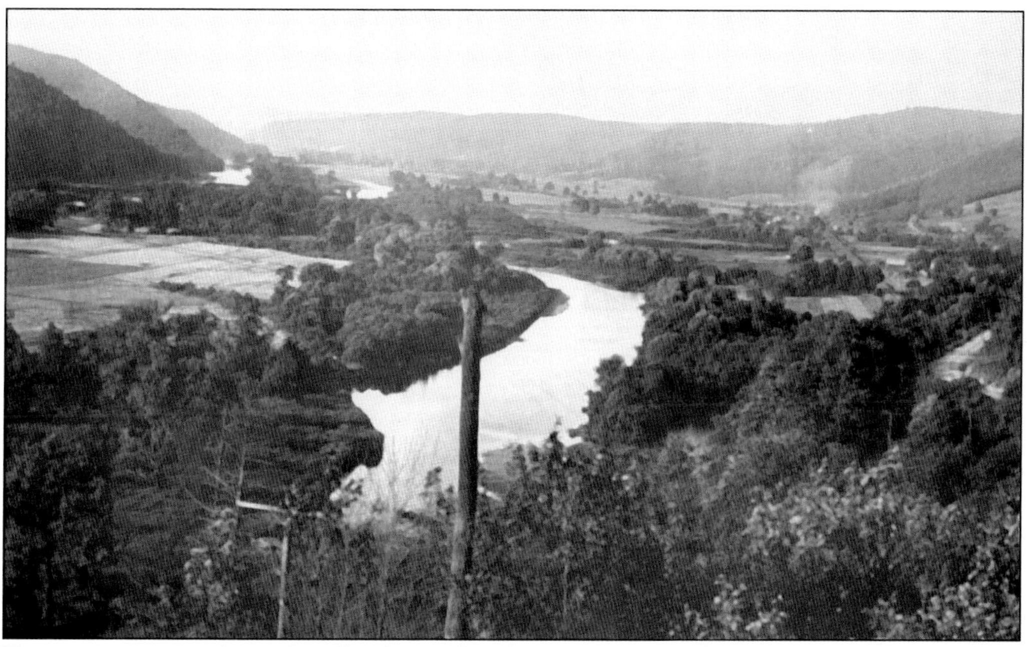

Kinzua was very similar to Corydon, being that the two were in such proximity. Corydon, though, was much more built up, while Kinzua remained forestlike. In 1801, James Morrison became the first white settler in Kinzua. Kinzua officially became a township on March 8, 1821, and was first called Number 8. The main industry in Kinzua was lumbering due to the abundant forest. There were, however, other businesses in Kinzua besides lumbering. Kinzua had a hotel, a harness shop, and a "square" with many businesses.

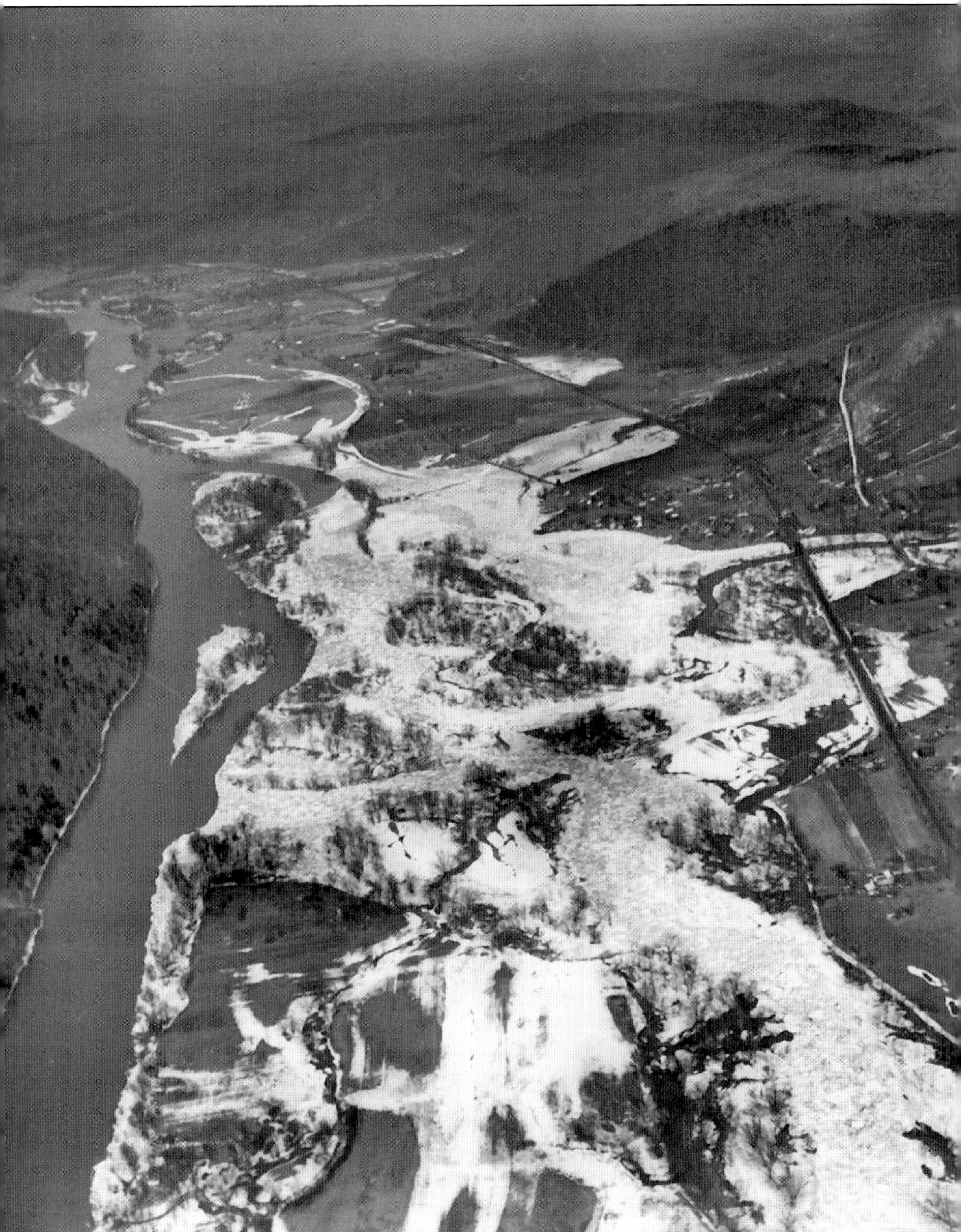

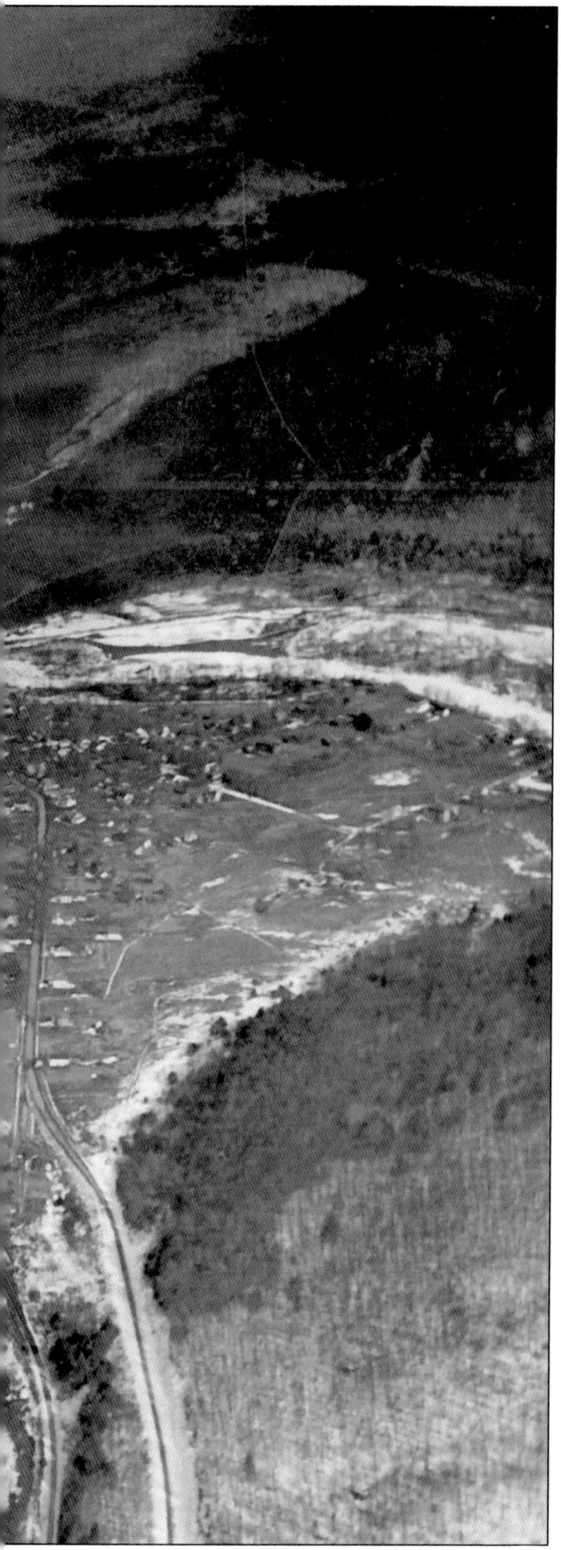

Kinzua had many schoolhouses throughout the years, similar to Corydon. Kinzua's first schoolhouse was built in 1825 and was used until it burned down in 1829. The second school was a large schoolhouse built in 1882. Kinzua also had various churches throughout the years. The first was St. Luke's Church, built in 1886 but burned in 1900. A new church was built of native stone and was used until 1962. There was also a Methodist church in Kinzua, built in 1848. Kinzua was a close community that enjoyed silent movies at the Community House on Saturday nights. In 1960, construction of the Kinzua Dam began and big changes came to Corydon and Kinzua. In this time, cemeteries, businesses, and families were moved to different locations. The Allegheny Reservoir flooded the area that was once Kinzua and Corydon. (Courtesy of the Everett Stoke aerial collection.)

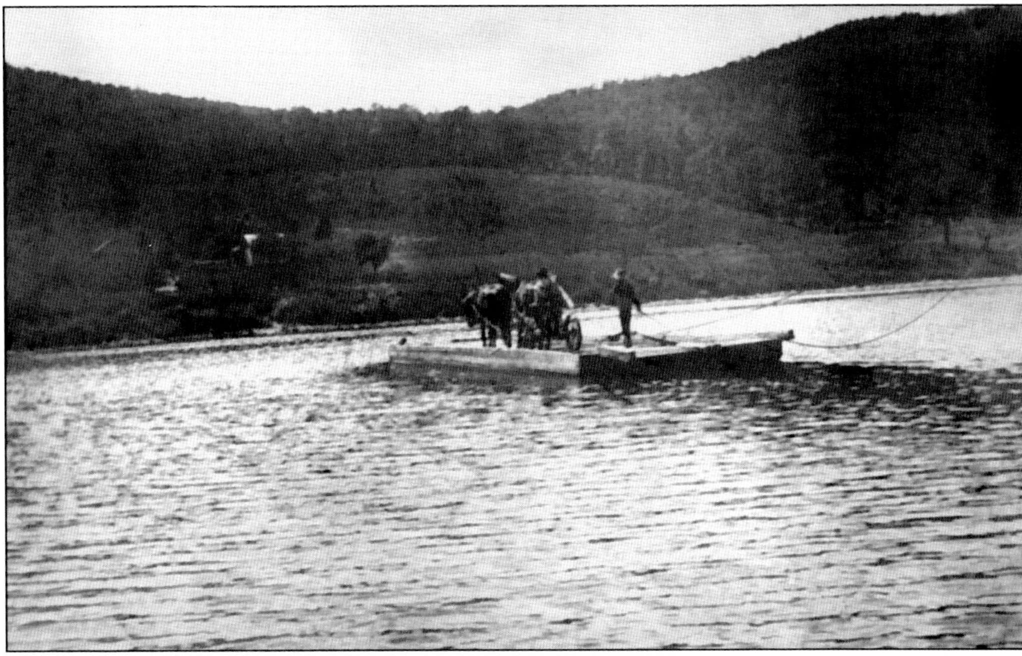

Corydon was a busy little town in the later part of the 1800s, according to Robert J. Clawson. There was a dam built primarily for the lumber operation; it was shaped like an *L* and provided spillways to the mills on the island and banks of the Allegheny River. Charles Sparks and John Taggert were ferrymen who took many passengers across the river. The Onoville Bridge across the Allegheny was built about 1902 and may have replaced the ferry.

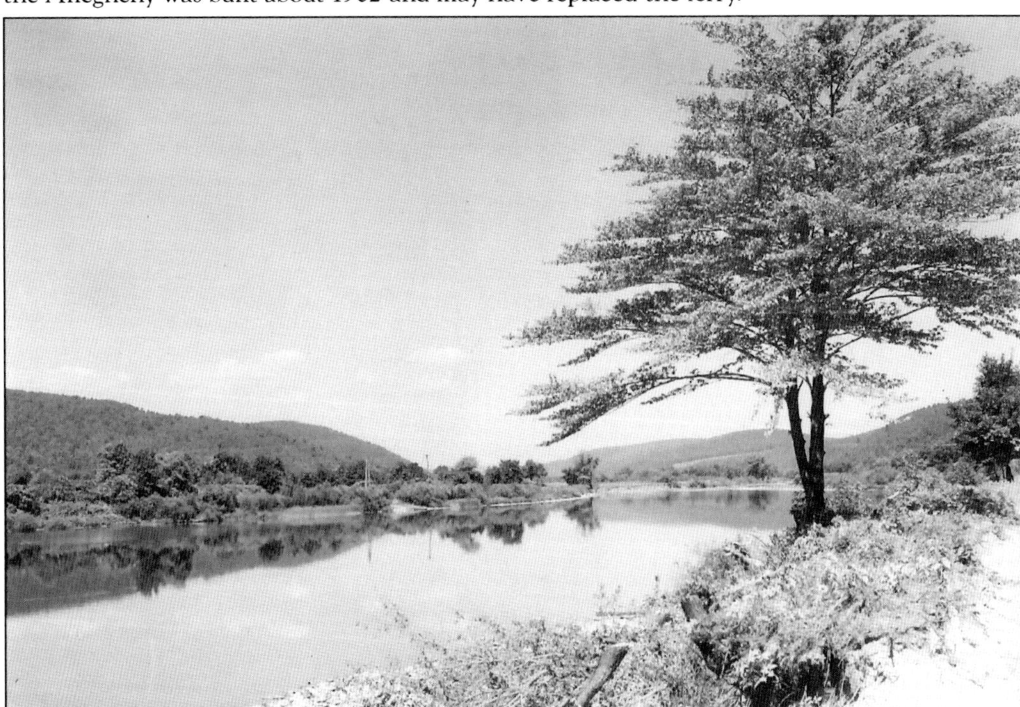

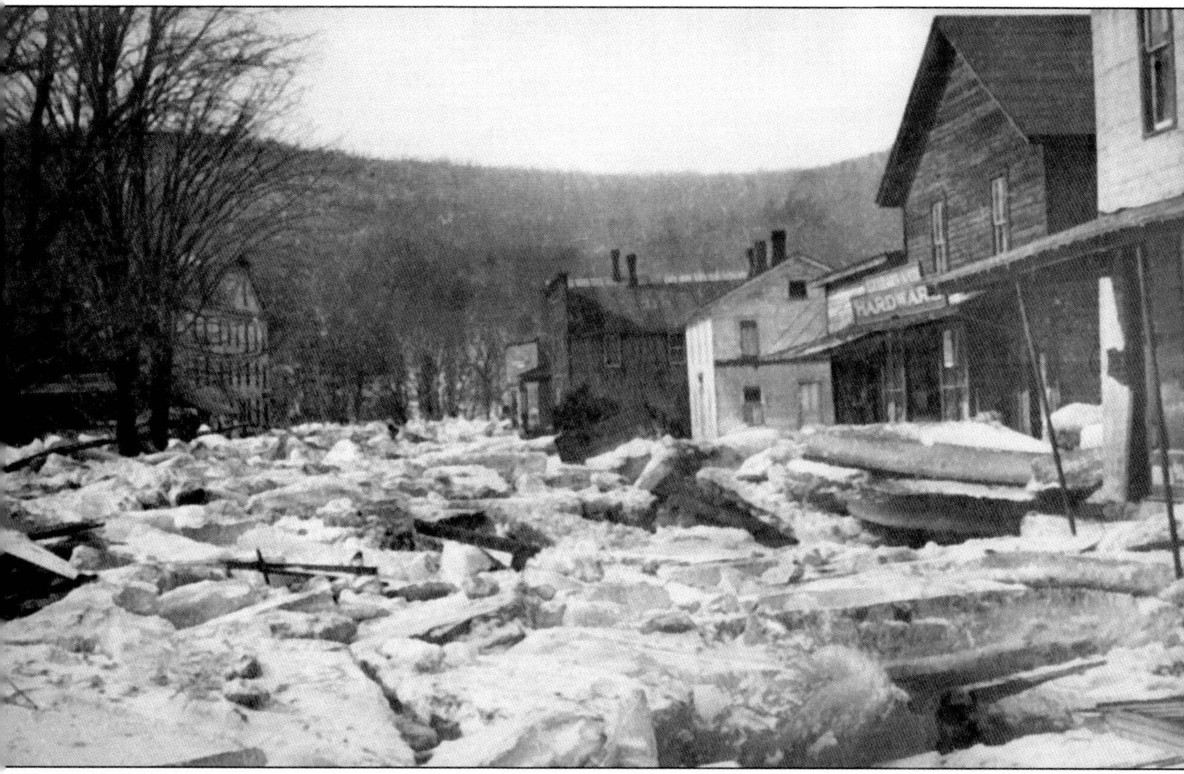

In the spring of 1918, Corydon suffered a disastrous flood that included an ice jam through the center of town. It destroyed many homes entirely and parts of others. McClintock's store and house and Evert's store and house were destroyed. The Fitzpatrick, Caldwell, White, and Reeves families all suffered damage to their homes.

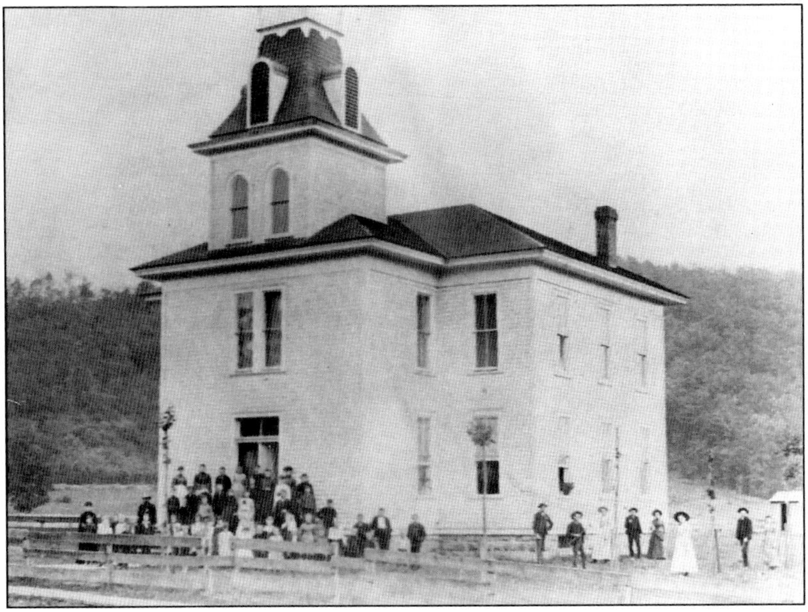

The first school building in Corydon was built in 1828, but due to an increase in population, a larger school was built in 1831. After many years of use, an even larger school building was built in 1883. By 1936, the high school had closed in Corydon, and students were displaced to other schools in the area.

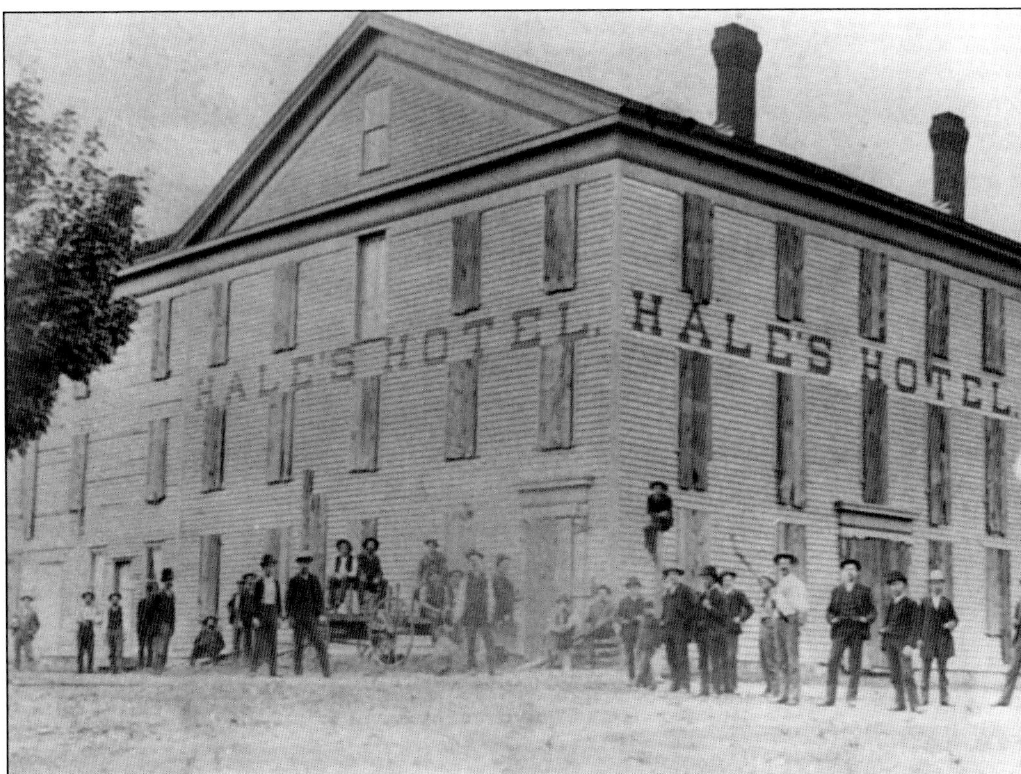

Hale's Hotel was built by Jacob McCall not long after the formation of Corydon Township. Samuel Boyer kept it for some time and was succeeded by Joseph McCollister, who entertained the traveling public for many years with good satisfaction. Joseph H. Hale came into the house on the first day of October 1885 and entirely renovated, refitted, and rebuilt it. He enlarged its capacity so that there were 45 beds for guests.

Index